19.99

New Thinking in Organizational Behaviour

D0269077

the last date

15

WITHDRAWN

L/R
STZ

658
TSO

Books in the Management Readers Series

New Thinking in Organizational Behaviour

From social engineering to reflective action

Haridimos Tsoukas

Butterworth-Heinemann Ltd
Linacre House, Jordan Hill, Oxford OX2 8DP

℞ A member of the Reed Elsevier plc group

OXFORD   LONDON   BOSTON
MUNICH   NEW DELHI   SINGAPORE   SYDNEY
TOKYO   TORONTO   WELLINGTON

First published 1994
Reprinted 1995

British Library Cataloguing in Publication Data
Tsoukas, Haridimos
   New Thinking in Organizational Behaviour:
   From social engineering to reflective
   action. – (Management Reader Series)
   I. Title II. Series
   302.3

ISBN 0 7506 1763 2

Composition by Genesis Typesetting, Rochester, Kent
Printed in Great Britain by Clays Ltd, St Ives plc

To Yow Moy

for being a difference that made a difference!

Contents

Foreword

Three props and the pit

Haridimos Tsoukas ends his introduction to this book with the words '*Bon Voyage*'. As I write, in June 1993, Dr Tsoukas is packing his bags in preparation for his national service in the Greek Armed Forces. The situation in the Balkans is still very unstable and the involvement of Greece in the conflict is by no means unthinkable. His colleagues wish Haridimos well and look forward to his safe return to Warwick University.

But this is not only a biographical comment. It is central to understanding the analysis found in this book. Dr Tsoukas draws out the key distinction between 'social engineering' and 'reflective action' in the study of organizations. Objectivity, detachment and control versus openness, ambiguity and interpretation; mechanisms versus self-organization. In discernible ways these tensions run through the current situation in the Balkans as well as in organization theory.

There is a low tolerance in Western European thought for ambiguity and undecidability. In a misuse of the term we tend to utilize the word 'anarchy' to describe situations in which we cannot fully grasp the presence, never mind the identity, of principles of organization. Where there is an absence of control, where there is a gap in our understanding, where we cannot apprehend the presence of neat, clear-cut linkages between events, and where cast-iron mechanisms demonstrably do not exist, then our anxiety mounts as we look deep into the pit of chaos. As Umberto Eco (1989:95), the novelist and semiologist, says: 'I have come to believe that the whole world is an enigma. A harmless enigma that is made terrible by our own mad attempt to interpret it as though it had an underlying truth.'

So does this mean that we 'give it up'? This is the title of a half-page 'novel' written by Franz Kafka in which the search for truth appears to be a game not worth playing. It is a stressful, disconcerting quest, and liable to be fruitless. Yet, in this volume, Dr Tsoukas and several other authors attempt to eschew nihilism and impose order on organizational life. Not through the clamping of some iron template upon our everyday behaviour in work organizations so as to impress our lines into false cavities and voids, but through a free-ranging examination of our language and discourse. If many modern human beings do seek to impose order on a disordered world there is much to be learnt from understanding the vocabularies they use and the linguistic conventions they employ in carrying out their highly predictable day-to-day timetables and itineraries. Indeed, timetabling and maps are very obvious organizational props upon which much of social order is built. But here we are back to social engineering. There *are* mechanical devices to shore up organizations but one cannot believe that they alone constitute life in large bureaucracies. They are scaffolding for the facade of order but mask much uncertainty. Several papers in this book reveal that behind the props lies a void which can only offer an 'impossibility of closure' and the certainty of ambiguity in organizational life.

What does this mean for those charged with the management of organizations? Well, it certainly explains the popularity of management 'handbooks' which provide supposedly easy-to-read guides to understanding and career-enhancing success. On these shelves the metaphors of the timetable and the map abound. The *One Minute Manager* and *In Search Of Excellence*, for example, offer fixity in time and space, and eschew ambiguity and the role of interpretation. Unlike honest medieval maps there is no '*terra incognita*' or '*tempora incognita*'. These guiding texts, of course, do not offer, nor could they offer, the secrets of wisdom. What each provides in reality is a prop. It is in two senses at least that the management gurus of the late twentieth century offer props. Like the elephants in Terry Pratchett's *Discworld*, they offer support in the sense of fixing an undecidable world securely and safely above the precipice. But in another way these books are also props for, in the well known sense of theatre, they allow us to carry around a smallish object which fixes more concretely and visibly our current role. A fashionable 'handbook' is a very useful prop in both these senses to many managerial groupings.

Dr Tsoukas has not produced a handbook which uses props in either of these two senses. His third, textual 'prop' is much more in the tradition of agitprop in which he seeks unremittingly to propagandize and agitate for a less rigid and falsely supportive view of organizational life than that found upon growing and groaning shelves of Heathrow Organization Theory. Haridimos Tsoukas and most authors in this book agitate persuasively for an acceptance of the reality of openness, ambiguity, self-reflection, enactment and self-organization – in short for the importance of reflective action, and not for social engineering.

In a world where the epithet 'post-modern' is taken seriously, the pit of chaos seems ever more gaping. A shoring up of our crumbling cognitive and organizational edifices and the need to hold on firmly to something to hide our own fears has produced a whole set of intellectual props. Dr Tsoukas shows us, however, that real wisdom, knowledge and understanding are not simple, they are not exclusively positive and they are not exclusively supportive. Knowledge is dangerous. It not only elevates, it destabilizes, it is often 'im-proper'. But he has edited a text which is challenging, threatening, stimulating and unnerving. Do not look in it for simple answers to simple questions. It offers complexity of argument, subtleties of disputation and much of insight. As a text it keeps us from falling into the pit where nothing can be known. In it, while we certainly peer deep into an undecidable underworld, the book offers progress away from nihilism. It offers hope but not panaceas, thoughtfulness not cant, fundamentals not formulae. You will find here challenge not comfort.

Reference

Eco, U. (1989) *Foucault's Pendulum*, Secker & Warburg, London.

Gibson Burrell
Professor of Organizational Behaviour
Warwick Business School, University of Warwick

Acknowledgements

I would like to thank Gibson Burrell for his unremitting encouragement throughout this project and Alan B. Thomas who was kind enough to offer me plenty of useful comments that helped me improve the introductory essay. I would also like to thank Robert Cooper and the three anonymous reviewers commissioned by the publisher who made very constructive comments on the whole project. Finally, I would like to extend my thanks to the authors and publishers for their permission to reproduce the chapters and articles which follow.

Introduction: From social engineering to reflective action in organizational behaviour

Haridimos Tsoukas

What this book is about

This volume aims to introduce you to some of the latest thinking in organizational behaviour. It is not so much the desire to include fresh material, whose sell-by date is a few months or years away, that is the main motive for this book, but the message that aims to communicate. 'What is the message?' In a nutshell, it is the increasing appreciation of language and, thus, interpretation in the shaping of social reality (Morgan, 1986, 1993; Watzlawick, 1984; Weick, 1979). 'What has it got to do with management?' A lot. To the extent that management is a social activity, that is to say, it is an activity that involves the action of purposeful human beings, management is inescapably shaped by the ideas, meanings and interpretations that human beings have of themselves and of their surroundings.

'Fine, we already know that, but are you sure this is going to help me to understand organizations better and, thus, be a better manager?' True, we have known it since the classical Greeks first emphasized the importance of *logos* (reason, discourse, speech) in the conduct of human affairs, but we have been terribly slow to appreciate fully its consequences for organization and management. The kind of thinking that places *interpretation* right at the centre of management is relatively new and its consequences are important. Management is no longer seen, as the old thinking has it, as a mechanical activity undertaken by a few fully knowledgeable individuals who are concerned primarily with the control of an objective social reality. Instead, new thinking in organization theory conceives of management as an open-ended process of coordinating purposeful individuals whose actions stem from applying their unique interpretations to the particular situations confronting them. These actions give rise to often unintended and ambiguous circumstances, the meaning of which is open to further interpretations and further actions, and so on.

'That's pretty vague, isn't it?' Yes, it admittedly is, but don't be surprised or discouraged. Look at it like a text written in a foreign language which, although you speak to some extent, you are not fluent in yet – some parts of the text you can understand but others, at the moment, you can't. New thinking in organizational behaviour challenges commonly accepted assumptions and may occasionally appear, indeed, counter-intuitive or strange. As I aim to show you in this introduction its implications are important and liberating for it highlights the active human contribution into shaping the world around us.

I call the old thinking in organization theory *social engineering* for I want to draw attention to its mechanistic view of organization and management. By contrast, wishing to underscore the active construction of the social world by human beings, I use the term *reflective action* for the new thinking in organizational behaviour. The social engineering perspective emphasizes objectivity, detachment and control. I argue here that there is another way of looking at organization and management which is more realistic, humane and creative. The reflective action perspective, for which I argue here, and which permeates the work of all authors in this volume, highlights the intrinsic openness of organizations (which is based on a view of the latter as self-organized systems of distributed knowledge), underscores the constructed (enacted) nature of organizational phenomena, and it looks at the latter as being inherently ambiguous and in need of interpretation. *Openness, ambiguity, meaning* and *interpretation, narrative understanding, self-reflection, enactment* and *self-organization* are the key themes discussed in this book. I will try below to expand on each one of them and, thus, prepare the ground for a more detailed discussion of these themes by the authors themselves. If you can't wait to see what the collected papers are about, you may go straight to the last section of this introduction where you will find a guide to the papers. I would urge you, however, to read this introduction to the end for it will supply you with a basic understanding of the key concepts discussed in this book.

The social engineering image of organization and management – 'don't you just love being in control?'

Imagine that you are the governor of a prison and that you are particularly concerned to manage it in such a way as to minimize the likelihood of prisoners rioting. You know that law and order are values strongly upheld by the media and the population at large; you also know that although riots are relatively rare, when they do occur they tend to attract a lot of bad publicity.

The only time the media seem to be interested in what is going on in a prison is when things go wrong. Almost always they point the finger at the way the prison has been managed and blame those in charge for not preventing the riot in the first place. In our modern societies, you see, prevention is deeply valued; we don't like to be taken by surprise!

Wouldn't it be wonderful if you had a system to warn you whether and when your prisoners were going to riot, so that you could take preventive measures, rather than wait until a riot broke out and then quell it? Well, your dream may have come true, or so at least some psychologists would like us to believe! 'Prison officers and psychologists,' writes a reporter in *The Times* (26 March 1992), 'are working on a computer base that will carry data on the populations of individual prisons including details of prisoners' behaviour, their records of assault against staff and fellow inmates, and any escape attempts. Prison staff will be trained to observe inmates more systematically.'

The usefulness of such a system, as Quentin Miller, a senior psychologist at Whitemoor prion, explains in the same article, is that 'it will give us a measure of an individual's badness, if you like. If you have a certain number of individuals with a high score, what we would say is don't be surprised if you have trouble'. In other words, the computer will be able to warn you of the chance of an imminent riot, very much like a weather bulletin informs motorists of likely bad weather – remember that both motorists and prison officers do not like surprises!

Although this case may sound extreme, and indeed to some extent it is, it does capture the most salient feature of the traditional view of management. To manage is like being in a control room checking certain variables on a panel of instruments and pressing buttons or pulling levers in order to bring any deviating variables within their normal range of operation. This image of management, which I call here *social engineering*, has been fairly widespread not only in total institutions like prisons, but also, in a more palatable form of course, in business firms and government agencies (Vickers, 1983).

What exactly is the social engineering image of management? Simply put, it equates management with control. More specifically, it conceives of management as a regulatory process consisting of four elements (see Figure 1). First, objectives for the management of a social system or an organization (these two terms will be used interchangeably here) must be explicitly spelled out (in Figure 1, a social system is designated as a 'process'). Second, the outcome of managing must be measurable in terms which are consistent with the objectives. Third, the manager must have a predictive model of the social system under control specifying causes and effects. In case the outcome deviates from the objectives stated, such a model will tell managers the causes responsible for the deviations observed. And fourth, deviations will subsequently be reduced via taking corrective action (see also Vickers, 1983:36).

Managing a social system is a practical activity which is inextricably bound up with making two assumptions. First, assumptions about the nature of a

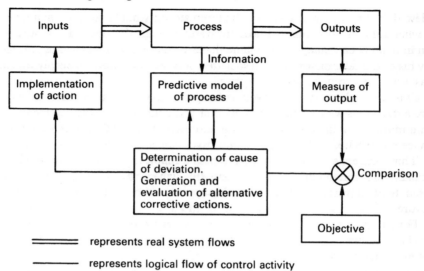

Figure 1   *The social engineering image of management. Source: Emmanuel and Otley, 1985:8*

social system as well as about the relationship between the latter and a manager. Second, assumptions about a manager's knowledge of a social system as well as about the types of knowledge that are desirable in assisting its management. In other words, managing presupposes answers to two fundamental questions: What are the salient properties of the social system I am supposed to manage? What do I need to know about this system, and how can I increase my knowledge of it so that I become more effective?

To these questions, those subscribing to the social engineering image are not short of providing answers. First, organizations are viewed as orderly entities by design. Indeed, most mainstream scholars in organizational behaviour concern themselves with designing organizations rationally so that their internal coherence and external match to their environments are both maximised (see, for example, Donaldson, 1985; Galbraith, 1977; Mintzberg, 1979). Organizational order is empirically manifested as a set of stable regularities which are linguistically expressed in the form of propositional statements. *If*, for example, prisoners appear to share certain features which, according to our experience in the past, are deemed to be conducive to anti-social behaviour, *then* rioting will probably occur. If one knows what these regularities are, one can attempt to influence them at will so that certain desirable outcomes accrue in the future (Cooper and Burrell, 1988).

Second, a social system is assumed to be independent of a manager and, thus, the relationship between the two is ignored or construed as *external*. A relationship between two social entities is regarded as external when it is viewed much like the relationship between an individual and a stone or a tree – what each one of them is or does is not affected by the other and, therefore, an individual can map faithfully the outside world in a way that is not affected by his or her relationship with it. What the system under regulation consists of (as well as information about the state in which it is), and the objectives which it aims to achieve (as well as information about how well it does achieve them), are either taken for granted or regarded as being imposed by the outside world in a manner that is independent from individuals' beliefs and interpretations (Vickers, 1983:39–42).

Third, the orderly nature of social systems enables a manager to accumulate explanatory and predictive knowledge about them. Such knowledge can be used to steer them towards the achievement of desirable objectives in the future.

Fourth, knowledge about organizations is reliable and, therefore, can be trusted only if it is, ideally, scientific knowledge, that is knowledge that has been formally produced according to the classical canons of the scientific method. Lay knowledge, obtained in the course of one's organizational and social lives, is not to be taken seriously and ought, ideally, to be replaced by formal knowledge (see Robbins, 1989:4). Thus, organizational behaviour, broadly understood as the discipline of the social sciences concerned with the human side of organization and management, is supposed to search for the regularities exhibited by social systems, establish their validity and codify them in the form of rules (that is, 'if, then' statements) which managers would then be able to put into practice with confidence (Thompson, 1956; Lupton, 1983).

The trouble with social engineering

The social engineering image of management is not necessarily wrong but it is heavily one-sided. It is certainly true that organizations are replete with patterns and regularities (see Berger and Luckmann, 1966). Can you imagine what would happen if a bank treated each and every one of its clients as an absolutely unique case for whom different procedures had to be set up and different policies had to apply? It would be madness! It is also true that organizations have a certain solidity which is relatively independent (but only *relatively*!) of what individuals think of them. If I begin thinking and, therefore, behaving towards my bank differently than before, the bank is not necessarily going to change its lending policies because of me. No, organizations are relatively enduring entities constructed to ensure predictability and the occurrence of certain events time and again. That is their strength but also their weakness!

All this is true but only in so far as it goes. There is another side to organizations and their management which remains untouched by the social-engineering image. The other side is that there is an *internal* relationship between a knowing manager and the system he or she manages, which messes things up: the models through which one views the world are not mere mirrors upon which the world is passively reflected but, in an important sense, our models also help *constitute* the world we experience (Beer, 1973; Watzlawick, 1984; Taylor, 1985). This may sound unrevealing, so let me illustrate it with an example.

Every year, beginning in 1993, each local authority in the UK has to publish in the local press 152 performance indicators covering a variety of issues of local concern, from how accessible public buildings are to people in wheelchairs to the number of potholes in their area. The Audit Commission will collate the information nationally and produce a national league table. Allowing citizens to compare the indicators over time and across the country, the objective of this exercise is to make councils' performance transparent and, thus, offer them an incentive to improve their services. The idea is that an informed electorate would be able to use their votes to reprimand under-performing councils (see *The Economist*, 19 September 1992).

So far so good, but what is underestimated in exercises of this kind is precisely the internal relationship between a policy-maker's view of a social system and the latter's behaviour. Indicators are supposed to reflect and reveal a true and objective reality (i.e. councils' performance). But what is often ignored is that the very same reality is crucially shaped by the indicators. Sounds strange? Maybe, but that's how it is in real life. Councils, you see, are bound to want to look good in the league table, for how else can local politicians confront the criticism of their opponents – numbers matter in politics! Wanting to look good in the league table, councils may thus choose to abandon sensible policies if they think that they do not give councils enough of a high profile, opting instead for policies which will enhance a council's standing in the league table.

Imagine, for example, the case of a council in which elderly residents would rather have a deep freeze and a microwave than have their food delivered to them daily by home helps. 'If the authority responds to what people want and cuts down on home helps it will look terrible in the league table which merely asks how many home helps there are per thousand of the population. It could be tempted to abandon its policy and hire more home helps simply for the sake of appearances' (Margaret Hodge, vice-chairman of the Association of Metropolitan Authorities quoted in *The Independent*, 11 September 1992).

Reflecting on this example (and several others like it) one is alarmed by the realization that, quite often, systems formally set up to serve laudable objectives may end up doing more harm than good – the solution often becomes the problem (Watzlawick *et al.*, 1974)! In their desire to map social reality for the purpose of influencing it at will, social engineers end up erecting systems of bureaucratic regulation which are in constant oscillation and are permeated by paradoxes (more about this in a moment).

Notice the internal relationship between the social engineering model of a social system and the nature of the system itself: the regularities in the latter are captured via propositional statements ('if, then' statements) which are then translated into explicit rules of action, and vice versa. In other words, the more we hold a propositional model of knowledge about the functioning of a social system, the more the latter's functioning will be formulated in terms of explicit bureaucratic rules, and vice versa. The more, in turn, this loop is in operation the more the management of a social system will be oscillatory (Beer, 1966, 1973; Clemson, 1984). The reason is, as Bateson (1979:63) explained, that the 'if, then' of causality contains time, but the 'if, then' of propositional statements is timeless. The application of timeless propositional logic to time-dependent phenomena leads to paradoxes. Let me explain this point in a little more detail.

Let us return to our example of local authorities? The more elderly residents demand a bespoken solution to their demands for daily food the more a council is likely to respond by using home helps (that is, by not meeting their demands). In other words, if the elderly residents' demands are met, then they are not 'met'; if they are 'met', then they are not met! When time is introduced, the paradox turns into an oscillation. This paradox is created because of a confusion of logical levels induced by timeless propositional logic. One logical level is that of the elderly residents' *real* demands (that is, what *they* want: a deep freeze and a microwave). A logically higher level is that of elderly residents' demands as these are *represented* by (or reduced to) a standardized indicator: home helps per thousand of the population. Collapsing one level into the other, that is to say conflating meeting elderly residents' demands with 'meeting' their demands as the league table prescribes (which is what the social engineering image of management and the concomitant bureaucratic regulation do), creates paradoxes, and makes the management of a system oscillatory.

The problem with oscillatory management is similar to that of trying to regulate the temperature of a room via a thermostat (Clemson, 1984:109). Suppose, for example, that it takes one minute to heat a room by one degree. Suppose also that it takes the thermostat in the room five minutes to transmit the signal that the room was adequately warm, and the heating should stop. Under these conditions, the room would get at least five degrees too hot before the heating stopped. If you open the windows to cool the place down, it would again take at least five minutes before the thermostat switched the heating on, by which time it would be too cold.

A system that is in oscillation cannot be managed effectively, it is never quite right: it sways between extreme positions. What is even more important is that such a social system leads eventually to the management of problematic 'solutions' (i.e. managing league tables) instead of the management of the original problems which the system was set up to deal with (i.e. managing the problem of helping elderly residents). Pushing the logic of the social engineering image to the extreme, management becomes tantamount to keeping up appearances and fighting shadows: managing *via* league tables leads to managing *the* league tables themselves! (See Chapter 3.)

Social systems are different: from social engineering to reflective action

By identifying organizations with stable regularities manifested *in* organizations, the social engineering image *reduces* the complexity and wholeness of organizations to a set of dimensions about which propositional knowledge can be generated (see Chapter 1). However, as several researchers have shown (Payne 1975; Starbuck, 1982, 1985; Webster and Starbuck, 1988) knowledge that has captured stable regularities in organizations across time and space is at best tentative, fragmented and unrevealing, while at worst it simply does not exist. Why is this so? The answer may be found in that social systems have certain specific (*sui generis*) features which social engineers tend to ignore or underestimate. These features are: openness; concept-dependence; self-reflection; ambiguity; and self-organization. Taken together they imply that management is a social activity that consists of interpretation, narrative understanding, enacting organization and recognizing patterns. In this section I will discuss and illustrate each one of these themes at some length.

The impossibility of closure

Social systems are intrinsically *open* – not in the traditional sense that they interact with their environments (that in itself is not terribly illuminating), but in the sense that it is impossible to obtain stable regularities across space and time. Regularities are generated by repeated individual actions (namely, acting similarly in similar circumstances) and are possible only within closed systems. For closure to occur the following two conditions must be met (Sayer, 1984; Tsoukas, 1992).

First, the mechanisms (that is, individual actions) producing regularities must not undergo qualitative change (this is the intrinsic condition of closure). And second, the relationship between mechanisms and the external conditions that matter for their operation must remain constant (this is the extrinsic condition of closure). To the extent that individuals' meanings, interpretations and models differ across contexts, and change over time, social systems violate both conditions of closure. Individuals have the potential of learning and developing – indeed they have to learn and develop if they are to be effective (see Chapter 1), thus violating the intrinsic condition for closure.

We understand social events and comprehend experiences only when we are able to locate them within a familiar context. Raising my hand, for example, is an act of voting, a sign of greeting, a manifestation of anger, or a symbol of worshipping depending on the context within which it happens. The physiological act itself is rather meaningless and possibly uninteresting. What matters is the intentions that are manifested through it, which are identified via understanding the context of action. Given, therefore, that individuals' actions are essentially context-dependent and that contexts change in ways that are not always predictable or even intelligible, the extrinsic condition of closure is also violated.

IBM's current plight is a good case to illustrate this point. The company that set the standards in the market for personal computers and, for most of the 1980s, was the biggest PC maker, eventually failed to adjust to a state of affairs that it had *itself* helped to generate. The actions of competitors, technological advances and changes in the behaviour of customers throughout the 1980s (over which IBM could not have had effective control), all gave rise to a new context in which earlier policies, no matter how successful they had been, were no longer appropriate (see *The Economist*, 16 January 1993, pp. 18–19 and 23–25). The same old policies in a new context acquire new significance and result in different effectiveness.

The concept-dependent character of social systems

As well as social systems being intrinsically open they are also concept-dependent (or as some philosophers put it, they are linguistically constructed). What this means is that unlike most natural systems, social systems do not have an existence independent of human beings, but are (in part at least) what they are because of the particular ways human communities define them. As Taylor (1985:34) observed: 'The language is constitutive of the reality, is essential to its being the kind of reality it is.'

Imagine, for example, that you were a manager of a manufacturing company in the USA around the beginning of this century. What notion of management do you think you would probably have? What would managing mean to you? Considering the context of ideas and ways of thinking that were dominant at that time, managing would probably mean a set of activities concerned with maximizing the efficiency of the workplace through the relentless control of subordinates via rewards and punishments. Like F. W. Taylor (1911), you would probably have viewed workers as anthropoid automata performing entirely mechanical tasks which should be carried out in an optimal manner. Production at all costs would probably have been your credo!

I bet that what you would see when looking at people performing manual work some ninety years ago would be very different from what you would see today. It is not only that the technology and methods of production have changed remarkably in most industries, but more fundamentally (and ironically, less perceptibly), *we* as society have changed. Partly as a result of our hitherto experiences of management, and partly because of a host of other social and intellectual changes that we have seen in the twentieth century, we now use a different vocabulary to describe what management consists of. We have come, for example, to appreciate the meaningful character of work and the importance of symbols. We begun to see the workplace as consisting of loops of relationships and feedback mechanisms (with all the unpredictability these imply) rather than solid events and fixed objects. We also begun to conceive of organizations not as unitary entities but as coalitions of diverse interests, and so on (Morgan, 1986). Thus it turns out that to the extent our language is different today, the practice of management is also different as a result (see also Chapter 3).

The manner in which different languages constitute different realities can also be seen if one looks at the 'same' phenomenon across different societal contexts. What an organization *is* depends to a large extent on what an organization *does* in the socioeconomic and cultural contexts in which it is embedded. In a socioeconomic system such as, for example, communism, firms were conceived as instruments of the State, thereby serving explicit political, ideological, and moral functions which are usually unknown in most market economies (Tsoukas, 1994). Similarly, while 'authority' in most Western industrial countries is primarily defined in legal–rational terms, 'authority' in, say, Hong Kong and Taiwan is quite a different phenomenon (meaning that it is based on different assumptions and has different implications) for it is primarily defined in moral, Confucian terms (Whitley, 1992).

Ambiguity, interpretation and narrative understanding

If the meaning of aspects of organizational life depends on the context in which they are located it follows that, placed in different contexts, the 'same' aspects acquire different meanings. Put differently, events, processes and experiences in organizations are rarely transparent, self-evident or completely fixed, but are intrinsically *ambiguous* and, therefore, open-ended in the interpretations that can be attached to them. Indeed, as Feldman (1991:146) observed: 'Ambiguity occurs when there is no clear interpretation of a phenomenon or set of events. It is different from uncertainty in that it cannot be clarified by gathering more facts. The facts that are, or could be, available support more than one interpretation.' (See also Chapters 3, 5 and 6.)

Consider, for example, Morgan's article in Part One of this volume. In it Morgan recounts the events that led to the failure of a senior mechanic to meet certain crucial quality standards in a product he was working on, and his subsequent dismissal by his boss. There is nothing exceptional in this account *per se*: events of this kind are pretty common in business organizations. What Morgan masterfully does, however, is demonstrate how such an unexceptional outcome (i.e. the mechanic's dismissal) turns out to be sufficiently ambiguous when one attempts to explain it. Approached from a variety of different angles one discovers different reasons for it happening.

At the organizational level of analysis, there are four sources of ambiguity: organizations are often unclear what their intentions are; they do not know unequivocally what is appropriate for them to do; they are usually unable to identify exactly what they did in the past and why; and it is not always clear who in the organization is responsible for what (March and Olsen, 1976; Feldman, 1991). Obviously, organizational ambiguity is a matter of degree. Those responsible for making strategic decisions are typically faced with higher ambiguity than those who are involved in routine, low level decisions. Moreover, organizations that process non-human objects are permeated by less ambiguity than organizations that 'process' human beings (e.g. hospitals, schools, prisons, etc.). It is easier and clearer to make a car than to educate people. In the former case we have a more or less reliable technology for achieving a relatively clear (although not fixed) objective, whereas in the latter case we, as society, *keep changing our minds* both about what is the purpose of education (e.g. is it to encourage pupils to know themselves or to impart to them a body of given knowledge?) and about what is the best way of realizing it (e.g. should there be nationwide standardized exams or is it better to leave assessment to the initiative of teachers?).

However, ambiguity can never be eliminated altogether. This is due mainly to the open-ended and concept-dependent character of social systems: the human capacity for self-reflection and reinterpretation, and thus for *novel* action, imply that one cannot offer a fixed description of a social system. There will always be an ineradicable *indeterminacy* in what the action of (or in) a social system is about and where it leads to. As Vickers (1983:43) remarked: 'In so far as [a practitioner's] actions are directed to other human agents, as they almost all are, they carry a load of meaning greater than their overt content.' The rise and recent decline of IBM helps illustrate this point pretty well (see *The Economist*, 16 January 1993, pp. 23–25).

IBM's entry into the personal computer market was viewed by the company as an undoubtedly sensible move at the time and, indeed, it was. IBM had originally thought PCs would actually boost the demand for its mainframes because it believed its customers would like to have the two connected. Alas, that is not how the market reacted! IBM's action may have been intelligent from a technical-cum-commercial point of view (what Vickers calls 'the overt content' of actions), but it inevitably had other aspects (in Vickers' terms, it carried a 'greater load of meaning') which were interpreted by the market in ways IBM had not thought of. The entry into the PC market, for instance, *legitimized* the PC for thousands of big companies that previously had been wary of them (see *The Economist,* 16 January 1993, p. 24). Consequently, several ripples (not all of them intended by IBM) followed the initial move into the PC market. The market exploded and IBM became the biggest PC maker while, ironically at the same time, demand for PCs began to undercut the demand for its mainframes and, naturally, attracted by the phenomenal success of the PC and the relatively low barriers to entry, new competitors made their appearance. The corporation that in 1985 looked invincible, in 1993 announced the biggest annual corporate loss ever recorded!

Ambiguity is inextricably bound with narrative sense making. Applying to the same set of events a variety of plausible interpretations, an inquirer attempts to build a convincing narrative (a story) which will attempt to show the coherence between the actions of the individuals involved and the meaning of the situation for them (Taylor, 1985; Ricouer, 1991). Moreover, making sense of organizational events in a narrative manner preserves their contextuality and draws upon both relevant organizational rules and on relevant past experiences in the form of stories shared by a community of practitioners (see Chapters 8, 11 and 13).

In their discussion of the role of directive documentation (i.e. machine manuals) in helping service technicians, Brown and Duguid (Chapter 9) observe that the machine manuals issued to service technicians contain an abstract image of their practice which is only remotely related to the informal practices technicians frequently employ to deal with a variety of local problems. For the designers of photocopier manuals, for example, a 'broken machine' is of central importance and manuals contain rules for repairing such a fixed entity. Repairing a machine, however, occurs in an open social context, the details of which cannot be exhaustively known *ex ante* to designers. Although certain rules can certainly be established and codified ('If this error is displayed then check this, or do that'), it does not mean that such rules can be exhaustive or even adequately descriptive. The technician, for example, needs to fix not only the machine but also the dissatisfied customer. He/she also strives not to lose the customer's trust in him/her as well as to maintain his/her reputation in the community of technicians. Stories of best practice or of particularly awkward problems shared by the community of technicians help preserve collective memory, and facilitate coping with the open-ended and local character of practical problems.

The organization is in the mind: enacting organizational reality

We usually think of organizations as static, fixed entities. Try for a moment to think of them in terms of processes of *organizing* – the processes that transform haphazard collections of individuals into organized entities. Understood this way, an organization can be seen as an *emergent* phenomenon: it emerges from the coherent and constrained interaction of several individuals. Weick's (1977, 1979) work has been enormously important in directing attention to the cognitive processes by which organization is formed. For him an 'organization' is not a given, objective structure confronting an equally given and objective entity called the 'environment' to which it ought to adapt in a rational manner. Although 'organizations' and 'environments' can be said to exist independently of individual beliefs and interpretations, this is only one side of the coin. The other side is that they are subjectively constructed entities which may change once individuals' understandings and interpretations change: it is individuals within organizations that *interpret* whatever they think their environments consists of and act upon their interpretations (see Part Four).

Individuals try to make sense of their environments (or, in Weick's terms, to reduce equivocality) and in so doing they undertake routine, habitual actions (Weick calls this stage *enactment*) the results of which they subsequently confront as their 'environment' and they seek to understand through *reflection*. In other words, individuals in organizations grapple with problems of their own making. Reflecting on their enacted environment, individuals try to identify systematic covariations among the variables that make it up. Such knowledge is *retained* in their minds in the form of causal maps indicating the variables that are crucial for carrying out their tasks and how they are interconnected. Through sustained interaction, individuals interlock their behaviour over time and in so doing they deal with residual equivocality, which they seek to remove through negotiating a consensus about their common task and how it ought to be handled. Individual causal maps, thus, converge and a group of individuals can then be said to have become organized. In other words, organization is the outcome of a process of sense making through which equivocality (ambiguity) is progressively removed and causal clarity is increased. For something to be said to be organized it implies that it is made sense of.

Thus for Weick, organization begins with individuals *first* enacting their environment which they *subsequently* seek to understand through reflection. Reflection, namely chopping experiences into meaningful chunks, labelling them and connecting them, removes equivocality from individuals' interaction, and this leads them to form a relatively homogeneous view of their task and how it ought to be carried out. At the stage of enactment, individual activities are partly blind: there is no prior knowledge about how they will fit the final outcome since it is not clear what the final outcome will look like. Individuals act according to the local knowledge they alone possess, and within the limits of the received knowledge by which they are constituted. In this sense, organizations are irremediably open systems within which chance events and quasi-blind actions are not only possible but inevitable. Sense making (and thus organization) gradually forms as a result of the 'raw data' generated by the quasi-blind process of enactment being plastically controlled (i.e. chopped and connected) by reflection.

Let us illustrate this process of enacting organization with an example of how a group of musicians become gradually organized to form an orchestra. Weick's (1977:291–2) account is very helpful and is worth quoting here in full:

> There are numerous sources of equivocality when new music is rehearsed. The music itself is equivocal because it is unknown, it contains some amount of musical complexity, it contains certain amounts of calculated or intentional disorder, many of its performance characteristics (such as the tempo where it plays well) have to be established, it is equivocal relative to the style in which the band prefers to play, and the tune shows a greater or lesser departure from convention in music. These and other questions are what an orchestra tries to resolve when it rehearses.
>
> The environment that the orchestra members face is not simply the composition placed in front of them, but rather what they do with the composition when they play it through for the first time. The musicians don't react to an environment, they *enact* the environment. In the credibility study the enacted environment available to the musicians after their first play was an undifferentiated 'soup'. As observers, we might label this soup with nouns such as 'sounds', 'tempos', 'themes', 'shadings' and 'errors'. The first play-through of the composition could be made sensible by participants in a variety of ways. The crucial point is that the play-through, not the sheets of music, was the environment the musicians tried to make sensible.
>
> Once musicians enact an environment, they then punctuate or break that environment into discrete events that are available for relating (e.g. 'those twelve notes are thrilling', 'those six bars are impossible', 'that portion is ugly', 'the notes are hard to read', 'the tempo at which we start seems to be crucial'). Essentially, the musicians punctuate the stream of enacted music into reasonable nouns and then try to relate or connect the nouns in a reasonable manner . . . . Once a musician parses the stream of experience into a set of variables, he is able to make the inference that some of these punctuated variables co-vary . . . . It is crucial to note that this act of connection is based on the experience of recurrent co-movement among the variables of interest and takes place in the mind of an individual participant. In a like manner, the organization is in the mind.

Order without design: self-organization

As well as being emergent, organization is also a very complex phenomenon. Its complexity (or variety), measured by the number of distinguishable states it is capable of having, is phenomenal and well beyond the conscious control of any individual. By way of illustration, consider Figure 2 (Beer, 1966:246–252) in which seven dissimilar parts are systematically connected. Moreover, each relationship has a switch capable of having two states: on and off. The switches make this pattern a *system*, namely a coherent, patterned and

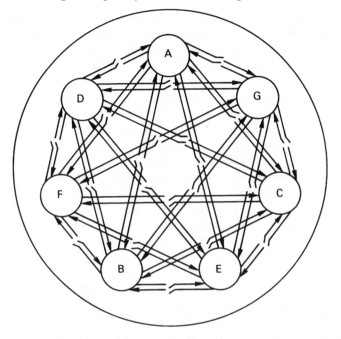

Figure 2 *Variety in a mechanical, dynamic system. Source: Beer, 1966, 251*

purposive entity that *does* things (i.e. its switches go on and off). The elements of such a system are the states the system is capable of having. Given that there are forty-two lines in it, a little mathematical calculation reveals that the number of distinguishable states is 2^{42} – well above one trillion!

We assumed in this exercise that the system was merely a mechanical one. The variability of each one of its elements was both limited and well known in advance – each one of the forty-two inter-connected switches was capable of having only two positions. We were also able to offer a description of the system which was independent of the observer – whoever undertook this exercise would come up with the same answer.

Imagine now the variety likely to be found in a system that includes human beings. Although rules and regulations help circumscribe the variability of each individual, the fact remains that the latter's repertoire of potential responses (which is the human analogue of the states of a switch) is very large indeed. If nothing else, an individual's 'reading' of a shared reality is bound to depend on how he or she experiences it. What is even more important is that, due to self-reflection and potential reinterpretation, it is impossible to know in advance the entire range of responses an individual is capable of. Moreover, as we saw in the example of the local authorities, the internal relationship between a knowing manager and the system he or she manages influences what the system does. If all the above are accepted, it may be concluded that the number of distinguishable states in an organization (i.e. its variety) is not only colossal, but also, as Hayek (1982:14–15) observed, it is inherently impossible to assemble as a surveyable whole all the data which make up its variety.

Organizations, therefore, are distributed knowledge systems, whose effective action is the result not so much of individuals acquiring more and more knowledge as of finding ways of *utilizing* widely distributed organizational knowledge. Thus the question of managing an intrinsically open-ended, concept-dependent, and self-reflective social entity leads on to the question of how one can undertake deliberate action without possessing all the requisite knowledge. Endlessly proliferating organizational variety can be controlled only if it is matched by an organizational design which possesses the capability of utilizing highly dispersed knowledge. This is, in effect, the law of requisite variety developed by Ashby (1956), which can also be stated, more simply, as follows: only variety can destroy variety (see also Chapter 8).

Utilizing organizational knowledge not possessed by anyone in its entirety implies that individuals adapt themselves to circumstances which directly affect, or are appreciated by, only them (Hayek, 1982). Thus, the requisite variety of an organization is enhanced through the intrinsic capacity of its members for self-organization. An organization is a 'spontaneous order' (Hayek, 1982: Chapter 2) which, without precise instructions from a central command, can enact novel responses to hitherto unknown stimuli. The output of an organization (namely its unique pattern of actions over time) is not programmed in advance, but it *emerges* as an interaction between the rules followed by organizational members and the latter's response to the particular conditions each one of them finds himself or herself in.

Thus, to return to an earlier example, the pattern of responses of the photocopier service technicians emerges as they try to repair machine breakdowns in open-ended social contexts in which a unique configuration of local contingencies is bound to exist. The machine is broken now, but it may also have had a history of breakdowns which the technician ought to investigate. The customer complains and, while it is not the first time they do so, it may be that their handling of the machine has had something to do with the machine's breakdown – the technician must also investigate this possibility. The technician's employer is concerned to preserve their image of high quality service, and the technician must show that he or she adheres to the same aims. The list of local contingencies can, of course, go on and on.

It is noteworthy that only the technicians themselves can have specific knowledge of the local context in which their work takes place. They clearly apply certain rules in their actions to put the problems right, but in a perennially incomplete and experimental way – they read the situation, try to form coherent interpretations of it, undertake action, observe the results, try afresh, and so on (see Chapter 13 for a brilliant description of this process; see also Schön, 1983). A coherent pattern of problem solving eventually emerges which was not designed by anyone in advance, but represents the technician's attempts to adapt to particular circumstances, unknown in their totality to anyone but to the individual technician.

Mintzberg and Waters (see Chapter 10) make a similar point about the process of strategy making in organizations. Strategies, they argue, are patterns of actions that emerge in a manner that is usually beyond an organization's rational control. In the 1950s, for example, the National Film Board of Canada found itself pursuing a strategy of making films for television which it did not consciously choose. A film-maker had set a precedent by making a film for television and many of his colleagues followed suit. A stream of actions thus emerged which was followed for about a decade.

Similarly, 3M found itself producing millions of one of its best known products, the Post-it notepads, but the idea for this product came about in a serendipitous way. Arthur Fry, a scientist working for 3M, needed a sticky, yet easily removable, note to mark the pages in his book of religious hymns while singing in a choir. The Post-it notepad emerged as a result of the interaction between 3M's technical competence on flat products and the context of experimentation that the company had institutionalized on the one hand, with the particular circumstances and experiences facing one of the company's employees (see also Peters and Waterman, 1982).

A guide to the papers

Part One presents several conceptual frameworks for understanding organizations. The basic premise underlying both papers is simple: we understand a phenomenon better when we are able to describe it from several different angles. Gharajedaghi and Ackoff discuss three ways of looking at organizations: as mechanisms; as organisms; and as social systems. Although all of them are valuable, it is only the latter, the authors argue, that does justice to the specific features of organizations, namely their constitution through language, meaning and human freedom. Morgan offers the reader a brief but effective introduction to his pioneering approach to analyzing organizations in terms of different metaphors. In a short case study he shows the depth of what otherwise seem to be fairly simple organizational phenomena, such as the dismissal of a senior mechanic. The more perspectives and metaphors one brings to the analysis of a situation, Morgan argues, the more meaning one discovers and, thus, the more skilful one is at 'reading' and acting in a situation.

Building on the implicit theme of ambiguity and the explicit need for practitioners to be effective interpreters that underlie Part One, the papers in Part Two move the discussion from the level of individual interpretations for making sense of ambiguous situations to the organizational level at which ambiguity and interpretation are also located. Probably more than anyone else, March has done much to bring to our attention the organizational sources of ambiguity. Although his paper here provides, in effect, an accessible summary of most of his work, he particularly underscores the fact that the traditional emphasis on clear goals and on the rational evaluation of alternatives, that has underpinned most work on decision making, underestimates the irreducible ambiguity of goals and intentions in organizations. Organizational ambiguity makes instrumental action far less effective than is conventionally assumed. Instead, much of management, March argues, is symbolic – a way of interpreting organizational life that allows individuals to place their experiences in a meaningful context. Daft and Weick similarly argue that organizations are interpretation systems which differ in the way they understand themselves and their environments and, thus, differ in the kind of information they collect and how they interpret it. The authors suggest an enlightening typology in which four distinct types of 'organizations-as-interpretation-systems' are described.

In Part Three the symbolic texture of organizing is explored. Organizations are viewed as webs of meaning located within wider webs of meaning. Meyerson and Martin address the first part of the equation – organizations are described as cultures and three different perspectives are reviewed. Organizational culture may be viewed as a monolithic entity, as a set of monolithic subcultures or as a very loose context that embodies ambiguities. The last perspective makes a fruitful connection with the papers in Part Two. Locating organization within a wider web of society-based meanings, Bolman and Deal offer a fascinating analysis of how organizations are concerned with legitimacy and how, therefore, they adopt the symbols and meanings of the wider society in their structures as a way of enhancing the chances of their survival. The organization is, effectively, like theatre – key members play to the popular orthodoxies and beliefs of their time and context, and reproduce them in their practices. Organizations, in other words, are structured the way they are because of the way the wider society expects them to be.

The circularity of organizational behaviour that is implicit in Bolman and Deal's macroanalysis (organizations reproduce the beliefs of the wider society and in so doing help perpetuate them) is the key theme of Part Four. Focusing on the microprocesses which give rise to organization, it is the basic premise of both papers here that the key concepts of 'organization' and 'environment' should not be understood as external, objective, fixed entities but rather as subjective constructions that are enacted by the coherent and constrained interaction of purposeful human beings. Drawing on the biological concept of autopoiesis (self-production, self-making), Morgan illustrates wonderfully how individuals in organizations deal with the outside world in terms of how *they* understand it, not in terms of how the world allegedly is. Interfacing with the 'environment' is not like confronting an independent, external entity, but a process whereby an organization creates opportunities for understanding itself, and in so doing it shapes its links with other organizations in its own image. Like individual action, organizational action is never purely instrumental – it is also like a display or a mirror at which organizations look to find out what they are. Weick's account of organizing is similar. The organization, he argues, is the outcome of a process originating with routine actions which are subsequently reflected upon and turned into meaningful information. The latter consists of systematically co-varied (i.e. organized) variables that make up an individual's experience of a situation. Weick illustrates this process by looking at how air-traffic controllers do their job. His account also includes a discussion of ambiguity (or, in his terms, equivocality) and self-organization.

The topic of self-organization is an important theme (although it is mostly implicit) in the papers included in Part Five. Self-organization is possible, even inevitable, because organizational knowledge is widely distributed. Rules in an organization are never enough to tackle problems, as Brown and Duguid elegantly show in their discussion of the work of photocopier service technicians. Technicians can tackle machine breakdowns only if they go beyond the rules of the organization to take account of (and thus interpret) the configuration of local contingencies of which only they, being on the front line, are aware. Unless technicians can do that organizational action will be pretty ineffective. This is a rich paper whose analysis also deals with the process of enactment, the role of ambiguity and the need for practitioners to build plausible narratives (interpretations) around the problems they encounter drawing on a variety of stories they share with fellow technicians. Mintzberg and Waters' paper has been very influential in reconsidering the concept of strategy. The authors describe eight different ways in which business strategies form. The gist of their argument is that, to a greater or lesser extent, most strategies are irreducibly emergent. More generally, the order one finds in organizations is only partly intended (namely, shaped by central direction). Organizations are compelled to act without full information or understanding and, thus, their actions are bound to be different from their plans. Organizations are open systems in which effective action is based on knowledge that is not possessed in its entirety by anyone. What is important, Mintzberg and Waters argue, is for managers to be able to recognize and shape patterns. Since things cannot be controlled from the centre, managers can at least turn the inherent openness of organizational life to their advantage by recognizing emergent strategies (patterns never intended), learning from them, and formalizing them when appropriate.

In Part Six the implications of the new thinking in organizational behaviour and management are outlined. What does it mean to be a reflective manager? Weick argues convincingly that reflective practitioners understand that their maps of the territory are only artefacts to aid understanding and not the territory itself. Don't be bewitched by your models, he seems to be saying –

develop the ability to construct and hold different accounts of a situation in your mind. Insisting on rational thinking at all costs is itself irrational. Reality is always more complex than we think – play with it, experiment with it, act. Schön's brilliant analysis defines reflective action as an experimental activity. Reflective practitioners first bring to a situation spontaneous, routinized responses. Almost invariably, routinized responses produce a surprise which gets their attention. Surprise leads to reflection and critical inquiry, which in turn gives rise to experimentation. Further action is undertaken and the whole cycle is activated again. Vargish, in his provocative paper, makes the point that practical action without an ethical dimension is unthinkable. Morality is deeply involved in what we do, irrespective of whether we like it or not. Humanities and the arts, claims Vargish, can help practitioners grapple with broader questions of human existence which tend to be obscured by the instrumental logic of bureaucratic organization. Thinking about values and moral issues is less served by participating in courses on business ethics (a typically bureaucratic response to a very important issue) and more by practitioners cultivating the habit of critical reflection and interpretation through their acquaintance with the major works of art and literature.

A final word. In my experience few people these days read a book of this kind from cover to cover. That isn't necessarily bad. Without loss, your point of entry into this volume may be anywhere you like. Although the book has a linear structure, the themes it covers form a *network* which can be traversed in any direction one likes. All papers are rich, elegantly written, and several of them make references to each other. What is important, of course, is what connections *you* make between these themes. This introduction and the organization of the material reflect my understanding of what these connections are. However, as I argued earlier, meaning is inherently open-ended; it depends on how a message is experienced by the recipient – in this case you. Having read the preceding summary of the papers and/or depending on your interests and mood you may start with any paper you choose. You may then begin your trip around the network exploring more and more nodes and, who knows, you may find that you have read the entire book! *Bon voyage!*

References

Ashby, R. (1956) *An Introduction to Cybernetics*, Chapman & Hall, London.
Beer, S. (1966) *Decision and Control*, J. Wiley & Sons, Chichester.
Beer, S. (1973) The surrogate world we manage, *Behavioral Science*, **18**, 198–209.
Bateson, G. (1979) *Mind and Nature*, Bantam Books, New York.
Berger, P. and Luckmann, T. (1966) *The Social Construction of Reality*, Penguin, London.

Clemson, B. (1984) *Cybernetics*, Abacus, Cambridge, MA.

Cooper, R. and Burrell, G. (1988) Modernism, postmodernism and organizational analysis. An introduction. *Organization Studies*, **9**, 91–112.

Donaldson, L. (1985) *In Defence of Organization Theory*, Cambridge University Press, Cambridge.

Emmanuel, C. and Otley, C. (1985) *Accounting for Management Control*, Van Nostrand Reinhold, Wokingham.

Feldman, M. (1991) The meanings of ambiguity: Learning from stories and metaphors. In P. Frost, L. Moore, M. R. Louis, C. Lundberg, and J. Martin (eds), *Reframing Organizational Culture*, Sage, Newbury Park, California, pp. 145–156.

Galbraith, J. R. (1977) *Organization Design*, Addison-Wesley, Reading, Mass.

Hayek, F. A. (1982) *Law, Legislation and Liberty*, Routledge & Kegan Paul, London.

Lupton, T. (1983) *Management and the Social Sciences* (3rd edn), Penguin, London.

March, J. G.and Olsen, J. P. (1976) *Ambiguity and Choice in Organizations*, Universitesforlaget, Bergen, Norway.

Mintzberg, H. (1979) *The Structuring of Organizations*, Prentice-Hall, Englewood Cliffs, NJ.

Morgan, G. (1986) *Images of Organization*, Sage, London.

Morgan, G. (1993) *Imaginization*, Sage, Newbury Park, California.

Payne, R. (1975) Truisms in organizational behaviour. *Interpersonal Development*, **6**, 203–220.

Peters, T. and Waterman, R. (1982) *In Search of Excellence*, Harper & Row, London.

Ricouer, P. (1991) *From Text to Reality: Essays in Hermeneutics, II* (Translation: K. Blamey and J. B. Thompson.). The Athlone Press, London.

Robbins, S. (1989) *Organizational Behavior* (4th edn), Prentice-Hall, Englewood Cliffs, NJ.

Sayer, A. (1984) *Method in Social Science*, Hutchinson, London.

Schon, D. (1983) *The Reflective Practitioner*, Avebury, Aldershot.

Starbuck, W. H. (1982) Congealing oil: Inventing ideologies to justify acting ideologies out. *Journal of Management Studies*, **19**, 3–27.

Starbuck, W. H. (1985) Acting first and thinking later: Theory versus reality in strategic change. In J. Pennings and Associates (eds), *Organizational Strategy and Change*, Jossey-Bass, San Francisco, pp. 336–372.

Taylor, C. (1985) *Philosophy and the Human Sciences: Philosophical Papers* (vol. 2), Cambridge University Press, Cambridge.

Taylor, F. W. (1911) *Principles of Scientific Management*, Harper & Row, New York.

Thomas, A. B. (1993) *Controversies in Management*, Routledge, London.

Thompson, J. D. (1956) On building an administrative science. *Administrative Science Quarterly*, **1**, 102–111.

Tsoukas, H. (1992) The relativity of organizing: Its knowledge presuppositions and its pedagogical implications for comparative management. *Journal of Management Education*, **16**, Special Issue S147–S162.

Tsoukas, H. (1994) Socio-economic systems and organisational management: An institutional perspective on the socialist firm, *Organization Studies*, **15**, in press.

Vickers, G. (1983) *The Art of Judgement*, Harper & Row, London.

Watzlawick, P. Weakland, J. and Fisch, R. (1974) *Change*, W. W. Norton, New York.

Watzlawick, P. (ed) (1984) *The Invented Reality*, W. W. Norton, New York.

Webster, J. and Starbuck, W. (1988) Theory building in industrial and organizational psychology. In C. Cooper and I. Robertson (eds) *International Review of Industrial and Organizational Psychology*, J. Wiley & Sons, London, pp. 93–138.

Weick, K.(1977) Enactment processes in organizations. In B. M. Staw and G. R. Salancik (eds), *New Directions in Organizational Behavior*, St Clair Press, Chicago, pp. 267–300.

Weick, K.(1979) *The Social Psychology of Organizing* (2nd edn), Addison-Wesley, Reading, Mass.

Whitley, R. (1992) *Business Systems in South East Asia*, Sage, London.

Part One

Of Maps and Territories: Frameworks for Understanding Organizations

---

Give me a place to stand and I shall turn the earth around.

Archimedes

1 Mechanisms, organisms and social systems

Jamshid Gharajedaghi and Russell L. Ackoff

We live in an age of accelerating change, increasing uncertainty and growing complexity. People are being pushed and pulled by forces that previously did not seem to be part of their environment. They respond by acquiring more information and knowledge, *but not understanding*. In fact, many futurists (e.g. Naisbitt, 1982) characterize the post-industrial era we are entering as an age of information or knowledge, not as an age of understanding. Information is *descriptive*; it is contained in answers to questions that begin with such words as *what, which, who, how many, when* and *where*. Knowledge is *instructive*; it is conveyed by answers to *how-to* questions. Understanding is *explanatory*; it is transmitted by answers to *why* questions. To understand a system is to be able to explain its properties and behaviour, and to reveal why it is what it is and why it behaves the way it does.

Information, knowledge and understanding form a hierarchy. Information presupposes neither knowledge nor understanding. Knowledge presupposes information and understanding presupposes both. One can survive without understanding, but not thrive. Without understanding one cannot control causes; only treat effects, suppress symptoms. With understanding one can *design and create the future*.

To think about anything requires an image or concept of it, a model. To think about a thing as complex as a social system most people use a model of something similar, simpler and more familiar. Traditionally, two types of model have been used in efforts to acquire information, knowledge and understanding of social systems: *mechanistic* and *organismic*. But in a world of accelerating change, increasing uncertainty and growing complexity it is becoming apparent that these are inadequate as guides to decision and action. Alienation, hopelessness, frustration, insecurity, corruption, tyranny and social unrest are only a few of the many symptoms of deeply rooted malfunctioning of societies and their institutions. Commonly prescribed remedies are increasingly ineffective and often make things worse. The growing number of social crises and dilemmas that we face should be clear evidence that something is fundamentally wrong with the way we think about social systems.

Here we describe and try to explain the deficiencies of the two traditional ways of thinking about social systems. The principal deficiency is the limited yield of understanding. We then develop a third type of model, one we believe does not suffer from these inadequacies, a *social system* model.

The mechanistic model

Mechanistic models of the world conceptualize it as a machine that works with a regularity dictated by its internal structure and the causal laws of nature. The world, like a hermetically sealed clock, is taken to be made up of purposeless and passive parts that operate predictably. Any deviation from regularity is reacted to with changes that restore it; the system is believed to tend in the long run towards a static equilibrium.

This type of model is based on two assumptions: that the world can be *completely understood* and that such understanding can be obtained by *analysis*. Analysis is a three-step thought process. First, it takes apart that which it seeks to understand. Then it attempts to explain the behaviour of the parts taken separately. Finally, it tries to aggregate understanding of the parts into an explanation of the whole.

Since understanding something mechanistically requires understanding its parts, the parts also have to be taken apart. This process stops only when indivisible parts, elements, are reached. These, when understood, are believed to make understanding everything else possible. This doctrine, called *reductionism*, is responsible for the prominence in science of such irreducibles as atoms, chemical elements, cells, basic needs, instincts, direct observations and phonemes.

Once the elements are understood, their explanations have to be aggregated into an understanding of the whole. This requires establishing a relationship between the parts. The relationship that is assumed to be sufficient to explain all actions and interactions of the parts is *cause–effect*. One thing is taken to be the cause of another if it is both necessary and sufficient for the other.

The exclusive commitment to cause–effect has three important consequences. First, because identification of causes provides *complete* explanations of their effects, the environment is not required to explain anything. This environment-free concept of explanation is reflected in such natural laws as that of *freely* falling bodies, which apply only in the absence of an environment. It is also reflected in the predisposition to conduct research in laboratories, places from which the environment can be excluded.

Secondly, causes themselves require explanation. This is done by treating them as effects and finding their causes, which must also be explained. Is there an end to this regression? Given the mechanist's assumption that the world is completely comprehensible, the answer must be 'yes'; there has to be a *first cause*. This was generally taken to be God and, naturally, He was taken to be the *Creator*. God alone is uncaused and, therefore, not subject to explanation. He must be accepted on faith.

Thirdly, because of the assumed comprehensibility of the world, everything other than God has to be assumed to be the effect of some cause and, therefore, to be *determined* by that cause. Such determinism leaves no room for choice, hence purpose, in the natural world.

The effects of applying mechanistic models to social systems are manifested by adherents to the so-called classical or traditional school of management. The way they organize work is a direct consequence of analytical thinking. They begin by reducing work to elementary tasks, tasks so simple that they can be performed by one person alone. The simplicity of these tasks facilitates their mechanization. Only those tasks that are too expensive or complex to be mechanized are assigned to people. Work is reduced to machine-like behaviour and workers are treated like replaceable machine parts.

Adherence by parts to rules and regulations is made an end-in-itself either by rewarding compliance or punishing non-compliance. By this means, human responses to stimuli are made to approximate mindless physical reactions.

Control and co-ordination are also analysed and reduced to tasks requiring the minimal amount of power and judgement at each organizational level. Judgement is further reduced by establishing policies that offer virtually no choice except to determine which policy applies to which situation.

Like the universe, believed, by some, to have been created by God to do His work, organizations are taken to be instruments of their owners with no purposes of their own. Corporations, for example, are considered to be instruments for producing profit for their owners.

Mechanistically modelled organizations are structured hierarchically and are centrally controlled by a completely autonomous authority. Such an authority can affect any part of the system without being affected by any of them. This separates the ultimate authority from the system making that authority an external controller.

All members of the system other than the one with ultimate authority are deprived of all information except that required to do their jobs. Instructions from above are not explained or justified. Blind adherence is expected: 'Theirs not to reason why, theirs but to do and die'. People are kept apart as much as possible. Their interactions are minimized to depersonalize their relations. Even non-work-related interactions are discouraged.

The operations of an ideal machine do not vary. Therefore, as long as its input does not vary, its output will not vary. For this reason controllers of mechanistically modelled social systems focus on inputs rather than outputs. For example, they assume that control of costs is equivalent to control of outputs. The quantity of output is assumed to be determined by the quantity of input. The system is thought of much as a vending machine.

A mechanistically conceived social system is inflexible. Therefore, it can operate effectively only if its environment is static or has little effect on it; that is, where it can operate as a *closed* system. However, a rapidly changing environment requires continuous adaptation and learning by organizations if they are to remain effective. Adaptation and learning require a readiness, willingness and ability to change, but these are precisely what mechanistically managed and structured organizations lack.

The larger social system of which every organization is a part, and other organizations that are part of that containing system, no longer permit an organization to ignore its effects on, and the effects on it of, its environment. Recognition of this interaction poses a severe dilemma to mechanistically conceptualized organizations. They find it difficult or impossible to be responsive to environmental changes. As a result, their effectiveness suffers. Increasing ineffectiveness leads to reinforcement of their rigidity, closer adherence to rules and regulations. The result is a vicious circle in which such organizations become more and more dysfunctional (March and Simon, 1958).

The organismic model

A social system conceptualized as an organism has a purpose of its own: *survival* for which *growth* is taken to be essential. Contraction is believed to be synonymous with deterioration and decay, with eventual death. Such a system is taken to be dependent on its environment for essential inputs (resources). Therefore, if that environment is believed to be changing, to survive the system must be capable of learning and adaptation.

Growth is necessary but not sufficient for survival. Nothing can preclude eventual death, but continuity through reproduction can keep death from being terminal. Therefore, such systems try to reproduce themselves either by spawning new organizations (e.g. establishing colonies) or by acquiring old ones (imperialism).

In an organismically conceptualized corporation, profit, like oxygen in the case of an organism, is taken to be necessary for survival but not the reason for it. Profit is taken as a means; growth as an end. With survival as the ultimate end, planning becomes prediction of environmental changes and preparation for them.

Preoccupation with growth creates certain problems: first, the fact that things can grow only at the expense of other systems and their environments and, secondly, that exponential growth, the best kind, cannot be sustained forever. Moreover, there seems to be an optimal size for each type of organization beyond which an increase in size leads to a decline in efficiency and effectiveness (Boulding, 1970).

Because changes in their environments are considered to be inevitable and relevant, organismically conceptualized social systems seek a dynamic rather than a static equilibrium. They operate homeostatically, adjusting the behaviour of their parts to maintain the properties of the whole within acceptable limits. Their parts are thought of as organs, each with a function the performance of which contributes to the survival and growth of the whole. Individuals are regarded as cells whose function it is to serve the organs and the organism of which they are part. Organs and cells are more difficult to replace than machines or machine parts.

The executive function is thought of as the brain of the system (Beer, 1981). It is linked to the parts of the system by a communication network through which it receives information from a variety of sensing organs (e.g. diplomatic corps, intelligence services and marketing departments), and issues directives that activate and deactivate the parts of the system.

An organismically conceived social system is organized hierarchically but, since thinking and sensing are separated, control is not as completely centralized as it is in a mechanistically conceived system. Different parts have some degree of self-control, but they do not control the functions they are intended to carry out. Some parts can interact directly with and, in some cases, react directly to environmental changes without intervention of 'the brain'. As well as formal structure, organismic social systems have an informal one that is maintained by direct communication between parts. There is also more two-way communication between and within different levels of the hierarchy in an organismic social system than in a mechanistic one. Moreover, conformity and obedience of the parts is not taken to be as essential as long as they perform well. They are managed by control of outputs rather than inputs.

Organismic organizations try to exercise control by specifying desired outputs, leaving the selection of means to the parts (management by objectives). The environment and organizational performance (outputs) are kept under surveillance to determine whether they are behaving as expected. If not, corrective action is taken. Thus, management engages in feedback control. This facilitates both learning and adaptation.

Although organismically conceived systems are capable of self-control, they can be influenced by other systems and, in some cases, can be controlled by them by the application of force. Force may be required to make such an organization act against its will. A horse, unlike an automobile, cannot be driven into a wall without compulsion. External control of an organism is easiest where there is submission or consent, both of which are matters of choice.

To treat an organization or other type of social system as an organism is to fail to recognize the ways in which these differ significantly. In contrast to an organism, which cannot change its structure more than a limited amount and still survive, a social system has almost complete control over its structure (Buckley, 1967). In addition, the relationship that exists between an organism and its cells and organs is very different from that between an organization and its parts. One's heart cannot decide for itself that it does not want to work or wants to work for someone else. The parts of a social system have purposes of their own and display choice. Therefore, an effective social system requires agreement among its parts and between its parts and the whole. It requires consensus; an organism does not.

An organismically conceived system devotes itself to making the best of a future that it believes to be largely out of its control, but is predictable. The fact is that in an environment characterized by accelerating change, increasing uncertainty and growing complexity, the possibility of accurate and reliable forecasts diminishes at an increasing rate. In such an environment the only hope for a social system lies in its ability to bring more and more of its future under its own control. To take such an approach requires a model of a social system different from the two we have reviewed.

The social systems model

A system is a whole that cannot be divided into independent parts; the behaviour of each part and its effect on the whole depend on the behaviour of other parts. Therefore, the essential properties of a system are lost when it is taken apart; for example, a disassembled automobile does not transport and a disassembled person does not live. Furthermore, the parts themselves lose their essential properties when they are separated from the whole; for example, a detached steering wheel does not steer and a detached eye does not see.

Recall that analysis takes a system apart and then tries to explain the behaviour of the parts taken separately. It is for this reason that it cannot yield understanding of a system, only knowledge of how it works. Put another way: it can reveal a system's structure but not its functions.

Because the parts of a system are interdependent, it can be shown that even if each part is independently made to perform as efficiently as possible, the system as a whole will not perform as effectively as possible. For example, all-star athletic teams are not known to be the best teams and may not be able to beat an average team in the league.

The performance of a system is not the sum of the independent performances of its parts. It is the product of their interactions. Therefore, effective management of a system requires management of the interactions of its parts, not their independent actions. Moreover, since a social system interacts with its environment, management of this interaction is also required for it to function effectively.

It follows, then, that to understand a system as a whole a new non-analytical approach is needed. Contrary to a widely held belief, a multidisciplinary approach does not fill this need for reasons revealed in the classical story of the blind men trying to identify an elephant, each by touching a different part of its body. The interesting point in this story is not the predicament of the blind men but the ability of the story-teller to see the whole. A different version of the same story found in old Persian literature (Molana Jalaledin Molavi) is about a group of men who encounter a strange animal in complete darkness. Their efforts to identify it, each by touching a different part, prove fruitless until someone arrives with a lamp. Light enables us to synthesize separate observations into a meaningful whole. This light must be provided by a way of thinking other than analysis.

To understand a system, its structure, processes and functions have to be examined. A system's structure is the way its work is divided among its parts and their efforts coordinated, that is the relationships between its parts. Structure can be understood only if observed in the functioning of a system. Therefore, analysis, which reveals only the structure of a system, not its functioning, cannot provide understanding, only knowledge. *Synthetic* thinking is required to complement analysis.

In the first step of analysis the thing to be explained is taken apart; in synthetic thinking it is taken as a part of a larger system. In the second step of analysis the contained parts are explained; in synthetic thinking the containing system is explained. In the third step of analysis an effort is made to aggregate understanding of the parts into an understanding of the whole; in synthetic thinking understanding of the containing whole is disaggregated to explain the parts by revealing their role or function in that whole. In the social systems model synthetic thinking and analysis are taken to be complementary; neither can replace the other. Both are necessary to understand a system.

To understand the functioning of a social system the cause–effect relationship is inadequate. The *producer–product* relationship (Singer, 1959) is required. A producer is only necessary, not sufficient, for its product. Therefore, a producer never completely explains its product; it does *not* determine its product. This makes it possible to treat choice, hence purpose, as an objectively observable property of system behaviour. Moreover, since a producer is not sufficient for its product, reference to its environment is required to explain its product. Therefore, explanation becomes *environment-full* rather than environment-free as it is in the mechanistic model.

As a consequence, knowledge of the processes by which parts of a system choose to respond to their environment is essential to understanding the dynamics of a system which changes its structure. Process, rather than initial conditions, is responsible for future states; similar conditions (initial states) can lead to dissimilar outcomes (end states).

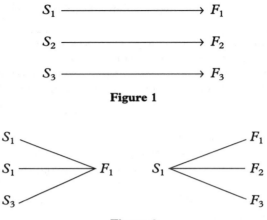

Figure 1

Figure 2

In a mechanistic conception of a system a specific structure (S) causes a particular function (F), and different structures cause different functions (Figure 1). Therefore, to understand a system, knowledge of its structure (the nature of its components and their relationships) is taken to be all that is required. This structuralist point of view is based on a deterministic conception of reality.

In a social systemic conception of a social system (1) different structures can yield the same function, and (2) the same structure can yield different functions (Figure 2). This makes it necessary to understand the relationship between structure and function keeping in mind that function is not a substitute for structure any more than form is a substitute for content. They are complements.

The time-telling function can be produced by such different structures as sundials, and sand, water, mechanical or electronic clocks. The transportation function can be produced by cars, ships, trains and automobiles. An educational system with a specific structure in a particular environment, in addition to its explicit educational function, also provides daytime child care. Clocks often have a decorative function as well as time-telling. Therefore, it is important to note that a redesign of a system to increase its efficiency with respect to one of its functions may, and often does, decrease its efficiency with regard to its other functions and, therefore, its overall effectiveness.

Now, what is a function? According to Ackoff and Emery (1972) a *functional class* is:

> . . . a set of structurally different individuals, systems or events, each of which is either a potential or actual producer of members (objects or events) of a specified class (Y) of any type.
>
> The function of such a class is Y-production, and each member of the class can be said to have Y-production as its function. If an individual displays a type of

structural behavior that is a member of a functional class of behavior displayed by other entities, then that individual or system can be said to have an *extrinsic function*. It is called extrinsic because the function is not one of its own but one it has by virtue of its membership in a class. The property that forms such a class is not structural but a common property of production . . . .

A person who can telephone a store, write to it, visit it, or get another to visit it displays a set of actions (events) that constitute a functional class defined by, say, acquiring a new shirt. In this case the individual displays an *intrinsic function* because its function can be attributed to it on the basis of *its behavior alone* (p. 26).

Using the difference between cause–effect and producer–product, Ackoff and Emery also distinguish between three types of system behavior: *reactions*, *responses* and *actions*.

A *reaction* of a system is a system event for which another event that occurs to the same system or its environment is *sufficient*. Thus, a reaction is an event that is (deterministically) caused by another event.

A *response* of a system is a system event for which another event that occurs to the same system or its environment is *necessary but not sufficient*. Thus, a response is an event of which the system itself is a *coproducer*. A person's turning on a light when it gets dark is a response to darkness, but the light's going on when the switch is turned is a reaction.

Table 1 Behavioural classification of systems

Type of system	*Behaviour* (*means, structure*)	*Outcome* (*ends, functions*)
Passive (tools)	*Fixed* One structure in all environments.	*Fixed* One function in all environments.
Reactive (self-maintaining system)	*Variable but determined* One structure in any one environment; different structures in different environments.	*Variable but determined* One function in any one environment, different functions in different environments.
Responsive (goal-seeking)	*Variable and chosen* Different structures in the same environment.	*Variable but determined* One function in any one environment, different functions in different environments.
Active (purposeful system)	*Variable and chosen* Different structures in the same environment.	*Variable and chosen* Different functions in the same environment.

An *act* of a system is a system event for the occurrence of which no change in the system's environment is either necessary or sufficient. Acts, therefore, are *self-determined* events, autonomous behaviour.

Systems, all of whose behaviour is reactive, responsive or active can be called reactive, responsive or active, respectively. However, most systems display some combination of these types of behaviour. Nevertheless, it should be noted that mechanically conceptualized systems are modelled as predominantly reactive; organismically conceptualized systems as predominantly responsive; and socially conceptualized systems as predominantly active (see Table 1).

Reactive, responsive, and active systems are also correlated with *state-maintaining, goal-seeking* and *purposeful* systems.

A *state-maintaining* system is one that *reacts* to changes so as to maintain its state under different environmental conditions. Such a system can react (not respond) because what it does is completely determined by the change in its environment, given the structure of the system. Nevertheless, it can be said to have the intrinsic function of maintaining the state it maintains because it can produce this state in a different way under different conditions.

For example, many heating systems are state-maintaining. An internal controller turns it on when the room temperature goes below a desired level, and turns it off when the temperature goes above this level. The state that is maintained is the room temperature. Such a system is able to adapt to changes but is not capable of learning because it cannot choose its behaviour. It cannot improve with experience.

A *goal-seeking* system is one that can *respond* differently to one or more different events in one or more different environments, and that can respond differently to a particular event in an unchanging environment until it produces a particular outcome (state). Production of this state is its goal. Such a system has a choice of behavior, hence is responsive rather than reactive. Response is voluntary; reaction is not.

For example, lower-level animals can try to get at food in different ways in different environments or even in the same environment at different times.

If a goal-seeking system has memory it can learn to pursue its goal more efficiently over time.

A *purposeful* system is one that can produce the same outcome in different ways in the same environment and can produce different outcomes in the same and different environments. It can change its ends under constant conditions. This ability to change ends under constant conditions is what exemplifies *free will*. Such systems not only learn and adapt, they can *create*. Human beings are examples of such systems.

Purposeful systems have all the capabilities of goal-seeking and state-maintaining systems, and goal-seeking systems have the capabilities of state-maintaining systems. The converse is not true. Therefore, they form a hierarchy.

Social systems are purposeful systems. Moreover, their parts are purposeful systems, and they are part of larger social, hence purposeful, systems. To understand a social system, then, one must not only know what the ends of the parts, system and containing system are, but how these affect their interactions. Managing a social system not only requires dealing with ends that may be in conflict at the different levels, but dealing with conflicting ends at any or all of the levels.

Recall that a mechanistically conceived system is not attributed with a purpose of its own even though it may serve the purpose of an external controller. Organismic systems have a purpose of their own: survival, for which growth is taken to be necessary. Then what is the appropriate purpose of a system conceptualized as a social system? *Development.*

Development

Growth and development are not the same thing and are not even necessarily associated. Either can take place with or without the other. A cemetery can grow without developing and a person may continue to develop long after he or she has stopped growing. This, of course, is obvious. What is not so obvious is that many of the problems associated with development derive from the assumption that economic growth is necessary if not sufficient for development and that limits to growth limit development.

Growth, strictly speaking, is an increase in size or number. Its principal, but not exclusive, domain of relevance is biological, as in the growth of plants and animals. Social systems are said to grow when they increase in size or number. Economies are said to grow when the economic value of their product or the amount of income they generate increases. Growth, however, is often used metaphorically or figuratively and, in such cases, it is frequently and incorrectly taken literally. For example, when we speak of a person 'growing up' we refer to increased maturity. Maturity has no size or number. It would be nonsensical to speak of a growing culture or quality of life because size and number are not relevant to them. A social system, like an individual, can grow by increasing in size or, unlike an individual, in number without developing. It can also develop without growing.

Growth occurs naturally, without choice, in most biological systems. In human beings and social systems, however, choices can deter or accelerate growth as, for example, in choice of diet or investment portfolio. If someone has a compulsion to grow, to increase in size, we are likely to consider this person to be a pathological case. For example, medical science increasingly views obesity as the product of a psychiatric disorder. However, if an organization has a compulsion to grow we generally consider it to be natural, even laudable. Why? Because we assume that physical or economic growth is necessary, if not sufficient, for development. This, as we will try to show, is not the case. Nevertheless, if limits to growth threatened an organization's survival, one could understand its preoccupation with such limits, but not even the authors of *The Limits to Growth* (Meadows *et al.*, 1972) claim that this is so. Unfortunately, many have incorrectly drawn the inference from this book that retarded growth implies retarded development. Such an error, we believe, is based on a misconception of the nature of development.

Development of a person, contrary to what many believe, is not a condition or a state defined by what or how much that person has. For example, if the products and services available in the most affluent nation were suddenly showered on an aborigine, he would not thereby be developed. Development has less to do with how much a person has than with *how much he or she can do with what he does have*. For this reason, Robinson Crusoe and the Swiss Family Robinson are better paradigms of development than J. P. Morgan and John D. Rockefeller.

Development is the process in which individuals increase their abilities and desires to satisfy their own needs and legitimate desires, and those of others. It is at least as much a matter of motivation, information, knowledge, understanding, and wisdom as it is of wealth. An individual's *level of development* is his current ability and desire to satisfy his own needs and legitimate desires, and those of others.

This definition requires clarification of the distinction between *needs* and *desires*, and of the meaning of *legitimate*. By a *need* we mean something that is necessary for survival, for example, food and oxygen. What is needed may or may not be desired; for example, a person who is unaware of his need for roughage does not desire it. On the other hand, as is obvious, a person may desire something he does not need.

By a *legitimate desire* we mean one the pursuit or fulfillment of which does not reduce the likelihood of other individuals fulfilling their needs or (legitimate) desires. This does not preclude interfering with a person who interferes with others' pursuit of their needs or legitimate desires.

Development, as we define it, is reflected at least as much in quality of life as in standard of living. To be developed is to have the desire and capacity to use effectively whatever has to improve one's own quality of life and standard of living, and those of others.

It has become more and more apparent that continued economic growth of a nation may increase the standard of living, but not necessarily improve the quality of life. Many argue that at least some of the economically most advanced nations today are increasing their standards of living at the expense of quality of life. Many American Indians, for example, assert that although their assimilation into the surrounding white culture has brought them a higher standard of living, their quality of life has deteriorated.

All this is *not* to say that wealth is irrelevant to development or quality of life; it is very relevant. How much people can actually improve their quality of life and that of others depends not only on their motivation, information, knowledge, understanding, and wisdom, but also on what instruments and resources are available to them. For example, a man can build a better house with good tools and materials than he can without them. On the other hand, a developed man can build a better house with whatever tools and materials he has than a less developed man with the same resources. Furthermore, a developed man with limited resources can often improve his quality of life and that of others more than a less developed man with unlimited resources.

It should also be borne in mind that resources are more often *taken* than given. The more developed a person or an organization, the more resources he or it can find or develop. The more dependent one is on resources that are given, the less developed that person is. Put another way: resources are created by what man does with what nature provides. What nature provides is not a resource until man has transformed it or learns how to use it. The more developed man is, the more resources he can create or extract out of nature's offerings.

Because development involves an increase of ability (i.e. learning) and one person cannot learn for another, one person or organization cannot develop another. One can only encourage and facilitate that development. There is only one type of development: *self-development*. One who tries to induce development in another must act like a teacher, not a doctor. It is not so much a matter of diagnosis and prescription as it is of encouragement and facilitation.

Therefore, social systems cannot develop their members and other stakeholders, but *they can and should encourage and facilitate such development.* The development of such systems consists of *an increase in their desire and ability to encourage and facilitate the development of their stakeholders.* Effective planning for development requires a major reorientation of organizations or governments that assume they can develop their members. Development is not a matter of what an organization or government does, but of what it encourages and enables its members to do.

The quality of life (including work life) that a person can realize is the joint product of his development and the resources available to him. Although this implies that limited resources may limit improvement of quality of life, it does not imply that they limit development. Desires and abilities can increase without an increase of resources. Put another way: development is *potentiality* for satisfaction of needs and desires, not the satisfaction (quality of life or standard of living) actually obtained.

A limit is a point, line, surface, quantity or other boundary that a variable cannot exceed. For example, nothing can move faster than the speed of light which, therefore, is a limit. The maximum speed at which an automobile can travel is also a limit. Nevertheless, we speak of speed limits which automobiles obviously exceed. Here 'limit' denotes a quantity that one is not supposed to but can exceed. Such a limit is better referred to as a *constraint* or *restriction*.

Even the limit to the speed of an automobile need not limit its driver. He can take an aeroplane if he wants to travel faster, or he might find something more desirable than travel. The effect of limits on purposeful individuals and systems can be evaded either by changing intent or by using better technology. A limited resource limits us only if we want to do something that requires more of that resource than is available and there is no suitable substitute in greater supply. A limited resource ceases to be limiting if our need for it decreases or *if we learn how to use it more effectively*; that is, *if we develop*.

Limits to and constraints on a social system's growth are found primarily in its environment; but the principal limits to and constraints on its development are found within the system itself. The key to unlimited development is freedom of choice that is limited only to those who do not limit the choice of others; that is, freedom that is exercised morally.

Conclusion

We have tried to show that there are three different ways of looking at and thinking about social systems: as mechanistic, organismic or social systems. We have argued that the first two types of modelling severely limit our ability to understand such systems, hence to control them. A mechanistic model yields a description of the actions and interactions of the parts of a social system and, therefore, knowledge of its structure. It does not yield understanding of the behaviour of either the parts or the whole. Organismic models of social systems lead to identification of the functions of the parts in the wholes and, therefore, to understanding of the parts, but not the whole. The social model conceptualizes a social system as a part of a larger purposeful system as well as a system with purposeful parts. It focuses on both the functions of the parts in the whole and of the whole in the larger containing system of which it is part. Therefore, it can yield understanding of both the behaviour of the parts and the whole.

Mechanistic management strives for efficiency and tries to construct social systems that behave like machines, and to train people to behave like machine parts. This results in a bureaucratic structure that is capable of neither learning nor adapting. In an environment characterized by an increasing rate of change, uncertainty and complexity, mechanistically managed organizations tend to become increasingly dysfunctional, to lose effectiveness, and often to die although burial may be postponed.

Organismic management strives for growth as necessary for survival. It conceptualizes the parts of a social system as organs with essential functions but no purposes of their own. Their only reason for existence is their service to the whole. Their environments are seen as purposeless and passive providers of necessary inputs to, and outputs of, organisms. Such organizations tend to be managed more permissively than bureaucracies, focusing on meeting assigned goals, leaving choice of means by which these goals are to be pursued to the parts that have responsibility for their attainment. They give more attention to efficiency than effectiveness. For them, planning consists of predicting a future environment believed to be beyond their control, and preparing for it.

Social-system management is concerned with development and tries to serve the purposes of the system, its parts, and its containing systems. There may be conflict between these levels or within them. Therefore, resolution or dissolution of conflict is one of management's principal responsibilities. A social system should be viewed as an instrument of those it affects. Its principal function is to encourage and facilitate their development. For management of social systems, planning should consist of designing a desirable future and inventing or finding ways of approximating it as closely as possible. Such management should attempt to maximize the freedom of choice of those it affects. Only from experience of choice can one learn, hence develop.

References

Ackoff, R. L. and F. E. Emery. *On Purposeful Systems*, Interscience Publications, Seaside, California, 1972.

Beer, Stafford. *Brain of the Firm*, 2nd edn, Wiley, Chichester, 1981.

Boulding, Kenneth. *Beyond Economics*, University of Michigan Press, Ann Arbor, Michigan, 1970.

Buckley, Walter. *Sociology and Modern Systems Theory*, Prentice Hall, Englewood Cliffs, New Jersey, 1967.

March, J. E. and H. A. Simon. *Organizations*, Wiley, New York, 1958.

Meadows, D. H., D. L. Meadows, J. Randers and W. W. Behrens III. *The Limits to Growth*, Universe Books, New York, 1972.

Naisbitt, John. *Megatrends*, Warner Books, New York, 1982.

Singer, E. A., Jr. *Experience and Reflection*, University of Pennsylvania Press, Philadelphia, 1959.

Source: Gharajedaghi, Jamshid and Ackoff, Russell. (1984) Mechanisms, organisms and social systems. *Strategic Management Journal*, 5, 289–300.

2 Teaching MBAs transformational thinking

Gareth Morgan

Paradox and transformation can be important concepts and tools in the helping professions. This is particularly true in teaching. At least, it is true when the teacher's intention is to change the capacity to understand and comprehend rather than just impart information and facts to be comprehended. If the intention of a teacher or any other kind of helper is to modify the assumptions, deep structures, or paradigms of another person, then 'telling' is a futile method. In this paper I wish to explore how paradox can be used to transform thinking about organization and management, with particular reference to my experience in teaching organizational analysis to MBA students.

I work from the hypothesis that there are strong parallels between the mindset of the 'average MBA' and that of the typical bureaucrat. Thinking tends to be fragmented in that knowledge of organization is 'departmentalized': into distinctions between organizational behavior (OB), strategy, accounting, finance, marketing, etc. And, as a result, expectations about legitimate spheres of discourse, perceived relevance, and the relationship between problems and solutions tend to fall in line with an over-bureaucratized view of the world. In addition, MBA conceptions of organization are often dominated by a bureaucratic view, gleaned from early work experience, introductory courses on management, or familiarity with texts that equate organization with a clarity of structure and control. This often leads them to see the process of 'getting organized' as one of developing clear, rational structures of tasks and activities, rather than of understanding organization as an open-ended, flowing process that demands the management of many contradictory strains and tensions.

My primary aim in teaching the art of organizational analysis is to transform this fragmented and over-bureaucratized view into a more open-ended appreciation that will allow the student to understand the complex and paradoxical nature of organizations and the problems of managing them. In essence, I strive to teach a style of critical thinking that recognizes how analysis and management are always based on an interpretative process that can take many forms according to the paradigms, images, or metaphors that are used to frame inquiry (Burrell and Morgan 1979; Morgan 1986).

My favored approach is to use the method of 'reading' developed in *Images of Organization* (Morgan 1986), which encourages students to generate multiple views and interpretations of situations before arriving at judgments and prescriptions. The aim is to create an element of paradox and tension that will challenge their taken-for-granted assumptions, and lead them to entertain and develop new ways of thinking, and eventually, new ways of organizing and managing.

It is impossible to describe the complete method in a short chapter such as this (the author can provide further details on request). Its essence rests in the attempt to transform thinking by getting students to appreciate that:

1 our favored ways of seeing are based on images or metaphors that provide partial and one-sided viewpoints;
2 a comprehensive understanding of any situation always rests in an ability 'to see' from multiple perspectives; and
3 it is necessary to integrate the insights thus provided.

The subject matter of the course is organized around readings and cases that illustrate the role of different metaphors in organizational analysis, integrated through a practical project applying all the ideas to the analysis of a real organization (usually the one in which the students work, or have worked in the recent past).

To illustrate the approach and the kind of transformation in thinking that I try to achieve, the rest of this chapter focuses on the very first class of my course, which uses a case study designed to help students reveal their taken-for-granted ways of thinking about organization, and some alternatives. The function is to show how we typically impose assumptions, biases, and knowledge on the situations that we are attempting to understand, and how a fuller understanding, or 'reading of the situation', requires that we remain open to the possibility of other interpretations as well.

To illustrate, consider the following case, which I typically introduce with the question: *How would you explain the events at Eagle Smelting?*[1]

The Eagle Smelting case

The Eagle Smelting Company has a number of smelting and refining operations in various sites across North America. The firm usually ships its finished product – aluminum ingot of various qualities – directly from its smelters to its customers, heavy industry manufacturers around the world.

Eagle's Northtown smelter is just outside a small port town on the Pacific coast. Raw materials are brought in by ship to the all-weather harbor and unloaded at the company dock, which is linked to the smelter by a private railroad. Any breakdown in the railway is a very serious matter, as it can disrupt both production and shipping schedules. Also important to the smelter's operations is the firm's fleet of land vehicles which are, for the most part, maintained on-site. To keep all this machinery in repair the company has a full-time crew of mechanics and a well-equipped machine shop, capable of fabricating most needed parts.

Don Macrae, a professional engineer, is the plant manager. Macrae, fifty-three, has been with the company for twenty-four years. He was plant engineer for four years before being named plant manager eighteen months ago.

The current plant engineer is John Holt, also a professional engineer. Holt, thirty-six, has been with Eagle for thirteen years. He was transferred to the Northtown smelter when Macrae became plant manager.

Holt is responsible for all engineering-related activities at Northtown, and is therefore involved in a variety of tasks, both at the plant and the nearby town site. Sometimes his work takes him even farther afield. One of his responsibilities is the plant's machine shop, but only a fraction of his time is actually spent there.

Ed Smith, a master mechanic, is foreman of the machine shop. Under him are three trainers, a half dozen semiskilled workers, and five fully qualified mechanics. The machine shop operates regular daytime hours, except when overtime work becomes necessary. Job requests are usually submitted to the shop by section heads, and requests are often supported by drawings or lists of specifications. Smith assigns tasks each day, but usually the work itself requires only a minimum of supervision.

One sunny Friday morning in June, events at Northtown got off to a bad start. The smelter's locomotive broke down while carrying a 'rush order' to the dock. The breakdown was reported to the dock captain, Luke Hardy, just as he was leaving for the 'morning conference', a short daily meeting with the plant engineer and the plant manager, held to discuss and deal with routine operational problems. Hardy raised the matter immediately when the meeting began. Holt, after hearing details, realized a part would have to be fabricated, and promised delivery of it by 1:45 that afternoon. Allowing for proper installation, this meant that the locomotive would be running again in time to catch the final shipment of the day.

The arrangement called for swift action, but Holt was confident that his target could be achieved even though special problems were involved in the fabrication of the required part. The special lathe needed for the job had recently become unreliable. While still functioning well at low RPMs, it tended to vibrate badly when operated at normal or high speeds. This vibration made precision work difficult and would, Holt feared, soon ruin the machine itself. The service representative from the manufacturer was due to visit the smelter to repair this lathe the following week, and Holt had hoped to keep it out of service until then. The present emergency, of course, made its use unavoidable. He felt, however, that the job could be done satisfactorily at low speed without risk to the machine and thus did not raise the problem for fear of lengthening the meeting.

As the job was urgent, Holt decided to leave the meeting early, and went straight to the machine shop to get work started. Foreman Smith, having made his daily work assignments, was over at the payroll department looking into a complaint by his men that too much was being deducted from their paychecks for the company's pension plan. Knowing that he was likely to be there a while, Holt decided that the work being done by Lee Curtis, one of the senior mechanics, was not urgent, and assigned Curtis to the job.

Curtis, a fully qualified mechanic and one of the most experienced and skilled men in the shop, had at one time been considered for the post of machine shop foreman. However, Macrae and Holt both preferred Ed Smith, another excellent mechanic who, at forty-eight, was just a few years younger than Curtis. At first, Curtis had taken the missed promotion badly, but he soon seemed to settle down and accept the situation.

In assigning the priority job to Curtis, Holt specified that the machining should be done at a low speed. Curtis knew the machine well and had, in fact, reported the problems in operating the lathe just two weeks before. Holt was thus quite confident that Curtis could do a high quality job, as he had on so many other 'rescue operations' in the past.

After giving Curtis his directions, Holt left the machine shop to attend to his other duties. Most Friday mornings took him to Northtown, where it was his custom to stop by his bank to deposit his weekly paycheck, and sometimes do a little shopping for the weekend. He felt free to do this as he often started early and worked late into the evening without overtime when his job required.

In the late morning, Macrae, on one of his frequent walks through the smelter, happened to stop by the machine shop. Seeing that Curtis was at work on the locomotive part, he stopped at his work station, where he discovered that Curtis was operating his machinery at low speed.

'Where's your foreman?' asked Macrae.

Curtis said he didn't know.

'How about Mr Holt?'

Curtis replied that he didn't know where he was either. Macrae muttered to himself, told Curtis to 'speed up the damn job,' and hurriedly took off for his office.

Holt returned to the machine shop a little after noon, and dropped in on Smith, who, after returning from the Payroll Department and making a rapid tour of the machine shop, had gone straight to his office to deal with a backlog of paperwork. Holt explained the trouble with the locomotive, and after a brief conversation they decided to visit Curtis's work station to check on progress.

The lathe was vibrating badly, and making an unpleasant whining sound. The part being tooled by Curtis was obviously not going to meet the required specifications.

'You knew the lathe shouldn't be run at this speed,' said Holt in a fury. 'You've messed up this job on purpose. You're fired.' Turning to the foreman he told him to make arrangements for Curtis's severance pay and to see that someone else took over the priority job. He then returned to his office.

A few minutes later Smith sought him out there, and told him that he was not justified in firing Curtis.

'He speeded up the job because Macrae ordered him to,' explained the foreman. 'He says Macrae is the boss, and he did what he was told.'

Holt, on hearing this explanation, strode over to Macrae's office and burst in without knocking. 'By sticking your nose in this morning you've ruined the rush job on the locomotive part and probably scrapped an expensive lathe to boot. If that's the way you run things here, then I quit.'

'You're right,' Macrae shouted back. 'That locomotive job was a top priority, so why weren't you or Smith overseeing it? Was it in danger of interfering with your personal business? I know your Friday morning routine! I accept your resignation.'

A case analysis

How, then, are we to explain the events at Eagle Smelting?

The case is a very rich one, and many different interpretations are possible, each suggesting different kinds of managerial solutions. Consider, for example, the following:

1 *A case of chaotic organization and poor communications?* Shaped by assumptions that Eagle Smelting is a bureaucratic organization that is functioning inefficiently, various problems can be highlighted, for example, violation of the chain of command, poor information exchange, overlapping job responsibilities, and sloppy adherence to prescribed roles. The solutions to the perceived problems are, of course, *bureaucratic* ones: 'tighten up' the organization in all these respects.
2 *A case of poor planning?* The failure and problems can be subscribed to the machine breakdown, and the lack of an effective stock of spare parts, or set of contingency plans. The solutions thus become highly *technical* ones: better machinery, more spare parts or better inventory control, clear emergency procedures, etc.
3 *A case illustrating the dysfunctions of authoritative management?* Macrae is a highly authoritarian manager. Holt also likes to give instructions. No one asks questions. There is no evidence of participation or 'bottom-up' influence. Curtis has been conditioned to a 'do as you're told' mentality.

This analysis leads toward some kind of *human relations* solution to the problems at hand, involving more participation, a 'flatter', less hierarchical form of organization, a better match between individual and organizational needs, or to some form of *contingency approach* emphasizing the importance of matching tasks, structure, and people to create 'good fit'.

4 *A case of the plant manager doing his old job?* Macrae is acting as the area engineer. He wants Holt to do the job exactly as he used to do it. He has interfered with his colleague's responsibilities. He is 'managing by walking about', but in a 'hands in' rather than 'hands off' style. This interpretation of the case sees the problem as resting with Macrae. He needs to change his *managerial style*, or be replaced by someone who can do the plant manager's job in a broader way.

5 *A case of 'awkward' or clashing personalities?* Relations between Macrae and Holt are frequently hot and emotional. Tempers are quick. Curtis may be seething with resentment about a missed promotion. Many managers would say he has 'an attitude problem'. Others might say he is alienated and fed up with his work, or dislikes authority. This kind of interpretation leads back to some kind of *human relations* solution calling for more participation and better communications, or to some kind of *fire and hire* solution.

6 *A case requiring a 'search for villains'?* Who's to blame? This approach leads one to prescribe solutions that involve *firing* key offenders. The trouble is that a case can usually be made against almost everyone. Macrae can be blamed for his meddling. Holt can be blamed for not staying on top of the job. Curtis can be blamed for deliberately wrecking the job. And even Smith can be 'fingered' for spending so much time away from the machine shop.

7 *A case of organizational politics?* Are Macrae and Holt in competition with each other? Does Holt have an eye on Macrae's job? Does Macrae feel insecure and threatened by his younger colleague, who does things in such a different way? Do they have personal dislikes and quarrels? Does this have an adverse influence on the work relations between the two managers? Is Curtis truly seething with resentment about the missed promotion? Is he looking for a way to get revenge? Has he deliberately engineered Holt's dismissal? Has he been waiting for an opportunity to use the conflict between Macrae and Holt for his own ends? Has he been waiting for the perfect opportunity to make his move? Are Smith and Curtis in collusion? Are their actions part of a preconceived plan to move against Holt and Macrae: disgruntled workers making a protest against incompetent management? Was Hardy involved in the plot? Was the locomotive sabotaged? Some of these questions may seem farfetched. The case is ambiguous and does not speak to these points in a specific way. But all identify possible situations. This line of questioning leads to a *political* interpretation of the case, favoring forms of conflict management that recognize competing interests and power relations.

8 *Is this a case of a fragmented corporate culture?* There appear to be few shared norms and values. Should those responsible for managing the organization attempt to develop an overarching sense of shared meaning that would bind people in the organization together in a meaningful way? This interpretation of the situation directs attention to solutions involving *the management of meaning*.

9 *Is this a case of a radicalized organization?* Are there deep divisions between management and workers? Even though there is no mention of a militant union, perhaps relations are antagonistic and conflictual. Are there divisions between the professional outsiders (Macrae and Holt) and the local workforce? Are there important social and cultural differences between management and workers? Such interpretations would lead to solutions that recognize the immediate problem to be *a symptom of a much deeper historical, socio-economic problem*, and lead to strategies that attempt to bridge the gulf in some way.

The above discussion is by no means exhaustive. But it does serve to illustrate the complexity and potentially paradoxical nature of what, at first sight, seems to be a relatively straightforward situation. All the above interpretations, which are all partial, and which all depend on a degree of 'reading into' the situation, especially where information is vague and incomplete, and may be simultaneously correct. They may all be combined in the very nature of the situation.

The task of the organizational analyst, or the reflective manager, is to unravel this complexity in the best way he or she can. It involves an awareness of the fact that we typically read and understand situations in partial ways, and that a comprehensive understanding demands the kind of framing and reframing process evident in the line of questioning posed above.

Effective managers and organizational analysts often develop the knack of reading situations intuitively. Some talk about gaining 'a feel' for a situation, or 'grabbing it with their guts', or trying to 'smell' its key dimensions. Each case involves an interpretative process that attempts to understand the essence of the situation at hand. The process simulated above, and explored in further detail in Morgan (1986), can be used to achieve the same results. By being open to the possibility of making multiple interpretations of any given situation, we create alternative models for understanding, alternative patterns of explanation, and set the basis for alternative modes of action, problem formulation, and problem solutions.

For example, mechanistic interpretations of a situation almost always result in mechanistic approaches to problem solving. The manager whose basic conception of organization is bureaucratic almost always looks for solutions that involve changes in the structure and design of organizational tasks and activities. The manager who is more open to negative thinking will be much more sensitive to issues of 'process,' the conditions required for evolution and change, and unsatisfied needs. The manager who has been influenced by the latest books on corporate culture is more likely to tune into the symbolism, and the construction and management of meaning. And those with a political bent will probably see wheeling and dealing everywhere.

The problem is to provide ways of balancing and integrating these insights, and of knowing when they provide the basis for effective action. By broadening one's ability to understand the different dimensions of the situations with which one is dealing, one's approach to management can become much more reflective, and transformative in its effects. New and broader forms of understanding can provide the basis for new kinds of organization to emerge.

Transformation in the classroom

The seeds for this kind of transformation begin in the class setting in the disjuncture between the views of organization brought into the classroom and the views with which the students leave. The typical student analysis of the Eagle Smelting case is usually a very limited one. Most often, students interpret the case as presenting a problem that must be solved, and proceed to analyze the case in terms of a quasi-mechanistic frame of reference identifying problems with the organization's systems of communication, job design, line of command, definitions of responsibility and authority, managerial styles, and poor human relations. Sometimes discussion points towards the politics of the situation, especially in terms of 'personality conflicts' and 'feelings of alienation'. But when it comes to 'solution time', the political problems are usually seen as a product of the structural problems referred to above. Solutions thus focus on clarifying structures, lines of command, job responsibilities, improving human relations skills, and so on.

The learning generated by this case really gets underway when the students have formulated their solutions, and the instructor begins to use the case analysis as a kind of mirror in which they can see their own assumptions and biases. For example, as the models and metaphors of organization that have been implicitly adopted as a basis for analysis and prescription are reflected back to the class, different interpretations of the case are quickly identified. And, as the paradoxes and contradictions highlighted by competing inter-pretations are explored, students quickly see that their prescriptions and solutions may be quite limited or inappropriate. The paradoxes can be clearly illustrated by focusing on the contrasts between quasi-mechanistic and political interpretations of the case. If the case is truly rooted in the kind of conflicts highlighted under points seven and nine of the earlier analysis, it is extremely unlikely that they can be resolved through the quasi-mechanistic or human relations approaches typically favored by the majority of the class. The political dynamic within the organization will merely take a new form.

This class session is often a dramatic one. Conventional assumptions are challenged. The existence of alternatives is clearly demonstrated. And the course is set on a voyage of discovery through which these alternatives will be explored. Subsequent weeks focus on the systematic interpretation and reinterpretation of organizations and organizational problems through the variety of metaphors explored in *Images of Organization*. The process, illustrated each week through case-based discussions in class, is also grounded in student projects involving the ongoing analysis of a real organizational situation that must be interpreted from different viewpoints. After each alternative perspective is applied, it is not uncommon for students to feel that they have at last arrived at *the* answer, the one that truly makes sense of the situation. However, after the fifth or sixth week, the transformation glimpsed in that very first class, but usually pushed to the sidelines for ease of mind thereafter, at last reoccurs.

There is no one theoretical frame that can provide the definitive answer. There are usually many possible answers, or combinations of answers, that need to be carefully evaluated against the many possible meanings and interpretations inherent in the situation being studied. As this message hits home, students begin to realize that organizational analysis is ultimately a complex interpretive process that deals with paradoxes and tensions of many kinds. Rather than reach for simple 'off-the-shelf' interpretations and solutions, they are encouraged to realize that there is no substitute for solid diagnosis that grasps and integrates the various aspects of the situation.

This process also illustrates that the managers in everyday situations face similar problems. They too must arrive at appropriate interpretations and understandings of the situation being managed, and engage in actions that fit those situations. Students thus begin to appreciate the key role of interpretation in the management process, and how managers must learn to be their own theorists and diagnosticians, developing the kind of critical thinking that will broaden their range of understanding and action opportunities.

In this way, students are encouraged to understand and explore the paradoxes and ambiguities inherent in organizational analysis and the management process generally, and to broaden their capacity for creative thinking about situations that were previously taken for granted. And ultimately this transformation in thinking helps to provide a basis for a transformation of action. For seeing and understanding organizations in new ways helps to create a capacity for one to manage them in new ways.

Note

1 The case is introduced without any prior discussion about the course, and before any course outlines or handouts have been distributed. The case is

based on a description of unknown origin; key details have been changed; and the case has been written to place it in a North American context.

References

Burrell, G., and G. Morgan. 1979. *Sociological Paradigms and Organizational Analysis.* London and Portsmouth, N.H.: Heinemann Educational Books.
Morgan, G. 1986. *Images of Organization.* Newbury Park: Sage Publications.

Source: Morgan, Gareth (1988) Teaching MBAs transformational thinking. In R. Quinn and K. Cameron (eds), *Paradox and Transformation*, Ballinger, Cambridge, Mass, pp. 237–248.

Part Two

Ambiguity and Interpretation in Organizations

The King [Apollo], whose oracle is at Delphi, neither speaks nor conceals but signifies.

Heraclitus

3 How we talk and how we act: administrative theory and administrative life

James G. March

I am not an administrator. I believe I am only the second person without experience as a college president to be invited to deliver the David D. Henry Lecture. I am a student of organizations and administration, and it is from that point of view that I talk. Nevertheless, I hope that some comments from the ivory tower may be marginally useful to the real world of administration. Students of organizations are secretaries to people who live in organizations. Much of our time is spent talking to people in administrative roles, recording their behavior, and trying to develop descriptions of organizational theory. As best we can, we try to make sense of what we see.

Making sense of organizational life is complicated by the fact that organizations exist on two levels. The first is the level of action where we cope with the environment we face; the second is the level of interpretation where we fit our history into an understanding of life. The level of action is dominated by experience and learned routines; the level of interpretation is dominated by intellect and the metaphors of theory. Ordinary administrative life is a delicate combination of the two levels. Managers act. They make decisions, establish rules, issue directives. At the same time, they interpret the events they see. They try to understand their own behavior, as well as that of others, in terms of theories that they (and others) accept. They try to present themselves in understandable, even favorable, terms. They try to improve the way they act by contemplating its relation to the way they talk, and they try to modify their talk by considering how they act.

The process has elegance, but it also has traps. The interweaving of experience and theory often makes it difficult for the student of administration to disentangle the events of organizational life from the theories about those events that participants have. The same interweaving complicates the ways in which administrators learn from their experience to improve their organizations. I want to explore some aspects of those complications today. My intentions are not grand. I want to talk about some parts of administrative theory and administrative life, about the implications of recent thinking on organizations, and particularly about the possibility that some of our administrative precepts – the way we talk – may sometimes be less sensible than our administrative behavior – the way we act.

Classical perspectives on administrative leadership are rich enough and varied enough to make any effort to describe them in broad terms ill informed. Nevertheless, there is a relatively standard portrayal of organizations and their leaders that is easily recognized and is implicit in most of our administrative theories. Without attempting to represent those theories in a comprehensive way, I want to focus on four assumptions of administrative thought that are important both to contemporary administrative action and the recent research on administrative life:

Assumption 1: The rigidity of organizations In the absence of decisive and imaginative action by administrative leaders, organizations resist change.

Assumption 2: The heterogeneity of managers Top managers vary substantially in their capabilities, and organizations that identify and reward distinctively able administrative leaders prosper.

Assumption 3: The clarity of objectives Intelligent administrative action presupposes clear goals, precise plans, and unambiguous criteria for evaluation.

Assumption 4: The instrumentality of action The justification for administrative action lies in the substantive outcomes it produces.

These assumptions permeate both our writings and our talk about organizations and administration. Although it is certainly possible to find counterexamples in the literature, they are part of generally received administrative doctrine. Moreover, they are not foolish. They reflect considerable good sense. One difficulty with them, however, is that they appear to capture only part of our experience. Most studies of administrative life present a somewhat different version of administrative roles. Although there is a tendency for some biographers of particular leaders to surround administrative life with grandeur, most studies and most reports from administrators present a different picture of what administrators do. Administrative life seems to be filled with minor things, short-time horizons, and seemingly pointless (and endless) commitments. The goals of an organization seem to be unclear and changing. Experience seems to be obscure. Life is filled with events of little apparent instrumental consequence. The ways in which administrative theory leads us to talk about administrative life seem to be partially inconsistent with the ways in which we have experienced and observed it.

Such an inconsistency is neither surprising nor, by itself, disturbing. Tensions between theory and experience are important sources of development for both. But in this case, I think our theories lead us astray in some important ways. In order to examine that thought, I want to note some observations about organizational life drawn from recent research. First, some observations about change; second, some observations about clarity; third, some observations about managers and managerial incentives; and fourth, some observations about instrumentality in administrative life. Taken together, these observations suggest some modest modifications in our assumptions of management.

Organizations and change

Recent literature on organizations often details the ways that hopes for change are frustrated by organizational behavior. The contrariness of organizations in confronting sensible efforts to change them fills our stories and our research. What most of those experiences tell us, however, is not that organizations are rigid and inflexible. Rather, they picture organizations as impressively imaginative. Organizations change in response to their environments, including their managements, but they rarely change in a way that fulfills the intentional plan of a single group of actors. Sometimes organizations ignore clear policies; sometimes they pursue them more forcefully than was intended. Sometimes they protect policymakers from the follies of foolish policies; sometimes they do not. Sometimes they stand still when we want them to move. Sometimes they move when we want them to stand still.

Organizational tendencies to frustrate arbitrary administrative intention, however, should not be confused with rigidity. Organizations change frequently. They adopt new products, new procedures, new objectives, new postures, new styles, new personnel, new beliefs. Even in a short perspective, the changes are often large. Some of them are sensible; some are not. Bureaucratic organizations are not always efficient. They can be exceptionally obtuse. Change is ubiquitous in organizations; and most change is the result neither of extraordinary organizational processes or forces, nor of uncommon imagination, persistence, or skill. It is a result of relatively stable processes that relate organizations to their environments. Organizational histories are written in dramatic form, and the drama reflects something important about the orchestration and mythology of organizational life, but substantial change results easily from the fact that many of the actions by an organization follow standard rules that are conditional on the environment. If economic, political, or social contexts change rapidly, organizations will change rapidly and routinely.

In such a spirit, recent efforts to understand organizations as routine adaptive systems emphasize six basic perspectives for interpreting organizational action:

1 Action can be seen as the application of standard operating procedures or other rules to appropriate situations. The terms of reference are duties, obligations, and roles. The model is a model of evolutionary selection.

2 Action can be seen as problem solving. The terms of reference are alternatives, consequences, and preferences. The model is one of intended rational choice.
3 Action can be seen as stemming from past learning. The terms of reference are actions and experiences. The model is one of trial and error learning.
4 Action can be seen as resulting from conflict among individuals or groups. The terms of reference are interests, activation, and resources. The model is one of politics – bargaining and power.
5 Action can be seen as spreading from one organization to another. The terms of reference are exposure and susceptibility. The model is one of diffusion.
6 Action can be seen as stemming from the mix of intentions and competencies found in organizational actors. The terms of reference are attitudes, abilities, and turnover. The model is one of regeneration.

These standard processes of organizational action are understandable and mostly reliable. Much of the time they are adaptive. They facilitate organizational survival. Sometimes organizations decline, and sometimes they die. Sometimes the changes that are produced seem little connected either to the intentions of organizational actors or to the manifest problems facing an organization. A propensity to change does not assure survival, and the processes of change are complicated by a variety of confusions and surprises. Solutions sometimes discover problems rather than the other way around. Organizations imitate each other, but innovations and organizations change in the process. Environments are responded to, but they are also affected. The efforts of organizations to adapt are entangled with the simultaneous efforts of individuals and larger systems of organizations. In these ways, the same processes that sustain the dull day-to-day activities of an organization produce unusual events.

These six perspectives portray an organization as coping with the environment routinely, actively adapting to it, avoiding it, seeking to change it, comprehend it, and contain it. An organization is neither unconditionally rigid nor unconditionally malleable; it is a relatively complicated collection of interests and beliefs acting in response to conflicting and ambiguous signals received from the environment and from the organization, acting in a manner that often makes sense and usually is intelligent. Organizations evolve, solve problems, learn, bargain, imitate, and regenerate. Under a variety of circumstances, the processes are conservative. That is, they tend to maintain stable relations, sustain existing rules, and reduce differences among similar organizations. But the fundamental logic is not one of stability in behavior; it is one of adaptation. The processes are stable; the resulting actions are not.

Organizations change routinely and continually, and the effectiveness of an organization in responding to its environment, as well as much of the effectiveness of management, is linked to the effectiveness of routine processes. As a result, much of the job of an administrator involves the mundane work of making a bureaucracy work. It is filled with activities quite distant from those implied in a conception of administration as heroic leadership. It profits from ordinary competence and a recognition of the ways in which organizations change by modest modifications of routines rather than by massive mucking around. Studies of managerial time and behavior consistently show an implicit managerial recognition of the importance of these activities. The daily activities of a manager are rather distant from grand conceptions of organizational leadership. Administrators spend time talking to people about minor things, making trivial decisions, holding meetings with unimportant agendas, and responding to the little irritants of organizational life. Memoirs of administrators confirm the picture of a rewarding life made busy by large numbers of inconsequential things.

These observations describe administrative life as uncomfortably distant from the precepts of administrative theory and from hopes for personal significance. They have led to efforts to change the ways managers behave. Numerous training programs attempt to teach managers to bring their personal time allocation closer to the ideal. They provide procedures designed to increase the time for decision making, planning, thinking, and other things that appear more characteristic of theories of administration than of administrative jobs. These efforts may be mistakes. Making bureaucracy work involves effectiveness in executing a large number of little things. Making bureaucracies change involves attention to the minor routines by which things happen. Rules need to be understood in order to be interpreted or broken; simple breakdowns in the flow of supplies need to be minimized; telephones and letters need to be answered; accounts and records need to be maintained.

The importance of simple competence in the routines of organizational life is often overlooked when we sing the grand arias of management, but effective bureaucracies are rarely dramatic. They are administrative organizations that require elementary efficiency as a necessary condition for quality. Efficiency as a concept has been subject to considerable sensible criticism on the grounds that it is either meaningless or misleading if we treat it independent of the objectives being pursued. The point is well taken as a critique of the 'cult of efficiency,' but it is much too simple if we take it as an assertion that all, or even most, efforts in an administrative organization need a clear specification of global goals to be done well. An administrative organization combines large numbers of tasks into some kinds of meaningful combinations, but much of the effectiveness of the combination depends on the relatively automatic, local correction of local inefficiencies without continuous attention to the 'big picture'.

Much of what distinguishes a good bureaucracy from a bad one is how well it accomplishes the trivia of day-to-day relations with clients and day-to-day problems in maintaining and operating its technology. Accomplishing these trivia may involve considerable planning, complex coordination, and central direction, but it is more commonly linked to the effectiveness of large numbers of people doing minor things competently. As a result, it is probably true that the conspicuous differences around the world in the quality of bureaucratic performance are due primarily to variance in the competence of the ordinary clerk, bureaucrat, and lower manager, and to the effectiveness of routine procedures for dealing with problems at a local level. This appears to be true of armies, factories, postal services, hotels, and universities.

Organizations and ambiguous preferences

The classical administrator acts on the basis of knowledge about objectives. Goals are presumed to be clear – or it is presumed to be a responsibility of administration to make them clear. Administrative life often seems to be filled with ambiguous preferences and goals, and this becomes particularly conspicuous as one nears the top of an organization. Objectives are hard to specify in a way that provides precise guidance. That is not to say that they are completely unknown or that all parts are equally obscure. Administrative goals are often unclear; when we try to make them clear, they often seem unacceptable.

Goal ambiguity is particularly troubling to a conception of rational administrative action. As we normally conceive it, rational action involves two kinds of guesses: guesses about future consequences and guesses about future preferences for those consequences. We try to imagine the future outcomes that will result from our present actions, and we try to imagine how we will evaluate those outcomes when they occur. Neither guess is necessarily easy. Anticipating future consequences of present decisions is often subject to substantial error. Anticipating future preferences is often confusing. Theories of rational choice are primarily theories of these two guesses and how we deal with their complications. Theories of choice under uncertainty emphasize the complications of guessing future preferences.

In standard prescriptive theories of choice:

Preferences are relevant   Prescriptive theories of choice require that action be taken in terms of preferences, that decisions be consistent with objectives in the light of information about the probable consequences of alternatives for valued outcomes.

Preferences are stable   With few exceptions, prescriptive theories of choice require that tastes be stable. Current action is taken in terms of current preferences. The implicit assumption is that preferences will be unchanged when the outcomes of current actions are realized.

Preferences are consistent   Prescriptive theories of choice allow mutually inconsistent preferences only insofar as they can be made irrelevant by the absence of scarcity or by the specification of tradeoffs.

Preferences are precise Prescriptive theories of choice eliminate ambiguity about the extent to which a particular outcome will satisfy preferences, at least insofar as possible resolutions of ambiguity might affect the choice.

Preferences are exogenous Prescriptive theories of choice presume that preferences, by whatever process they may be created, are not themselves affected by the choices they control.

Each of these theoretical features of proper preferences seems inconsistent with some observations of administrative behavior. Administrators often ignore their own, fully conscious preferences in making decisions. They follow rules, traditions, hunches, and the advice and actions of others. Preferences often change over time in such a way that predicting future preferences is often difficult. Preferences are often inconsistent. Managers and others in organizations are often aware of the extent to which some of their preferences conflict with other of their preferences, yet they do nothing to resolve the conflict. Many preferences are stated in forms that lack precision. It is difficult to make them reliably operational in evaluating possible outcomes. While preferences are used to choose among actions, it is often also true that actions and experiences with their consequences affect preferences. Preferences are determined partly endogenously.

It is possible, of course, that such portrayals of administrative behavior are perverse. They may be perverse because they systematically misrepresent the actual behavior of administrators, or they may be perverse because the administrators they describe are, insofar as the description applies, stupid. It is also possible that the description is accurate and the behavior is intelligent, that the ambiguous way administrators sometimes deal with preferences is, in fact, sensible. If such a thing can be imagined, then perhaps we treat preferences inadequately in administrative theory.

The disparity between administrative objectives, as they appear in administrative theory, and administrative objectives, as we observe them in organizational life, has led to efforts to 'improve' the way administrators act. These characteristically emphasize the importance of goal clarity and of tying actions clearly to prior objectives. Deviations from the goal precision anticipated by decision theory have been treated as errors to be corrected. The strategy has led to important advances in management, and it has had its successes. But it also has had failures. Stories of disasters attributable to the introduction of decision technology are clichés of recent administrative experience.

As a result, students of administrative theory have been led to ask whether it is possible that goal ambiguity is not always a defect to be eliminated from administration, whether perhaps it may sometimes reflect a form of intelligence that is obscured by our models of rationality. For example, there are good reasons for moderating an enthusiasm for precise performance measures in organizations. The introduction of precision into the evaluation of performance involves a trade-off between the gains in outcomes attributable to closer articulation between action and measured objectives and the losses attributable to misrepresentation of goals, reduced motivation for development of goals, and concentration of effort on irrelevant ways of beating the index. Whether we are considering a performance evaluation scheme for managers or a testing procedure for students, there is likely to be a difference between the *maximum* clarity of goals and the *optimum* clarity.

The complications of performance measures are, however, only an illustration of the general issue of goal ambiguity in administrative action. In order to examine the more general issue, we probably need to ask why an intelligent administrator might deliberately choose – or sensibly learn – to have ambiguous goals. In fact, rationalizing ambiguity is neither difficult nor novel, but it depends on perspectives somewhat more familiar to human understanding as it is found in literature, philosophy, and ordinary experience than as we see it in our theories of administration and choice. For example:

1 Many administrators engage in activities designed to manage their own preferences. These activities make little sense from the point of view of a conception of action that assumes administrators know what they want and will want, or a conception that assumes wants are morally equivalent. But ordinary human actors sense that they might come to want something they should not, or that they might make unwise or inappropriate choices under the influence of fleeting, but powerful, desires if they do not control the development of preferences or buffer action from preferences.
2 Many administrators are both proponents for preferences and observers of the process by which preferences are developed and acted upon. As observers of the process by which their beliefs have been formed and evoked, they recognize the good sense in perceptual and moral modesty.
3 Many administrators maintain a lack of coherence both within and among personal desires, social demands, and moral codes. Though they seek some consistency, they appear to see inconsistency as a normal, and necessary, aspect of the development and clarification of values.
4 Many administrators are conscious of the importance of preferences as beliefs independent of their immediate action consequences. They accept a degree of personal and social wisdom in ordinary hypocrisy.
5 Many administrators recognize the political nature of rational argument more clearly than the theory of choice does. They are unwilling to gamble that God made clever people uniquely virtuous. They protect themselves from cleverness by obscuring the nature of their preferences; they exploit cleverness by asking others to construct reasons for actions they wish to take.

If these characteristics of ambiguous preference processing by administrators make sense under rather general circumstances, our administrative theories based on ideas of clarity in objectives do not make as much sense as we sometimes attribute to them. Not only are they descriptively inadequate, they lead to attempts to clarify things that serve us better unclarified. Some of our standard dicta that managers should define and pursue clear objectives need to be qualified by a recognition that clarity is sometimes a mistake.

Organizations, managerial ambitions and managerial incentives

In most conceptions of administration, administrators are assumed to be ambitious for promotion, position, and success. Managerial incentive schemes are efforts to link such personal ambitions of managers with the goals of the organization so that the behavior of self-interested managers contributes to achieving organizational objectives. As you move toward the top of an organization, however, some things happen that confuse ambition. Promotions are filters through which successful managers pass. Assuming that all promotions are based on similar attributes, each successive filter further refines the pool, reducing variation among managers. On attributes the organization considers important, vice-presidents are likely to be significantly more homogeneous than first-level managers. In addition, as we move up the organization, objectives usually become more conflicting and more ambiguous. Exactly what is expected of a manager sometimes seems obscure and changing, and it becomes harder to attribute specific outcomes to specific managerial actions.

Thus, as we move up the organization, evaluation procedures become less and less reliable, and the population of managers becomes more and more homogeneous. The joint result is that the noise level in evaluation approaches the variance in the pool of managers. At the limit, one vice-president cannot be reliably distinguished from another; quality distinctions among top executives, however consistent with their records, are less likely to be justified than distinctions made at a lower level. Toward the top of an organization, it is difficult to know unambiguously that a particular manager makes a difference. Notice that this is not the same as suggesting that management is unimportant. Management may be extremely important even though managers are indistinguishable. It is hard to tell the difference between two different light bulbs also; but if you take all light bulbs away, it is difficult to read in the dark. What is hard to demonstrate is the extent to which high-performing managers (or light bulbs that endure for an exceptionally long time) are something more than one extreme end of a probability distribution of results generated by essentially equivalent individuals.

Because it has such properties, a mobility system in an organization is a hierarchy of partial lotteries in which the expected values of the lotteries increase as we move up the organization, but control over their outcomes declines. Of course, if the objective is to recruit ambitious and talented people into management, it may not matter whether potential managers are able to control outcomes precisely, as long as the expected values of the games are higher than other opportunities. Ambitious people will seek such careers even if they believe – which they may not – that the outcomes are chance. What is less clear is exactly what kind of managerial behavior will be stimulated by management lotteries.

At the heart of a managerial promotion and reward scheme is normally some measure of managerial performance. Managers are seen as improving organizational outcomes by trying to improve their own measured performance, but every index of performance is an invitation to cleverness. Long before reaching the top, an intelligent manager learns that some of the more effective ways of improving measured performance have little to do with improving product, service, or technology. A system of rewards linked to precise measures is not an incentive to perform well; it is an incentive to obtain a good score. At the same time, since managers are engaged in a lottery in which it is difficult to associate specific outcomes with specific managerial behavior, it becomes important to be able to say, 'I did the things a good manager should do.' We develop a language for describing good managers and bad ones, and individual managers are able to learn social norms of management. Not all managers behave in exactly the same way, but they all learn the language, expectations, and styles. They are socialized into managerial roles.

These analyses of the consequences of managerial incentives at the top seem inconsistent with the way we talk about leadership in organizations. In effect, we now have two contending theories of how things happen in organizations. The first is considerably influenced by stories of great figures – Catherine the Great, Bismarck, Alfred Sloan – and elaborated by the drama of success and failure of individuals in bureaucratic settings. It portrays administration in relatively heroic ways. Such portrayals lead us to attribute a large share of the variance in organizational outcomes to special properties of specific individual managers. They are comfortably reassuring in the major role they assign to administrative leadership, but they seem to describe a world rather far from administrative experience or research.

The second theory (filled with metaphors of loose coupling, organized anarchy, and garbage can decision processes) seems to describe administrative reality better, but it appears uncomfortably pessimistic about the significance of administrators. Indeed, it seems potentially pernicious even if correct. Consider two general types of errors a manager might make in assessing the importance of intentional actions in controlling organizational outcomes. A manager might come to believe in considerable personal control over outcomes when, in fact, that control does not exist. A 'false positive' error. Such a belief would lead to (futile) attempts to control events, but it would not otherwise affect results. Alternatively, a manager might come to believe that significant personal control is not possible, when in fact, it is. A 'false negative' error. Such a belief would lead to self-confirming withdrawal from efforts to be effective. Either type of error is possible, but the social costs of the first seem small, relative to the second. Given a choice, we would generally prefer to err on the side of making false positive errors in assessing human significance, rather than false negative errors.

Perhaps fortunately, organizational life assures a managerial bias toward belief in managerial importance. Top managers are not random managers; they are successful managers. They rise to the top on the basis of a series of successful experiences. We know that individuals often find it easy to believe that successes in their lives are attributable to their talents and choices, while failures are due more to bad luck or malevolence. Promotion to the top on the basis of successes at lower levels results in top-level executives believing in the possibility of substantial intentional control over organizational events. Even though their experiences might have led managers to such beliefs erroneously, managerial experience is likely to be subjectively very persuasive. In effect, the system of managerial mobility is designed to make managers much more resistant to false beliefs in impotence than to false beliefs in control. Administrative experience, as well as managerial self-esteem, will usually give managers a greater sense of personal importance and uniqueness than the second theory suggests.

In fact, there is a third theory, and it is probably closer to the truth than either of the others. In this third view, managers *do* affect the ways in which organizations function. But as a result of the process by which managers are selected, motivated, and trained, variations in managers do not reliably produce variations in organizational outcomes. In such a conception, administrators are vital as a class but not as individuals. Administration is important, and the many things that administrators do are essential to keeping the organization functioning; but if those vital things are only done when there is an unusually gifted individual at the top, the organization will not thrive. What makes an organization function well is the density of administrative competence, the kind of selection procedures that make all vice-presidents look alike from the point of view of their probable success, and the motivation that leads managers to push themselves to the limit.

Earlier, I used the analogy of a light bulb. I think it is a good analogy. If the manufacture of light bulbs is so unreliable that only a few actually work, you will not be able to do much reading. On the other hand, if light bulbs are reliable, you can read whenever you want to, but you won't much care which light bulb you use. One problem with some conventional administrative thought is that it encourages us to glorify an organization that finds the unique working light bulb in a large shipment of defective bulbs, rather than an organization that persistently produces a supply of nearly indistinguishable good bulbs. It is the latter organization that functions better.

Organizations, rituals and symbols

Administrators and administrative decisions allocate scarce resources and are thereby of considerable social and individual importance, but decisions in organizations and the administration of them are important beyond their outcomes. They are also arenas for exercising social values, for displaying authority and position, and for exhibiting proper behavior and attitudes with respect to a central ideological construct of modern Western civilization – the concept of intelligent choice. Bureaucratic organizations are built on ideas of rationality, and rationality is built on ideas about the way decisions should be made. Indeed, it would be hard to find any institution in modern society more prototypically committed to systematic, rational action than a formal organization.

Thus, administrative action in an organization is a performance in which administrators try to behave in a normatively praiseworthy way. Making intelligent decisions is important, but the verification of intelligence in decision making is often difficult. As a result, it often becomes heavily procedural. For example, in the usual scenario for administrative performance, the gathering of information is not simply a basis for action; it is a representation of competence and a reaffirmation of personal virtue. Command of information and information sources enhances perceived competence and inspires confidence. The belief that more information characterizes better decisions and defensible decision processes engenders a conspicuous consumption of information. Information is flaunted but not used, collected but not considered.

Ideas about proper administrative behavior diffuse through a population of organizations and change over time. What makes a particular procedure appropriate for one manager is that it is being used in other successful organizations by other successful managers. What makes an administrative innovation new and promising is that it has been adopted by other organizations that are viewed as being intelligently innovative. Managerial procedures spread from successful organizations to unsuccessful ones, as the latter try to present themselves as equivalent to the former; the signal a particular procedure provides is gradually degraded by its adoption by organizations that are not 'well managed' or 'progressive,' thus stimulating the invention of new procedures.

This competition among managers and organizations for legitimacy and standing is endless. As managers attempt to establish and maintain reputations through the symbols of good management, social values are sustained and elaborated. For symbols of administrative competence are, of course, symbols simultaneously of social efficacy. Belief in the appropriateness of administrative actions, the process by which they are taken, and the roles played by the various actors involved is a key part of a social structure. It is not only important to decision makers that they be viewed as legitimate; it is also useful to society that leaders be imagined to control organizational outcomes and to act in a way that can be reconciled with a sense of human control over human destiny.

Ritual acknowledgement of managerial importance and appropriateness is part of a social ceremony by which social life is made meaningful and acceptable under conditions that would otherwise be problematic. For example, managerial capabilities for controlling events are likely to be more immediately obvious to managers than to others in the organization. Since most of the managers with whom managers must deal are themselves successful managers, the problem is somewhat concealed from daily managerial experience. Many of the people whom we see in administration, particularly in a growing organization, are people who see themselves as successful; but there are others, less conspicuous, who do not derive the same prejudices from their own experience. So, we construct various myths of management. The same mobility process that encourages top managers in a belief in their own control over events tends to teach some others that managerial successes and the events associated with them are more due to luck or corruption.

The stories, myths, and rituals of management are not merely ways some people fool other people or a waste of time. They are fundamental to our lives. We embrace the mythologies and symbols of life and could not otherwise easily endure. Executive behavior and management procedures contribute to myths about management that become the reality of managerial life and reinforce a belief in a human destiny subject to intentional human control. They may not be essential to such a belief – it is reinforced in many subtle ways throughout society – but executive rituals and executive life are parts of that large mosaic of mutually supporting myths by which an instrumental society brings hope and frustration to individual lives. Since managerial rituals are important to our faith, and our faith is important to the functioning of organizations as well as to the broader social and political order, these symbolic activities of administration are central to its success.

Most administrators seem ambivalent about symbol management. On the one hand, they recognize that they spend considerable time trying to sustain beliefs in the intelligence, coherence, importance, and uniqueness of their organizations (and themselves). At the same time, however, they seem to view the activity as either somewhat illegitimate or as an imposition on more important things – such as decision making, directing, or coordinating. They treat the rituals of administration as necessary, but they talk about them as a waste of time.

Partly, of course, the ambivalence is itself socially dictated. In a society that emphasizes instrumentality as much as Western society does, leaders would be less acceptable if they were to acknowledge the ritual activities of their jobs as central. One of their key symbolic responsibilities is to maintain an ideology that denies the legitimacy of symbol maintenance. Thus, they tend to do it but to deny they do it, or to bemoan the fact that they must do it. It is a careful dance along a narrow beam, and there is the possibility of much grace in it. But the elegance of the dance probably depends on a fine modulation between talk and action, as well as some administrative consciousness of the meaning of the dance. In order to achieve that consciousness, we probably need to recognize the ambivalence and to encourage administrators to see how the activities in which they participate are an essential part of a larger social ritual by which they, as well as others in society, reaffirm purpose and order in a potentially disorderly world.

Many managers, of course, recognize the many elements of storytelling by which they present themselves. Successful managers are usually adept at managing their own reputations. They know how to manage symbols for that purpose. The self-serving character of managerial symbol manipulation is easily seen as unattractive, and few would want to legitimize the self-aggrandizement and self-delusion that are its corollaries. Nor would many observers welcome an unconditional enthusiasm for using symbols to sustain the existing social order against all counterclaims. Critics of the establishment cannot be expected to embrace symbolic performances that have as their main consequence the reinforcement of an unacceptable social system.

These reasonable concerns about symbol manipulation are reminders of its administrative importance. Life is not just choice. It is also poetry. We live by the interpretations we make, becoming better or worse through the meanings we impute to events and institutions. Our lives change when our beliefs change. Administrators manage the way the sentiments, expectations, commitments, and faiths of individuals concerned with the organization fit into a structure of social beliefs about organizational life. Administrative theory probably underestimates the significance of this belief structure for effective organizations. As a result, it probably underestimates the extent to which the management of symbols is a part of effective administration. If we want to identify one single way in which administrators can affect organizations, it is through their effect on the world views that surround organizational life; those effects are managed through attention to the ritual and symbolic characteristics of organizations and their administration. Whether we wish to sustain the system or change it, management is a way of making a symbolic statement.

Round theories and flat experience

In general, these observations are not particularly surprising. In most ways, they are familiar to our experience. They are less familiar, however, to the way we talk about administration. I have tried to list four emphases of administrative theory that seem to be relatively distant from our observations and experience. First, the theoretical emphasis on change as produced by heroic leader action and the consequent emphasis on effectiveness (goal-oriented action) rather than efficiency (goal-free actions), on *leadership* rather than *management*. The theoretical rhetoric of change seems antithetical to routine, but I have argued that effective systems of routine behavior are the primary bases of organizational adaptation to an environment.

Second, the theoretical emphasis on problem-solving of a classical sort in which alternatives are assessed in terms of their consequences for prior goals that are stable, precise, and exogenous. I have argued that many situations in administration involve goals that are (and ought to be) ambiguous.

Third, the theoretical emphasis on explaining variations in organizational outcomes is due to variations in top leadership skills and commitment. I have argued that when an organizational system is working well, variations in outcomes will be due largely to variables unrelated to variations in attributes of top leaders. Where top leadership affects variation in outcomes, the system is probably not functioning well.

Fourth, the theoretical emphasis on administrative action as instrumental, is being justified by the way it produces substantive consequences for important outcomes. I have argued that much of administration is symbolic, a way of interpreting organizational life in a way that allows individuals in organizations to fit their experience to their visions of human existence. Administrative processes are sacred rituals at least as much as they are instrumental acts.

If informed opinion says the earth is round but we experience it flat, we are in danger of having to choose between our senses and our intellect. If we can, we want to discover behavior that is sensible but at the same time confirms our conventional probity – in the face of their apparent inconsistency. The usual procedure, of course, is to talk about a round world and use a flat map. In the case of the map and the earth, we are confident enough of the round theory to be willing to make a fairly precise rationalization of the map. In other cases, the issues are in greater doubt. If you experience planning as something you rarely do yet all the people you admire report that it is important, you might plausibly come to echo their comments without a clear understanding of why you talk about planning so much yet do it so little.

Like a person contemplating a naked emperor amidst courtiers exclaiming over the royal clothing, an administrator must simultaneously act intelligently and sustain a reputation for intelligence. Since theories of administration – and the talk that they generate – are part of the basis for reputation, their distance from ordinary administrative experience poses a problem. For most administrators, the difficulties are not likely to be seen as stemming from failures in administrative theory. What I have called 'administrative theory' is not some set of esoteric axioms propagated by a few high priests of academe; rather, it is an elaboration of very general cultural beliefs about organizations, change, leadership, and administration. Most reasonable people accept them with as much confidence as they accept the notion that the earth is round, even while at the same time finding them inconsistent with important parts of organizational life.

The argument is not that administrative theory and administrative life should coincide. In general, they should not. The criterion for good normative theory is not its descriptive accuracy. It is not necessary that the theory be correct, consistent, or even meaningful in conventional terms. It is not necessary that the theory resolve all the difficult trade-offs that impinge on administrative life. In most human domains, we maintain the maxims of a good life by violating them judiciously without claims of virtue; we pursue goals we would not want to achieve in hopes thereby of becoming better than we are. For our theories of administration to be useful in administrative life, we require that *pursuing* (without necessarily fulfilling) the precepts of the theory improves organizations and administration. In such a spirit, administrators may struggle to follow the precepts of administrative thought, even though they are impossible, inconsistent, or unwise. Intelligent administrators might well do such a thing in full consciousness, not in hopes of fulfilling the precepts – for they would not want to do that – but in hopes of acting in a better way than they would without the struggle.

Much of standard administrative theory, including parts that have long been criticized by behavioral students of organizations, seems to me to meet such criteria. There are numerous elementary – but vital – rules of thumb that help improve the management of an organization when applied with intelligence, even though they seem either trivial or contradictory. For example, the dictum that managers should minimize the span of control *and* minimize the number of levels of the organization is obviously nonsensical as a statement of an optimization problem. It is, however, not foolish as a statement of contradictory complications in organizing. Many of the things that ancient texts on administration say seem to me similarly sensible – but not all of them. The fact that administrative theory, like a moral code, does not have to be prima facie sensible in order to be useful should not lead us to assume immediately that incomplete, inconsistent, or incorrect maxims are *necessarily* helpful.

Sometimes our assumptions are wrong, and the worlds we experience as flat actually are, if not entirely flat, not entirely round either. Administrators who feel that their experiences with the way organizations change, with ambiguity in objectives and experience, with management incentives and careers, and with symbolic action are consistent with the kinds of research observations I have noted may well want to question conventional administrative thought and welcome alternative formulations. If these research observations capture a part of organizational truth, some of the apparently strange things that an administrator does are probably more sensible than administrative theory recognizes, and the struggle to fulfill the expectations of administrative virtue may result in actions that are less intelligent than they would have been in the absence of administrative dogma. Sometimes our theories are misleading, and the way we talk confuses the way we act.

Source: March, James G. (1984) How we talk and how we act: administrative theory and administrative life. In T. Sergiovanni and J. E. Corbally (eds), *Leadership and Organizational Cultures*, University of Illinois Press, Urbana, pp. 18–35.

4 Toward a model of organizations as interpretation systems

Richard L. Daft and Karl E. Weick

Consider the game of 20 questions. Normally in this game one person leaves the room, the remaining people select a word that the person is to guess when he/she returns, and the only clue given about the word is whether it signifies an animal, vegetable, or mineral. The person trying to guess the word asks up to 20 questions that can be answered yes or no in an effort to guess what the word is. Each question is designed to provide new information about the correct word. Together, the questions and answers are the process by which an interpretation is built up by the person who is 'it.'

Organizations play 20 questions. Organizations have limited time and questions, and they strive for the answer. The answer is discovering what consumers want that other organizations do not provide. The answer is finding that there is a market for pet rocks, roller skates, encounter groups, erasable ballpoint pens, or zero population growth. Many organizations presume that there is a correct answer to the puzzle of 20 questions. They query the environment with samples, market surveys, and test markets. They may establish specialized scanning departments that use trend analysis, media content analysis, and econometric modeling to obtain answers about the external environment. These organizations try to find an acceptable answer before their resources run out, before competitors corner the market, before people's interests change, or before more compelling opportunities in other environmental sectors dominate the search.

All of these activities, whether in organizations or in 20 questions, represent a form of interpretation. People are trying to interpret what they have done, define what they have learned, solve the problem of what they should do next. Building up interpretations about the environment is a basic requirement of individuals and organizations. The process of building the interpretation may be influenced by such things as the nature of the answer sought, the characteristics of the environment, the previous experience of the questioner, and the method used to acquire it.

Why interpretation?

Pondy and Mitroff (1979) recently reminded organizational scientists that organizations have characteristics typical of level 8 on Boulding's (1956) 9-level scale of system complexity. Boulding concluded that organizations are among the most complex systems imaginable. Organizations are vast, fragmented and multidimensional. Pondy and Mitroff argue that most empirical research is at Boulding's level 1 to 3, which assumes that organizations behave as static frameworks or mechanical systems.

One purpose of this paper is to propose a conceptualization of organizations that is at a higher level of system complexity and incorporates organizational activities and variables that have not been captured in other approaches (Weick & Daft, 1983). The critical issue for interpretation systems is to differentiate into highly specialized information receptors that interact with the environment. Information about the external world must be obtained, filtered, and processed into a central nervous system of sorts, in which choices are made. The organization must find ways to know the environment. Interpretation is a critical element that distinguishes human organizations from lower level systems.

A second purpose of this paper is to integrate diverse ideas and empirical facts that pertain to organizational interpretation of the environment. Pfeffer and Salancik (1978) reviewed the literature on organization and environment relationships. They concluded that scanning is a key topic for explaining organizational behavior, yet practically no research had been reported on environmental scanning processes. There also is little understanding of the interpretation process and the organizational configurations that may enhance interpretation. The scarcity of empirical studies remains, although a few findings have been reported in diverse areas, such as organization theory, policy and strategy, futures research, and planning. The consolidation of these ideas and the organization of them into a model of interpretation system characteristics may provide a stimulus for future research into scanning and interpretation processes.

Working assumptions

Any approach to the study of organizations is built on specific assumptions about the nature of organizations and how they are designed and function. Four specific assumptions underlie the model presented in this paper and clarify the logic and rationale on which the interpretation system approach is based.

The most basic assumption, consistent with Boulding's scale of system complexity, is that organizations are open social systems that process information from the environment. The environment contains some level of uncertainty, so the organization must seek information and then base organizational action on that information. Organizations must develop information processing mechanisms capable of detecting trends, events, competitors, markets, and technological developments relevant to their survival.

The second assumption concerns individual versus organizational interpretations. Individual human beings send and receive information and in other ways carry out the interpretation process. Organization theorists realize that organizations do not have mechanisms separate from individuals to set goals, process information, or perceive the environment. People do these things. Yet in this paper it is assumed that the organizational interpretation process is something more than what occurs by individuals. Organizations have cognitive systems and memories (Hedberg, 1981). Individuals come and go, but organizations preserve knowledge, behaviors, mental maps, norms, and values over time. The distinctive feature of organization level information activity is sharing. A piece of data, a perception, a cognitive map is shared among managers who constitute the interpretation system. Passing a startling observation among members, or discussing a puzzling development, enables managers to converge on an approximate interpretation. Managers may not agree fully about their perceptions (Starbuck, 1976), but the thread of coherence among managers is what characterizes organizational interpretations. Reaching convergence among members characterizes the act of organizing (Weick, 1979) and enables the organization to interpret as a system.

The third assumption is that strategic-level managers formulate the organization's interpretation. When one speaks of organizational interpretation one really means interpretation by a relatively small group at the top of the organizational hierarchy. A large number of people may span the boundary with the external environment (Aldrich & Herker, 1977; Leifer & Delbecq, 1978), and this information is channeled into the organization. Organizations can be conceptualized as a series of nested systems, and each subsystem may deal with a different external sector. Upper managers bring together and interpret information for the system as a whole. Many participants may play some part in scanning or data processing, but the point at which information converges and is interpreted for organization level action is assumed to be at the top manager level. This assumption is consistent with Aguilar's (1967) observation that below the vice presidential level, participants are not informed on issues pertaining to the organization as a whole.

The fourth assumption is that organizations differ systematically in the mode or process by which they interpret the environment. Organizations develop specific ways to know the environment. Interpretation processes are not random. Systematic variations occur based on organization and environmental characteristics, and the interpretation process may in turn influence organizational outcomes such as strategy, structure, and decision making. For example, Aguilar (1967) interviewed managers about their sources of environmental information. He concluded that scanning behavior might vary according to the breadth or narrowness of the organization's viewing and also by the extent of formal search. Other authors have suggested that institutional scanning can be classified as regular or irregular (Fahey & King, 1977; Leifer & Delbecq, 1978) or by the extent to which organizations passively perceive the environment versus creating or enacting external reality (Weick, 1979; Weick & Daft, 1983).

Definition of interpretation

Organizations must make interpretations. Managers literally must wade into the ocean of events that surround the organization and actively try to make sense of them. Organization participants physically act on these events, attending to some of them, ignoring most of them, and talking to other people to see what they are doing (Braybrooke, 1964). Interpretation is the process of translating these events, of developing models for understanding, of bringing out meaning, and of assembling conceptual schemes among key managers.

The interpretation process in organizations is neither simple nor well understood. There are many interpretation images in the literature, including scanning, monitoring, sense making, interpretation, understanding, and learning (Duncan & Weiss, 1979; Hedberg, 1981; Weick, 1979; Pfeffer & Salancik, 1978). These concepts can be roughly organized into three stages that constitute the overall learning process, as reflected in Figure 1. The first stage is *scanning*, which is defined as the process of monitoring the environment and providing environmental data to managers. Scanning is concerned with data collection. The organization may use formal data collection systems, or managers may acquire data about the environment through personal contacts.

Interpretation occurs in the second stage in Figure 1. Data are given meaning. Here the human mind is engaged. Perceptions are shared and cognitive maps are constructed. An information coalition of sorts is formed. The organization experiences interpretation when a new construct is introduced into the collective cognitive map of the organization. Organizational *interpretation* is formally defined as the process of translating events and

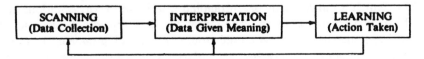

Figure 1 *Relationships among organizational scanning, interpretation and learning*

developing shared understanding and conceptual schemes among members of upper management. Interpretation gives meaning to data, but it occurs before organizational learning and action.

Learning, the third stage, is distinguished from interpretation by the concept of action. Learning involves a new response or action based on the interpretation (Argyris & Schon, 1978). Organizational *learning* is defined as the process by which knowledge about action-outcome relationships between the organization and the environment is developed (Duncan & Weiss, 1979). Learning is a process of putting cognitive theories into action (Argyris & Schon, 1978; Hedberg, 1981). Organizational interpretation is analogous to learning a new skill by an individual. The act of learning also provides new data for interpretation. Feedback from organizational actions may provide new collective insights for coalition members. Thus the three stages are inter-connected through a feedback loop in Figure 1.

Figure 1 and the definitions of scanning, interpretation, and learning oversimplify complex processes. Factors such as beliefs, politics, goals, and perceptions may complicate the organizational learning cycle (Staw, 1980). The purpose of Figure 1 is to illustrate the relationship of interpretation to scanning and learning as the basis for a model of organizational interpretation.

Toward a model of organizational interpretation

Two key dimensions are used here to explain organizational interpretation differences. They are: (1) management's beliefs about the analyzability of the external environment and (2) the extent to which the organization intrudes into the environment to understand it. The proposed model provides a way to describe and explain the diverse ways organizations may obtain knowledge about the environment.

Assumptions about the environment

Many organizations undoubtedly play the interpretation game with the goal of finding the correct answer, just as in the game of 20 questions. The game of 20 questions, however, is of limited value as a metaphor because there is one way in which it mocks many organizational worlds. Many organizations have nothing that corresponds to 'the answer.' In everyday life the act of questioning may be much more influential in determining the correct answer than is the case with the clear-cut roles of asking and answering and the fixed answer present in the conventional version of 20 questions.

The game, 20 questions, becomes more typical with a variation suggested by the physicist John Wheeler. Once the player leaves the room so that those remaining can choose the word, the game unfolds in a different fashion.

> While he is gone the other players decide to alter the rules. They will select no word at all; instead each of them will answer 'yes' or 'no' as he pleases – provided he has a word in mind that fits both his own reply and all the previous replies. The outsider returns and, unsuspecting, begins asking questions. At last he makes a guess: 'Is the word "clouds"?' Yes, comes the answer, and the players explain the game (*Newsweek*, 1979, p. 62).

When the questioner began, he assumed the answer already existed. Yet the answer was created through the questions raised. If the player asked different questions, a different answer would emerge.

If some organizations play 20 questions in the traditional way, seeking the correct answer already in the environment, and if others play 20 questions John Wheeler's way, constructing an answer, then there is an interesting difference in interpretation behavior. This difference reflects the organization's assumption about the analyzability of its environment.

If an organization assumes that the external environment is concrete, that events and processes are hard, measurable, and determinant, then it will play the traditional game to discover the 'correct' interpretation. The key for this organization is discovery through intelligence gathering, rational analysis, vigilance, and accurate measurement. This organization will utilize linear thinking and logic and will seek clear data and solutions.

When an organization assumes that the external environment is unanalyzable, an entirely different strategy will apply. The organization to some extent may create the external environment. The key is to construct, coerce, or enact a reasonable interpretation that makes previous action sensible and suggests some next steps. The interpretation may shape the environment more than the environment shapes the interpretation. The interpretation process is more personal, less linear, more ad hoc and improvisational than for other organizations. The outcome of this process may include the ability to deal with equivocality, to coerce an answer useful to the organization, to invent an environment and be part of the invention.

What factors explain differences in organizational beliefs about the environment? The answer is hypothesized to be characteristics of the environment combined with management's previous interpretation experience. When the environment is subjective, difficult to penetrate, or changing (Duncan, 1972), managers will see it as less analyzable (Perrow, 1967; Tung, 1979). Wilensky's (1967) work on intelligence gathering in government organizations detected major differences in the extent to which environments were seen as rationalized, that is subject to discernible, predictable uniformities in relationships among significant objects. In one organization studied by Aguilar (1967), managers assumed an analyzable environment because of previous experience. Accurate forecasts were possible because product demand was directly correlated to petroleum demand, which in turn was correlated to well defined trends such as population growth, auto sales, and gasoline consumption. However, for a similar organization in another industry, systematic data collection and analysis were not used. Statistical trends had no correlation with product demand or capital spending. Facts and figures were not consistent with the unanalyzable assumptions about the environment. Soft, qualitative data, along with judgment and intuition, had a larger role in the interpretation process.

Organizational intrusiveness

The second major difference among interpretation systems is the extent to which organizations actively intrude into the environment. Some organizations actively search the environment for an answer. They allocate resources to search activities. They hire technically oriented MBAs; build planning, forecasting, or special research departments; or even subscribe to monitoring services (Thomas, 1980). In extreme cases, organizations may send agents into the field (Wilenksy, 1967). Organizational search also may include testing or manipulating the environment. These organizations may leap before they look, perform trials in order to learn what an error is, and discover what is feasible by testing presumed constraints. Forceful organizations may break presumed rules, try to change the rules, or try to manipulate critical factors in the environment (Kotter, 1979; Pfeffer, 1976). A survey of major corporations found that many of them established departments and mechanisms for searching and/or creating environments (Thomas, 1980). These organizations might be called test makers (Weick & Daft, 1983), and they will develop interpretations quite different from organizations that behave in a passive way.

Passive organizations accept whatever information the environment gives them. These organizations do not engage in trial and error. They do not actively search for the answer in the environment. They do not have departments assigned to discover or manipulate the environment. They may set up receptors to sense whatever data happen to flow by the organization. By accepting the environment as given, these organizations become test avoiders (Weick, 1979). They interpret the environment within accepted limits.

Research evidence suggests that many organizations are informal and unsystematic in their interpretation of the environment (Fahey & King, 1977). These organizations tend to accept the environment as given and respond actively only when a crisis occurs. For a crisis, the organization might search out new information or consciously try to influence external events. Other organizations actively search the environment on a continuous basis (Aguilar, 1967; Wilensky, 1967). Organizations thus differ widely in the active versus passive approach toward interpretation.

One explanation of differential intrusion into the environment is conflict between organization and environment. Wilensky (1967) argued that when the environment is perceived as hostile or threatening, or when the organization depends heavily on the environment, more resources are allocated to the intelligence gathering function. Organizations attempt to develop multiple lines of inquiry into the environment. In the corporate world, intense competition or resource scarcity will lead to allocation of more resources into interpretation-related functions. Organizations in benevolent environments have weaker incentives to be intrusive (Child, 1974; Hedberg, 1981). Only rarely do organizations in benevolent environments use their slack resources for trial and error experimentation or formal search. A hostile environment generates increased search because of new problems and a perceived need to develop new opportunities and niches. More exhaustive information is needed.

Another explanation of different levels of intrusion is organizational age and size (Kimberly & Miles, 1980). New, young organizations typically begin their existence as test makers. They try new things and actively seek information about their limited environment. Gradually, over time, the organization interpretation system begins to accept the environment rather than searching or testing its boundaries. New organizations are disbelievers, are unin-doctrinated, and have less history to rely on. They are more likely to dive in and develop a niche that established organizations have failed to see. But as the organization grows and as time passes, the environment may be perceived as less threatening, so search will decrease.

The model

Based on the idea that organizations may vary in their beliefs about the environment and in their intrusiveness into the environment, organizations can be categorized according to interpretation modes. The two underlying dimensions are used as the basis for an interpretation system model, presented in Figure 2, which describes four categories of interpretation behavior.

The *enacting* mode reflects both an active, intrusive strategy and the assumption that the environment is unanalyzable. These organizations construct their own environments. They gather information by trying new behaviors and seeing what happens. They experiment, test, and stimulate, and they ignore precedent, rules, and traditional expectations. This organization is highly activated, perhaps under the belief that it must be so in order to succeed. This type of organization tends to develop and market a product, such as polaroid cameras, based on what it thinks it can sell. An organization in this mode tends to construct markets rather than waiting for an assessment of demand to tell it what to produce. These organizations, more than others, tend to display the enactment behavior described by Weick (1979).

	Passive	Active
Unanalyzable **Assumptions about environment**	**Undirected viewing** Constrained interpretations. Nonroutine, informal data. Hunch, rumor, chance opportunities.	**Enacting** Experimentation, testing, coercion, invent environment. Learn by doing.
Analyzable	**Conditioned viewing** Interprets within traditional boundaries. Passive detection. Routine, formal data.	**Discovering** Formal search, Questioning, surveys, data gathering. Active detection.

Passive   Active
Organizational intrusiveness

Figure 2   *Model of organizational interpretation modes*

The *discovering* mode also represents an intrusive organization, but the emphasis is on detecting the correct answer already in an analyzable environment rather than on shaping the answer. Carefully devised measurement probes are sent into the environment to relay information back to the organization. This organization uses market research, trend analysis, and forecasting to predict problems and opportunities. Formal data determine organizational interpretations about environmental characteristics and expectations. Discovering organizations are similar to organizations that rely on formal search procedures for information (Aguilar, 1967) and in which staff analysts are used extensively to gather and analyze data (Wilensky, 1967).

Organizations characterized as *conditioned viewing* (Aguilar, 1967) assume an analyzable environment and are not intrusive. They tend to rely on established data collection procedures, and the interpretations are developed within traditional boundaries. The environment is perceived as objective and benevolent, so the organization does not take unusual steps to learn about the environment. The viewing is conditioned in the sense that it is limited to the routine documents, reports, publications, and information systems that have grown up through the years. The view of the environment is limited to these traditional sources. At some time historically, these data were perceived as important, and the organization is now conditioned to them. Organizations in this category use procedures similar to the regular scanning of limited sectors described by Fahey and King (1977).

Undirected viewing (Aguilar, 1967) reflects a similar passive approach, but these organizations do not rely on hard, objective data because the environment is assumed to be unanalyzable. Managers act on limited, soft information to create their perceived environment. These organizations are not conditioned by formal management systems within the organization, and they are open to a variety of cues about the environment from many sources. Managers in these organizations are like the ones Aguilar (1967) found that relied on information obtained through personal contacts and casual information encounters. Fahey and King (1977) also found some organizational information gatherings to be irregular and based on chance opportunities.

Examples of conditioned and undirected viewing modes have been illustrated by clothing companies in England (Daft & Macintosh, 1978). These companies developed different interpretation systems over time, although they were in a similar industry. Top management in the conditioned viewing organization used a data collection system to record routinely such things as economic conditions, past sales, and weather forecasts. These data were used to predict sales and to schedule production. These systems had grown up over the years and were used routinely to interpret problems that occurred. The other company gathered information from personal contacts with a few store buyers, salesmen, and informants in other companies. Managers also visited a few stores to observe and discuss in a casual manner what seemed to be selling. This company used undirected viewing. Interpretation was based on a variety of subjective cues that happened to be available.

Another example of interpretation styles is illustrated by the relationship between corporations and their shareholders (Keim, 1981). A few corporations actively influence and shape shareholder attitudes. The enacting organization may try to manipulate shareholder perceptions toward itself, environmental issues, or political candidates by sending information to shareholders through various media. Discovery-oriented corporations actively stay in touch with shareholders to learn what they are thinking, and they conduct surveys or use other devices to discover attitudes. A few corporations handle the shareholder relationships through routine data transactions (stockholder voting, mailing out dividend checks), which is typical of conditioned viewing. Finally, some corporations rely on informal, personal contact with shareholders (undirected viewing). Managers use whatever opportunities arise (annual meetings, telephone contact about complaints and questions) to learn shareholders' opinions and to adapt to those opinions.

Other organizational characteristics

The model can be completed by making predictions about other organizational characteristics associated with interpretation modes. The predictions pertain to: (1) scanning and data characteristics; (2) the interpretation process within the organization; and (3) the strategy and decision processes that

Unanalyzable	**Undirected viewing** Scanning characteristics: 1 Data sources: external, personal. 2 Acquisition: no scanning department, irregular contacts and reports, casual information. Interpretation process: 1 Much equivocality reduction 2 Few rules, many cycles Strategy and Decision Making: 1 Strategy: reactor. 2 Decision process: coalition building.	**Enacting** Scanning characteristics: 1 Data sources: external, personal. 2 Acquisition: no department, irregular reports and feedback from environment, selective information. Interpretation process: 1 Some equivocality reduction 2 Moderate rules and cycles. Strategy and Decision Making 1 Strategy: prospector. 2 Decision process: incremental trial and error.
Assumptions about environment	**Conditioned viewing** Scanning characteristics: 1 Data sources: internal, impersonal 2 Acquisition: no department, although regular record keeping and information systems, routine information. Interpretation process: 1 Little equivocality reduction 2 Many rules, few cycles Strategy and Decision Making 1 Strategy: defender. 2 Decision process: programmed, problemistic search.	**Discovering** Scanning characteristics: 1 Data sources: internal, impersonal 2 Acquisition: Separate departments, special studies and reports, extensive information. Interpretation process: 1 Little equivocality reduction 2 Many rules, moderate cycles Strategy and Decision Making 1 Strategy: analyzer. 2 Decision process: systems analysis, computation.
Analyzable		

Passive   Active

Organizational intrusiveness

Figure 3 *Relationship between interpretation modes and organizational processes*

characterize each mode. The predicted relationships with interpretation modes are shown in Figure 3.

Scanning characteristics

Scanning characteristics pertain to the nature and acquisition of data for top management about the environment. The data may vary by source and acquisition, depending on the interpretation mode of the organization.

1. *Data Sources*. Data about the environment can come to managers from external or internal sources, and from personal or impersonal sources (Aguilar, 1967; Daft & Lengel, in press; Keegan, 1974). Sources are external when managers have direct contact with information outside the organization. Internal sources pertain to data collected about the environment by other people in the organization and then provided to managers through internal channels. Personal sources involve direct contact with other individuals. Impersonal sources pertain to written documentation such as newspapers and magazines or reports from the organization's information system.

Generally, the less analyzable the perceived external environment the greater the tendency for managers to use external information gained from personal contact with other managers. Organizations characterized as undirected viewing will obtain most of their information from the relationship of senior managers with colleagues in the environment (Keegan, 1974). Managers in enacting organizations also will use personal observations to a large extent, although this information often will be obtained through experimentation and from trying to impose ideas on the environment. When the environment is analyzable, a larger percentage of the data will be conveyed through the management information system. The discovering organization also will use internal, formal reports, although these reports are the outcome of specialized inquiries rather than a routine, periodic reporting system.

2. *Data Acquisition*. Organizational mechanisms for acquiring information and the regularity of acquisition are other distinguishing characteristics of organizational scanning (Fahey & King, 1977). Discovering organizations will allocate many resources to data acquisition. Special departments typically will be used to survey and study the environment. Regular reports and special studies will go to top managers. Conditioned viewing organizations will have regular reports available through the formal information system of the organization. These organizations will devote few resources to external scanning.

Undirected viewing organizations will make little use of formal management information. Data will tend to be irregular and casual. Scanning departments are not needed; formal reports will be ad hoc and irregular. The enacting organization also will use data that are somewhat irregular and will reflect feedback about selected environmental initiatives. The general pattern across organizations is that environmental information is more regular when the environment is analyzable, and more studies and information are available when the organization is active in information acquisition.

Interpretation process

Interpretation pertains to the process by which managers translate data into knowledge and understanding about the environment. This process will vary according to the means for equivocality reduction and the assembly rules that govern information processing behavior among managers.

1. *Equivocality Reduction.* Equivocality is the extent to which data are unclear and suggest multiple interpretations about the environment (Daft & Macintosh, 1981; Weick, 1979). Managers in all organizations will experience some equivocality in their data. Equivocality reduction will be greatest in organizations characterized as undirected viewing. External cues of a personal nature are subject to multiple interpretations. Managers will discuss these cues extensively to arrive at a common interpretation. Equivocality is reduced through shared observations and discussion until a common grammar and course of action can be agreed on (Weick, 1979). The enacting organization also will experience high equivocality, which will be reduced more on the basis of taking action to see what works than by interpreting events in the environment. Information equivocality generally is lower in the conditioned viewing and discovering organizations. Some equivocality reduction takes place before the data reach managers. Specialists will routinize the data for periodic reports and perform systematic analyses and special studies. The data thus provide a more uniform stimulus to managers, and less discussion is needed to reach a common interpretation.

2. *Assembly Rules.* Assembly rules are the procedures or guides that organizations use to process data into a collective interpretation. The content of these rules and the extent to which they are enforced depend on the organization. Generally, the greater the equivocality in the data, the fewer the number of rules used to arrive at an interpretation. Conversely, the smaller the perceived equivocality of data entering the organization, the greater the number of rules used to assemble the interpretation (Weick, 1979).

Fewer rules are used for equivocal information inputs because there is uncertainty as to exactly what the information means. Only a small number of rather general rules can be used to assemble the process. If the input is less equivocal, there is more certainty as to what the item is and how it should be handled. Hence a greater number of rules can be assigned to handle the data and assemble an interpretation (Putnam & Sorenson, 1982).

The number of information cycles among top management follows a similar logic. The greater the equivocality, the more times the data may be cycled among members before a common interpretation is reached. The lower the equivocality, the fewer cycles needed. The number of assembly rules and cycles tends to be inversely related.

Undirected viewing organizations, which receive equivocal information, will have few rules but will use many internal cycles during the course of assembling an interpretation. By contrast, managers within a directed viewing organization receive unequivocal information that will be handled according to numerous rules, but few cycles are needed to reach a common understanding. The discovering organization also will use many rules, although a moderate number of cycles may be needed because of some equivocality in the reports and data presented to managers. The equivocality in interpreting the success of initiatives in the enacting organization will be associated with the moderate number of assembly rules and information cycles.

Strategy formulation and decision making

The variables described above are directly related to the scanning and interpretation behaviors through which organizations learn about and make sense of the external environment. Two additional variables – strategy formulation and decision making – may be associated with interpretation modes. The hypothesized relationships with interpretation modes also are shown in Figure 3.

1. *Strategy Formulation.* Miles and Snow (1978) proposed that corporations can be organized according to four types of strategies: prospector, analyzer, defender, and reactor. Strategy formulation is the responsibility of top management and thus may be related to environmental conditions that are similar to interpretation modes. The prospector strategy reflects a high level of initiative with regard to the environment. The environment is seen as changing and as containing opportunities. The organization develops new products and undertakes new initiatives. This is consistent with the enacting mode of interpretation. The analyzer organization is more careful. It is concerned with maintaining a stable core of activities but with occasional innovations on the periphery if the environment permits. This strategy is consistent with the discovering orientation, in which the organization studies the environment and moves ahead only in a careful, constrained way.

The defender strategy is one in which top management perceives the environment as analyzable and stable and the management is determined to protect what it has. This organization is concerned with maintaining traditional markets and is focused on internal efficiency rather than on external relationships. The defender strategy will tend to be related to the conditioned viewing mode of interpretation. Finally, the reactor strategy is not really a strategy at all. The organization moves along, more or less accepting what comes. This organization will react to seemingly random changes in the environment. Scanning behavior in this organization is based on casual data from personal contact rather than from specialized information systems. The reactor strategy will be associated with the interpretation mode classified as undirected viewing.

2. *Decision making.* The organizational literature suggests that organizations make decisions in various ways. Organizational decisions may be influenced by coalition building and political processing (Cyert & March, 1963); by incremental decision steps (Lindblom, 1959; Mintzberg, Raisinghani, & Théoret, 1976); by systems analysis and rational procedures (Leavitt, 1975); and by programmed responses to routine problems (March & Simon, 1958; Simon, 1960). Decision making generally is part of the information and interpretation processes in organizations; it thus is posed that decision processes may be associated with interpretation modes.

In undirected viewing organizations, the environment is not analyzable. Factors cannot be rationalized to the point of using rational decision models. Managers respond to divergent, personal cues, and extensive discussion and coalition building are required to agree on a single interpretation and course of action. Managers will spend time making sense of what happened and reaching agreements about problems before proceeding to a solution.

In enacting organizations, by contrast, a more assertive decision style will appear. The enacting organization does not have precedent to follow. A good idea, arrived at subjectively, may be implemented to see if it works. Enacting organizations utilize the trial and error incremental process described by Mintzberg et al. (1976). When organizations decide on a course of action, they design a custom solution and try it. If the solution does not work, they have to recycle and try again. Enacting organizations move ahead incrementally and gain information about the environment by trying behaviors and seeing what works.

Discovering organizations also take an active approach, but they assume that the environment is analyzable. Here the emphasis is on rational understanding. Systems analysis will be an important decision tool. Operational researchers and other staff personnel will perform computations on environmental data and weigh alternatives before proceeding. This organization's decision process will be characterized by logic and analysis. Solutions will not be tried until alternatives have been carefully weighed.

Finally, directed viewing organizations may be considered the easiest situation for decision makers. The organization is passive and operates in an analyzable environment. Decision making by managers is programmed. Programs are built into the organization to describe reactions to external events based on previous experience. Rules and regulations cover most activities and are applied unless a genuine crisis erupts. Crises will be rare, but if one occurs, managers will respond with problemistic search (March & Simon, 1958). Problemistic search means that the organization performs a local search through its immediate memory bank for a solution. Only after exhausting traditional responses will the organization move toward a new response of some sort.

Implications

The purpose of this paper is to present a model of organizations as interpretation systems and to bring together a number of ideas that are related to interpretation behavior. The two variables underlying the model are (1) management's beliefs about the analyzability of the external environment and (2) organizational intrusiveness. These variables are consistent with empirical investigations of interpretation behavior (Aguilar, 1967; Wilensky, 1967), and they are the basis for four modes of interpretation – enacting, discovering, undirected viewing, and conditioned viewing. The model explains interpretation behaviors ranging from environmental enactment to passive observation. The model also makes predictions about scanning characteristics, interpretation processes, and top management strategy and decision behavior.

The model is proposed as a set of tentative hypotheses for future test. Evidence in the literature does support the general framework, but the specific predictions remain to be tested. The model might best be characterized as an initial organization of ideas about scanning and interpretation behavior, and it has implications for research and the practice of management.

Organizational Research. The implications of the interpretation system model for organizational research are two-fold. First, the interpretation system perspective is concerned with high level processes on Boulding's system hierarchy (Daft, 1980; Pondy & Mitroff, 1978). An organization might be viewed as a framework, control system, or open system by organization scholars. The interpretation system view is concerned with specialized information reception, equivocality reduction, and sensemaking. This perspective represents a move away from mechanical and biological metaphors of organizations. Organizations are more than transformation processes or control systems. To survive, organizations must have mechanisms to interpret ambiguous events and to provide meaning and direction for participants. Organizations are meaning systems, and this distinguishes them from lower level systems.

Perhaps the process of interpretation is so familiar that it is taken for granted, which may be why little research on this topic has been reported. But interpretation may be one of the most important functions organizations perform. Indeed, the second research implication of the interpretation system perspective is that scanning and sensemaking activities are at the center of things. Almost every other organizational activity or outcome is in some way contingent on interpretation. For example, one of the widely held tenets in organization theory is that the external environment will influence organization structure and design (Duncan, 1972; Pfeffer & Salancik, 1978; Tung, 1979). But that relationship can be manifested only if participants within the organization sense and interpret the environment and respond to it. Almost all outcomes in terms of organization structure and design, whether caused by the environment, technology, or size, depend on the interpretation of problems or opportunities by key decision makers. Once interpretation occurs, the organization can formulate a response. Many activities in organizations, whether under the heading of structure, decision making, strategy formulation, organizational learning, goal setting, or innovation and change, may be connected to the mode of interpreting the external environment.

The paradox is that research into environment-structure relationships gives scant attention to interpretation. An issue that seems crucial for explaining the why of organizational form has produced little systematic research. One value of the model proposed here, then, is the introduction of an interpretation model and set of relationships as candidates for empirical research in the future.

Management. The interpretation system model has two implications for managers. First, it says that the job of management is to interpret, not to do the operational work of the organization. The model calls attention to the need in organizations to make sense of things, to be aware of external events, and to translate cues into meaning for organizational participants. Managers, especially top managers, are responsible for this process and are actively involved in it. Managers may do interpretations spontaneously and intuitively, without realizing their role in defining the environment for other participants. One implication is for managers to think of organizations as interpretation systems and to take seriously their roles as interpreters.

The other implication of the model is that it provides a comparative perspective for managers. The model calls attention to interpretation modes managers may not have thought of before. If managers have spent their organizational lives in a discovery-oriented interpretation system, using relatively sophisticated monitoring systems, they might want to consider modifying these activities toward a more subjective approach. The external environment may not be as analyzable as they assume. Discovery-oriented managers could consider intuition and hunch in some situations and decide to launch test markets instead of market surveys. On the other hand, passive, conditioned viewers might be encouraged to try breaking established rules and patterns to see what happens. The value of any comparative model is that it provides new alternatives. Managers can understand where they are as opposed to where they would like to be. Managers may find that they can create a new and valuable display of the environment by adopting new interpretation assumptions and modes.

Conclusion

Any model is itself a somewhat arbitrary interpretation imposed on organized activity. Any model involves trade-offs and unavoidable weaknesses. The greatest weakness in the model presented in this paper is reflected in Thorngate's (1976) postulate of commensurate complexity. His postulate states that a theory of social behavior cannot be simultaneously general, accurate, and simple. Two of the three characteristics are possible, but only at a loss to the third. The model in this paper has attempted to be general and simple, and the trade-off is a model that is not very accurate at specifying details. The loss in precision may not be all bad, however. An interpretation system is an awesomely complex human social activity that may not be amenable to precise measurement at this point in development (Daft & Wiginton, 1979). To design a model that is precise and accurate may be to lose the phenomenon of interest.

Interpretation is the process through which information is given meaning and actions are chosen. Even in the most objective environments, the interpretation process may not be easy. People in organizations are talented at normalizing deviant events, at reconciling outliers to a central tendency, at producing plausible displays, at making do with scraps of information, at translating equivocality into feasible alternatives, and at treating as sufficient whatever information is at hand (Weick & Daft, 1983). The result of these human tendencies is that the organization can build up workable interpretations from scraps that consolidate and inform other bits and pieces of data. The process and the outcomes are a good deal less tidy than many have come to appreciate with current models and assumptions about organizations. The ideas proposed in this paper suggest a new viewpoint – perhaps a starting point of sorts – from which to interpret the richness and complexity of organizational activity.

References

Aguilar, F. *Scanning the business environment.* New York: Macmillan, 1967.
Aldrich, H., & Herker, D. Boundary spanning roles and organization structure. *Academy of Management Review,* 1977, 2, 217–230.
Argyris, C., & Schon, D. A. *Organizational learning: A theory of action perspective.* Reading, Mass.: Addison-Wesley, 1978.

Boulding, K. E. General systems theory: The skeleton of a science. *Management Science*, 1956, **2**, 197–207.

Braybrooke, D. The mystery of executive success re-examined. *Administrative Science Quarterly*, 1964, **8**, 533–560.

Child, J. Organization, management and adaptiveness. Working paper, University of Aston, 1974.

Cyert, R. M., & March, J. G. *A behavioral theory of the firm*. Englewood Cliffs, N. J.: Prentice-Hall, 1963.

Daft, R. L. The evolution of organization analysis in *ASQ*: 1959–1979. *Administrative Science Quarterly*, 1980, **25**, 623–636.

Daft, R. L., & Lengel, R. H. Information richness: A new approach to manager behavior and organization design. In B. Staw & L. L. Cummings (Eds.), *Research in organizational behavior* (Vol. 6). Greenwich, Conn.: JAI Press, in press.

Daft, R. L., & Macintosh, N. B. A new approach to design and use of management information. *California Management Review*, 1978, **21(1)**, 82–92.

Daft, R. L., & Macintosh, N. B. A tentative exploration into the amount and equivocality of information processing in organizational work units. *Administrative Science Quarterly*, 1981, **26**, 207–224.

Daft, R. L., & Wiginton, J. C. Language and organization. *Academy of Management Review*, 1979, **4**, 179–192.

Duncan, R. B. Characteristics of organizational environments and perceived environmental uncertainty. *Administrative Science Quarterly*, 1972, **17**, 313–327.

Duncan, R. B., & Weiss, A. Organizational learning: Implications for organizational design. In B. Staw (Ed.), *Research in organizational behavior* (Vol. 1). Greenwich, Conn.: JAI Press, 1979, 75–123.

Fahey, L., & King, W. R. Environmental scanning for corporate planning. *Business Horizons*, 1977, **20(4)**, 61–71.

Hedberg, B. How organizations learn and unlearn. In P. Nystrom & W. Starbuck (Eds.), *Handbook of organizational design*. New York: Oxford University Press, 1981, 1–27.

Keegan, W. J. Multinational scanning: A study of information sources utilized by headquarters executives in multinational companies. *Administrative Science Quarterly*, 1974, **19**, 411–421.

Keim, G. D. Foundations of a political strategy for business. *California Management Review*, 1981, **23**, 41–48.

Kimberly, J. R., & Miles, R. H. *The organizational life cycle*. San Francisco: Jossey-Bass, 1980.

Kotter, J. P. Managing external dependence. *Academy of Management Review*, 1979, **4**, 87–92.

Leavitt, H. J. Beyond the analytic manager: I. *California Management Review*, 1975, **17(3)**, 5–12.

Leifer, R. T., & Delbecq, A. Organizational/environmental interchange: A model of boundaries spanning activity. *Academy of Management Review*, 1978, **3**, 40–50.

Lindblom, C. The science of 'muddling through'. *Public Administration Review*, 1959, **19(2)**, 79–88.

March, J. G., & Simon, H. A. *Organizations*. New York: Wiley, 1958.

Miles, R. E., & Snow, C. C. *Organizational strategy, structure and process*. New York: McGraw-Hill, 1978.

Mintzberg, H., Raisinghani, D., & Theoret, A. The structure of 'unstructured' decision processes. *Administrative Science Quarterly*, 1976, **21**, 246–275.

Newsweek, March 12, 1979, 62.

Perrow, C. A framework for the comparative analysis of organizations. *American Sociological Review*, 1967, **32**, 194–208.

Pfeffer, J. Beyond management and the worker: The institutional function of management. *Academy of Management Review*, 1976, **1(2)**, 36–46.

Pfeffer, J., & Salancik, G. R. *The external control of organizations: A resource dependence perspective.* New York: Harper & Row, 1978.

Pondy, L. R., & Mitroff, I. I., Beyond open systems models of organizations. In B. M. Staw (Ed.), *Research in organizational behavior.* Greenwich, Conn.: JAI Press, 1979, 3–39.

Putnam, L. L., & Sorenson, R. L. Equivocal messages in organizations. *Human Communication Research*, 1982, **8(2)**, 114–132.

Simon, H. A. *The new science of management decision.* Englewood Cliffs, N.J.: Prentice-Hall, 1960.

Starbuck, W. H. Organizations and their environments. In M. D. Dunnette (Ed.), *Handbook of industrial and organizational psychology.* New York: Rand McNally, 1976, 1069–1123.

Staw, B. M. Rationality and justification in organizational life. In B. M. Staw & L. L. Cummings (Eds.), *Research in organizational behavior* (Vol. 2). Greenwich, Conn.: JAI Press, 1980, 45–80.

Thomas, T. S. Environmental scanning – The state of the art. *Long Range Planning*, 1980, **13(1)**, 20–28.

Thorngate, W. 'In general' vs. 'it depends': Some comments on the Gergen–Schlenker debate. *Personality and Social Psychology Bulletin*, 1976, **2**, 404–410.

Tung, R. L. Dimensions or organizational environment: An exploratory study of their impact on organization structure. *Academy of Management Journal*, 1979, **22**, 672–693.

Weick, K. *The social psychology of organizing.* Reading, Mass.: Addison-Wesley, 1979.

Weick, K. E., & Daft, R. L. The effectiveness of interpretation systems. In K. S. Cameron & D. A. Whetten (Eds.), *Organizational effectiveness: A comparison of multiple models.* New York: Academic Press, 1983, 71–93.

Wilensky, H. L. *Organizational intelligence.* New York: Basic Books, 1967.

Source: Daft, Richard L. and Weick, Karl E. (1984) Toward a model of organizations as interpretation systems. *Academy of Management Review*, **9**, 284–295.

Part Three

Webs of Meaning: The Symbolic Texture of Organizing

Human civilization differs essentially from nature in that it is not simply a place where capacities and powers work themselves out; man becomes what he is through what he does and how he behaves – i.e. he behaves in a certain way because of what he has become. Thus Aristotle sees ethos as differing from physis in being a sphere in which the laws of nature do not operate, yet not a sphere of lawlessness but of human institutions and human modes of behavior which are mutable, and like rules only to a limited degree.

Hans-Georg Gadamer (Truth and Method)

5 The organization as theater

Lee G. Bolman and Terrence E. Deal

> Theatre as an activity, as a staging of reality, depends on the ability of the audience to frame what they experience as theatre. It depends precisely on the audience recognizing, being aware, that they are an audience; they are witnesses to, not participants in, a performance. It depends further on a distinction between actors and the parts they play – characters may die on stage, but actors will live to take a bow. Finally, theatre depends on a recognition that performances play with reality in such a way as to turn the taken-for-granted into a plausible appearance [Mangham and Overington, 1987, p. 49].

Managers and organization theorists usually assume a linear, cause-effect connection between activities and outcomes. Decisions solve problems. Evaluations separate effective from ineffective programs and people. Leaders make things happen. Administrators administer. Structures coordinate activity. Planning shapes the future. The environment affects decision making, and decisions shape the environment. Such statements seem so obvious that they are rarely questioned.

Yet, these 'obvious' connections often fail in the everyday world. Decisions may not decide anything (March and Olsen, 1976). Evaluations rarely accomplish what they are supposed to (Dornbusch and Scott, 1975). Structures may have little to do with activities (Cohen, Deal, Meyer, and Scott, 1979; Weick, 1976a). Things make leaders happen instead of the other way around (Edelman, 1977). Change efforts reinforce the *status quo* (Baldridge and Deal, 1975; Deal and Ross, 1977). Planning produces no plans or produces plans that have no effect on the future.

The development in the United States of the Polaris Missile System was heralded as an example of government activity at its best. One of its distinctive characteristics was the introduction of modern management techniques – such as PERT charts and Program Planning and Budgeting System (PPBS) – into the public sector. Those techniques were reflected in several structural forms, such as specialist roles, technical divisions, management meetings, and a Special Projects Office. Since Polaris turned out to be a highly successful project, it was easy to conclude that the modern management techniques were a major causal factor of this success. The admiral in charge of the project received a plaque recognizing his contribution in bringing modern management techniques to the US Navy. A visiting team of British experts recommended PERT to the British Admiralty.

However, a later study of the Polaris project suggested a different interpretation of what really happened. The activities of the specialists were in fact only loosely coupled to other aspects of the project. The technical division produced plans and charts that were largely ignored. The management meetings served two primary purposes: they were arenas that the admiral used to publicly chide poor performers, and they were revival meetings that reinforced the religious fervor around the Polaris project. The Special Projects Office served as a briefing area in which members of Congress and other visiting dignitaries were informed about the progress of Polaris through an impressive series of diagrams and charts that had little to do with the actual status of the project. The team from the British navy apparently surmised this on their visit and therefore recommended a similar approach (Sapolsky, 1972).

Although the structural forms may not have served their ostensible purposes, they helped to foster a myth that maintained strong external support for the Polaris project and kept its critics at bay. The myth provided breathing space so that people could do their work on the basis of informal coordination, and it helped to keep their spirits and self-confidence high. The development of the Polaris missile demonstrates the power of theatre – for audiences both inside and outside the organization.

The idea that there can be activities without results casts doubt on a substantial proportion of human endeavor. At first glance, such a heresy might seem wholly negative – undermining the hope and morale of those who want to make a contribution to their organizations. The symbolic frame does argue that cause-and-effect relationships are often elusive or absent, but it offers a hopeful interpretation of this phenomenon. Organizational structures, activities, and events are more than simply instrumental. They are part of the organizational theatre, an ongoing expressive drama that entertains, creates meaning, and portrays the organization to itself. Geertz observed of Balinese pageants, 'The carefully scripted, assiduously enacted ritualism of court culture was, once more, "not merely the drapery of political order, but its substance"' (Mangham and Overington, 1987, p. 39).

Internal theater also plays to an audience outside the organization. It signals to the outside world that all is well. If management is making decisions, if plans are being formulated, if new units are being created in response to new problems, if sophisticated evaluation and control systems are in place, then the organization must be well managed and worthy of support. Getting the drama right is particularly critical in sectors where outputs are ambiguous and hard to measure, but good theater also is important even in highly technical organizations.

Theatre plays a role in a variety of situations. When external constituencies question the worth of existing practices, organizations promise reform and stage a drama called *Change*. If consumers complain about the quality of its current products, the organization creates a consumer affairs department and promises tighter quality standards. If the government questions the fairness of its personnel practices, the organization hires an affirmative action officer. If the organization is experiencing a crisis, a new leader is brought in who promises to make substantive changes. An example of this occurred during the crises that rocked Poland beginning in 1980: 'Poland's new Communist party leader, Stanislaw Kania, last night promised more democracy and pledged the party would work to regain the confidence of the disquieted Poles. In his first speech as national leader Kania promised less ceremony and more substance and called on the Poles to rally around the party after a summer of labor and political turmoil' (Soderlind, 1980, p. 1).

From the vantage point of the symbolic frame, organizational structures, activities, and events are secular theatre. They express our fears, joys, and expectations. They arouse our emotions and kindle our spirit. They reduce our uncertainty and soothe our bewilderment. They provide a shared basis for understanding events and for moving ahead.

Structure as theater

Traditionally, organizational structure is depicted as a network of interdependent roles and units coordinated through a variety of horizontal and vertical linkages. Since structure needs to be responsive to organizational purposes, the shape of an organization is determined by its goals, technologies, and environment (Woodward, 1970; Perrow, 1979; Lawrence and Lorsch, 1967). An alternative view is that structure is like stage design: an arrangement of space, lighting, props, and costumes to make the organizational drama vivid and credible to its audience. The dramatic perspective suggests that, at least in most organizations, structure may not have much to do with task and technology after all.

The symbolic view suggests a number of noninstrumental purposes that structure can serve. One purpose is to express the prevailing values and myths of the society. In many organizations, goals are multiple and elusive, the technology is underdeveloped, the linkages between means and ends are poorly understood, and effectiveness is almost impossible to determine. Schools, churches, mental health clinics, personnel departments, and management consulting firms all share these characteristics. One way for such organizations to achieve legitimacy is to maintain an appearance that conforms to the way society *thinks* they should look. The setting and costumes should be appropriate. Churches should have a building, religious artifacts, and a properly attired member of the clergy. Mental health clinics should have waiting rooms, uniformed nurses, and certified mental health professionals.

A study of elementary schools found no relationship between the structure of a school district and classroom instruction. The policies, efforts, and activities of administrators and specialists had little or no impact on how teachers taught: The research suggested that school districts had three major levels of personnel – central administrators, building administrators, and teachers – whose activities were mostly independent of one another. Other research on schools – both public and private – shows similar patterns (Abramowitz, Tenenbaum, Deal, and Stackhouse, 1978). Structure and activity seem to be unrelated to each other, and both are loosely linked with the environment.

Meyer and Rowan (1978) apply symbolic logic to the role of structure in public schools. They argue that a school will have difficulty sustaining public support unless it gives the right answer to three questions: First, does it offer appropriate topics (for example, third-grade English, American history)? Second, are the topics taught to age-graded students by certified teachers? Third, does the school look like a school (with classrooms, a gymnasium, a library, and a flag near the front door)? If the school is an institution of higher education its worth is likely to be measured by the size and beauty of its campus, the number of books in its library, its faculty-student ratio, and the number of professors who received Ph.D. degrees from high-prestige institutions.

Kamens (1977) applies this theme to higher education. First, the major function of colleges and universities is symbolic – to redefine students as graduates possessing special qualities or skills; second, the legitimacy of the transformation must be negotiated with important constituencies; third, this is done through legitimizing myths about the quality of education that are validated by the structural characteristics or appearance of the institution.

The appropriate structural form, in Kamens's view, depends on two major features of an institution: whether it is elite or non-elite and whether it allocates students to a specific corporate group in the society. Each type of institution will espouse a different myth and will dramatize different aspects of its structure. Size, complexity, formal curriculum, admissions procedures, and demographics all vary according to the symbolic messages that the institution attempts to communicate. The main considerations are having the right actors, a suitable script, and an appropriate stage. Elite schools, for example, will dramatize selectivity ('we will only accept one out of ten of the highly qualified candidates'); develop an attractive residential campus ('the residential experience is an essential feature of our total curriculum'); advertise a high ratio of faculty to students ('this provides for ongoing contact and dialogue between individual students and the many dedicated, outstanding faculty members'); develop a curriculum that restrains specialization ('we seek to educate the whole person, rather than to train narrow specialists').

If an institution or its environment changes, then some adaptation will be necessary for the institutional persona to mirror those shifts. A new audience may require a revision in actors, script, or setting. Since legitimacy and worth are judged by correspondence between structural characteristics and prevailing myths, organizations are frequently obliged to alter their appearance to produce consonance. In this view, organizational structures are built out of 'blocks' of contemporary myth, a reason why universities adopt core curricula or new programs in cognitive psychology.

Another purpose of organizational structure is to convey a 'modern' appearance, that is, to communicate to external audiences that this is not a horse-and-buggy operation, but one that is fully up-to-date. A modern drama must reflect contemporary issues and dilemmas. In response to legal and social pressures, business organizations create affirmative action policies and roles, even though their hiring practices may change very little. As economics becomes increasingly fashionable, banks hire sophisticated economists, but place them in departments well away from the mainstream of decision making. As laws are passed mandating education for children with special needs, schools hire psychologists and learning-disabilities specialists who are featured prominently but who then perform functions that classroom teachers rarely see or understand. In response to criticism of their antiquated management methods, universities adopt sophisticated control systems that produce elaborate printouts but have little effect on operations. Legislatures pass laws on occupational safety, and factories create safety units that post signs that are mostly ignored.

The new structures reflect legal and social expectations and represent a bid for acceptance and support from relevant constituencies. An organization that does not have an affirmative action program signals that it is out of step with prevailing expectations. Nonconformity invites questions, criticism, and inspection. At the same time, it is much easier to appoint an affirmative action officer than to change hiring practices that are deeply embedded in both individual beliefs and organizational culture. Since the presence of the affirmative action officer is much more visible than any given hiring decision, the new role may successfully signal to those outside the organization that a change has occurred, even if the change is only pro forma.

In government, administrative agencies often serve the same symbolic functions. Agencies are created to encapsulate existing ambivalence or conflicts. Conflict between shippers and railroads led to formation of the Interstate Commerce Commission. Conflict between labor and management produced the National Labor Relations Board. Conflict between consumers and producers of food and drugs resulted in the Food and Drug Administration. Concern over pollution led to the Environmental Protection Agency. Yet such agencies often serve mostly political and symbolic functions (Edelman, 1977).

Politically, regulatory agencies are often 'captured' by those whom they are supposed to regulate. Major drug companies are far more effective than the public in lobbying and influencing decisions about drug safety. In practice, agencies legitimize elite values, reassure the public that they are zealously protecting its interests, and struggle for continuing funding from the legislature. They reduce tension and uncertainty and increase the public's sense of confidence and security (Edelman, 1977).

From a symbolic perspective, organizations are judged not so much by their actions as by their appearance. The right formal structure provides a ceremonial stage for enacting the correct drama of the day for the appropriate audience. The drama provides reassurance, fosters belief in the purposes of the organization, cultivates and maintains the faith of the audience, and so forth. Structures may do little to coordinate activity or establish relationships among organizational participants, but they do provide internal symbols that help participants to cope, find meaning, and play their role in the drama without reading the wrong lines, upstaging the lead actors, or confusing a tragedy with a comedy.

Organizational process as theater

Structurally administrative and technical processes are the basic tools that organizations use to get work done. These processes include formal meetings, evaluation systems, accounting systems, management information systems, and labor negotiations. Technical processes vary with the task to be achieved. In industrial organizations, workers assemble parts into a salable product or conduct operations that result in a batch of something (such as petroleum or industrial chemicals). In what we might call people-processing organizations, a variety of technical activities can be observed. Professors give lectures to provide students with knowledge and wisdom that will help them in later life. Physicians diagnose illnesses and prescribe treatments to help people get well. Social workers write case reports to identify and remedy conditions that entrap individuals in a cycle of poverty.

People who work in organizations spend much of their time engaged in such processes. To justify the way they spend their time and to maintain a sense of self-worth, they (and others) must believe that the processes work and produce the intended outcomes. But effort does not always lead to effectiveness, and organizational processes often fail to produce what they are supposed to. Many meetings make no decisions, solve no problems, and lead only to a need for more meetings. Conflict is often ignored rather than resolved or managed (Deal and Nutt, 1980). Planning produces documents that no one uses.

Even at the technical core, particularly in people-processing organizations, there is considerable slippage between processes and intended outcomes.

Graduates often wonder why the things they learned at the university seem irrelevant or counterproductive in their new work setting. Patients wonder why symptoms linger after medication and treatment. Poor people see that the same problems persist despite the best efforts of social workers. However, even processes that produce no results may still play a vital role in the organizational drama. They serve as scripts and stage markings that provide opportunities for self-expression, forums for airing grievances, and arenas for negotiating new understandings and meanings.

Meetings

According to March and Olsen (1976), meetings serve as 'garbage cans' into which problems are dumped. At any moment in an organization, there are participants looking for places to expend time and energy, problems looking for solutions, and solutions looking for problems. A scheduled meeting attracts all three, and the outcome of the meeting depends on a complicated interplay among the inputs that happened to arrive: Who came? What problems, concerns, or needs did they bring with them? What solutions or suggestions did they have to offer? Meanwhile, the meeting soaks up excess time and energy. It provides an opportunity for new myths to be created and old ones to be renegotiated. It helps individuals become clearer about their role in the organizational drama and to practice and polish their lines.

A faculty meeting in a distinguished university exemplifies the garbage can logic. The agenda outlined three topics for a two-hour meeting: (1) whether to accept $300,000 to support an annual award for an outstanding woman educator; (2) whether to begin a new doctoral program; (3) whether to approve a new core curriculum in the school's largest department. The discussion of the $300,000 gift lasted one hour and thirty minutes and covered the following issues: sexism, longstanding conflicts between the social sciences and the professions, minority rights, academic freedom, excellence in the university, institutional autonomy, faculty integrity, and declining enroll-ments. The discussion produced a committee to explore the issue further. In contrast, the discussion of the new doctoral program lasted twenty minutes, and the program was approved unanimously. The discussion about the core curriculum lasted barely ten minutes. The chairman of the committee that developed the new curriculum gave a brief speech and answered one question. The curriculum was also approved unanimously.

The first item on the agenda – the award for a woman educator – elicited the same old topics, problems, and solutions that were carried by the same faculty members from meeting to meeting. The other two items came late in the meeting after some faculty members had already left and resulted in unanimous decisions with little debate or deliberation. Many of the important functions of garbage cans can be easily seen in the discussion of the first time. Older professors had an opportunity to deliver thoughtful speeches, and younger faculty members had a chance to offer new perspectives. The rights of women and minorities were highlighted and reinforced. Academic freedom and institutional autonomy were reaffirmed. The faculty members reminded themselves of the school's excellence. The diversity of the faculty was publicly displayed. A new committee gave vocal individuals an additional opportunity to render service. The school's history and ideology were recreated and reinforced.

Garbage cans are particularly likely to form around issues that are emotionally powerful and symbolically visible, but technically fuzzy. Normally, a discussion of organizational mission is likely to attract a much larger and more diverse set of inputs than a conversation about cost-accounting procedures. Examples of garbage cans in the organizational literature include studies of reorganization (Olsen, 1976b), the choice of a new chief administrator (Olsen, 1976a), and conflict over desegregation (Weiner, 1976). Garbage cans may not produce rational discourse or effective problem solving, but they serve symbolic functions that help to prevent individual and organizational disintegration.

Planning

This is an administrative process that has become increasingly prominent as a sign of good management. An organization that does not plan is thought to be reactive, shortsighted, and rudderless. Planning has become a ceremony that an organization must conduct periodically if it wants to maintain its legitimacy. A plan is a badge of honor that organizations wear conspicuously and with pride.

Cohen and March (1974) identify four major functions that plans serve in universities:

1 Plans are symbols. Academic organizations provide few 'real' pieces of feedback data. They have nothing analogous to profit or sales figures. How are we doing? Where are we going? An organization that is failing can announce that it has established a plan to revitalize itself. An institution that does not have a nuclear reactor, or an economics department, can announce a plan to get one, and may see its stock soar past that of rival institutions.

2 Plans become games. In an organization whose goals and technology are unclear, plans and the insistence on plans become an administrative test of will. If a department wants a new program badly enough, it will spend a substantial amount of effort to justify the expenditure by fitting it into a plan. If an administrator wishes to avoid saying yes to everything but has no basis for saying no to anything, asking the department to submit a plan is a way to test its commitment.

3 Plans become excuses for interaction. As several students of planning have noted, benefits come more from the process than from the plan itself. The development of a plan forces some discussion and may induce some interest in and commitment to relatively low priorities in departments and schools. Occasionally, that interaction yields positive results. But rarely does it yield an accurate forecast. As people engage in discussions of the future, they may modify each other's views about what should be done today, but their conclusions about next year are likely to be altered in the interim by changes in personnel, political climate, foundation policy, or student demand.

4 Plans become advertisements. What is frequently called a 'plan' by a university is really an investment brochure. It is an attempt to persuade private and public donors of the attractiveness of the institution. Such plans are characterized by glossy photographs, by *ex cathedra* pronouncements of excellence, and by the absence of relevant information.

When they surveyed college presidents, Cohen and March (1974, p. 113) asked about the linkage between plans and current decisions. The responses fell into four main categories:

Yes, we have a plan. It is used in capital project and physical location decisions.

Yes, we have a plan. Here it is. It was made during the administration of our last president. We are working on a new one.

No, we do not have a plan. We should. We are working on one.

I think there's a plan around here someplace. Miss Jones, do we have a copy of our comprehensive, ten-year plan?

A study of a large-scale planning project in a suburban school district (Edelfson, Johnson, and Stromquist, 1977) provides another illustration of the symbolic importance of planning. Project Redesign was a five-year planning effort, supported by federal funds, that involved a significant proportion of the district's professionals and citizens in creating a means for the school district to meet the challenges of the 1980s.

The plan produced no major decisions or changes in the district. But it did provide participants with the chance to participate and interact, which they liked. It provided a garbage can that attracted a variety of problems, solutions, and conflicts that might have caused more difficulty if they had surfaced in some other arena. It provided the district with another opportunity to present itself as a model district. It renewed faith in the virtues of participation, the merits of grass-roots democracy, the value of good ideas, and the efficacy of modern planning techniques.

Evaluation

Assessing the value of people, departments, and programs is a major activity in almost all organizations. Evaluation efforts often consume substantial time and effort and result in lengthy reports that are then presented with considerable ceremony in formal meetings. Universities convene visiting committees to evaluate schools or departments. The federal government mandates evaluations of many of its programs. Social service agencies commission studies or program audits when important problems or issues arise. Yet the results typically disappear into the recesses of people's minds or the shelves of administrators' offices.

Organizations need to undertake evaluations if they are to be viewed as responsible, serious, and well managed, even though the results of evaluations are rarely used for decision making. Evaluations are used for other purposes. Evaluation data can be used as a weapon in political battles or as justification for decisions that would have been made in any event (Weiss, 1980). Evaluation fosters belief, confidence, and support from external constituencies and benefactors.

In public organizations, Floden and Weiner (1978, p. 17) argue, '[e]valuation is a ritual whose function is to calm the anxieties of the citizenry and to perpetuate an image of government rationality, efficiency, and accountability. The very act of requiring and commissioning evaluations may create the impression that government is seriously committed to the pursuit of publicly espoused goals, such as increasing student achievement or reducing malnutrition. Evaluations lend credence to this image even when programs are created to appease interest groups.'

The picture of a committed government serves two functions. First, it improves the image of public officials. In both democratic and authoritarian systems, political leaders must appear to be confident, efficacious, and in control if they hope to produce any changes (Arnold, 1938; Ellul, 1965). The impression of government rationality also promotes a feeling of security in the citizenry. Societal problems are often magnified by the media to the point where a crisis seems imminent. The threat of crisis leads to a widespread sense of helplessness and hopelessness. Evaluations serve to combat this feeling by fostering the belief that the government is acting on everyone's behalf to find solutions to pressing problems. The publicity given to these efforts reduces the level of public anxiety, whether or not evaluations produce useful information. Evaluations may also serve as a means for reducing complex social problems to a choice between relatively well-defined alternatives. The reduction of apparent complexity acts both to make the problems seem more manageable and to give citizens the sense that they have a firm understanding of the issues involved (Ellul, 1965).

The evaluation process often takes the form of high drama. Prestigious evaluators are hired, and the process receives considerable publicity. Participants wear 'costumes' that are more formal than normal dress. New roles are enacted: evaluators ask penetrating questions, and respondents give answers that portray the world as it is supposed to be. The results are often presented dramatically, especially when they are favorable. Negative results, in contrast, are often couched in vacuous language with high-sounding recommendations that no one is likely to take very seriously. All attempts to solve the problems disappear after the ceremony is concluded.

Occasionally, an evaluator blows the whistle by producing a highly critical report. The drama then becomes a tragedy that is often injurious to both parties. In the United States, a widely publicized report on public education (the Coleman Report) argued the thesis that 'schools don't make a difference.' The report and the subsequent debate undermined public confidence in the schools at the same time as it raised questions about the cohesion and maturity of the social sciences.

Evaluation persists primarily because it serves significant symbolic purposes. Without it, we would worry about the efficiency and effectiveness of activities. Evaluation produces magic numbers to help us believe that things are working. An evaluation shows that organizations take goals seriously. It demonstrates that an organization cares about its performance and wants to improve itself. Evaluations provide opportunities for participants to share their opinions and to have them publicly heard and recognized. Evaluation results help people relabel old practices, provide opportunities for adventure outside the normal routine, and foster new beliefs (Rallis, 1980).

Collective bargaining

This is the most common process for resolving conflicts and achieving workable agreements between labor and management. Through a combination of persuasion and muscle flexing, the two sides reach an agreement on wages and working conditions. But collective bargaining can also be viewed as a drama: 'A young executive took the helm of a firm with the intention of eliminating the bickering and conflict between management and labor. He commissioned a study of the company's wage structure and went to the bargaining table to present his offer. He informed the union representatives what he had done, and offered them more than they had expected to get. The astonished union leaders berated the executive for undermining the process of collective bargaining and asked for another five cents an hour beyond his offer' (Blum, 1961, pp. 63–64).

The story supports the symbolic interpretation of collective bargaining as drama. When some actors fail to follow the script, others become angry because they cannot deliver their lines. The drama is played to an audience, and it represents a struggle designed to convince each side that the ending was the result of a heroic battle. The drama, if well acted, conveys the message that the two opponents fought hard and persistently for what they believed was right (Blum, 1961). It conceals the reality that, in many cases, the actors knew in advance exactly how the play would end.

Power

This is usually seen as an attribute that individuals or systems possess – an attribute based on the resources that they are able to control. Power is discussed as if it were real, that is, it is seen as something that can be seized, exercised, or redistributed. But power, like many other organizational phenomena, is often ambiguous. It is not always easy to determine who has power in a given organization. How one goes about getting power is often unclear. It is sometimes even hard to know when power is being exercised.

From a symbolic perspective, individuals have power if others believe that they do. Such beliefs are encouraged by events or outcomes that become linked to particular individuals. The unemployment rate improves, and incumbents take credit. A firm becomes more profitable, and we attribute its success to the chief executive. A new program is started at a time when things are getting better anyway, and the program gets credit.

The belief that certain individuals are powerful is often based on observing their interactions. Individuals with formal status who talk a lot, who belong to many committees, and who feel close to the action are likely to be perceived as having power. But there may be little relationship between those characteristics and the ability to get what one wants. The relationship may be negative. Those who are dissatisfied with an organization may plunge into all sorts of activities in an attempt to change it and still have no impact (Enderud, 1976).

Myths of leadership generally attribute power to individuals. Individuals cause important events to occur. Whether things are going well or badly, we like to think that we can legitimately hold someone responsible. Cohen and March (1974) have this to say about college presidents: 'Presidents negotiate with their audiences on the interpretations of their power. As a result, during recent years of campus troubles, many college presidents sought to emphasize the limitations of presidential control. During the more glorious days of conspicuous success, they solicited a recognition of their responsibility for events. This is likely to lead to popular impressions of strong presidents during good times and weak presidents during bad times. Persons who are primarily exposed to the symbolic presidency (for example, outsiders) will tend to exaggerate the power of the presidency. Those people who have tried to accomplish something in the institution with presidential support (for example, educational reforms) will tend to underestimate presidential power or presidential will' (pp. 198–199).

Edelman (1977) makes a similar point: 'Leaders lead, followers follow, and organizations prosper. While this logic is pervasive, it is somewhat misleading. Marching one step ahead of a crowd moving in a particular direction may define realistically the connection between leadership and followership. Successful leadership is having followers who believe in the leader. By believing, people are encouraged to link positive events with leadership behaviors. George Gallup once remarked, "People tend to judge a man by his goals, by what he is trying to do, and not necessarily by what he accomplishes or how well he succeeds" '(p. 73).

The effectiveness of leaders is judged on the basis of their style and their ability to cope. It also helps if they have the opportunity to participate in well-publicized but noncontroversial activities and to figure in dramatic performances that emphasize the traits popularly associated with leadership – traits such as forcefulness, responsibility, courage, and decency. The assumption that leaders can make a real difference is reassuring but often fallacious. Cohen and March (1974) compare the college president to the driver of a skidding automobile: 'The marginal judgments he makes, his skill, and his luck will probably make some difference to the life prospects of his riders. As a result, his responsibilities are heavy. But whether he is convicted of manslaughter or receives a medal for heroism is largely outside his control' (p. 203).

Leadership, therefore, is less a matter of action than of appearance. And when leaders do make a difference in a more proactive sense, it is usually by enriching and updating the script for the organizational drama – by constructing new myths that alter beliefs and generate faith among members of their audience.

Summary

In a world of chaos, ambiguity, and uncertainty, individuals search for order, predictability, and meaning. Rather than admit that the ambiguity may not be resolvable or the uncertainty reducible, individuals and societies create symbolic solutions. Organizational structure and processes then serve as theater: they become dramatic performances that promote cohesion inside organizations and bond organizations to their environment.

The symbolic frame introduces and elaborates concepts that in the past were rarely applied to organizations. These concepts sharply redefine organizational dynamics and have significant implications for managing and changing organizations. Historically, theories of management and organization have focused on instrumental issues. We see problems, try to develop and implement solutions, and then ask, What did we accomplish? Often, the answer is nothing or not much, and we find ourselves repeating the old saw that the more things change, the more they remain the same. Such a message is disheartening and disillusioning. It produces a sense of helplessness and a belief that things will never improve significantly.

The symbolic frame sounds a more hopeful note. For a variety of reasons, we have decided to reframe our organization. It may be that we are restless, frustrated, or feel the need to renew our faith in the organization. We therefore enact a new play called *Change*. At the end of the pageant, we can ask three questions:

1 What was expressed?
2 What was attracted?
3 What was legitimized?

The answers are often enormously uplifting. The drama allows us to resolve contradictions and envision a solution to our problems. Old conflicts, new blood, borrowed expertise, and vital issues are attracted into the arena of change where they combine and begin to produce new myths and beliefs. Change becomes exciting, uplifting, and vital. The message is heartening and spiritually invigorating. There is always hope. The world is always different. Each day is potentially more exciting and full of meaning than the next. If not, we can change the symbols, revise the drama, develop new myths, or dance.

References

Abramowitz, S., Tenenbaum, E., Deal, T. E., and Stackhouse, E.A. *High School, 1977.* Washington, D. C.: National Institute of Education, 1978.

Arnold, T.W. *The Folklore of Capitalism.* New Haven, Conn.: Yale University Press, 1938.

Baldridge, J. V., and Deal, T. E. *Managing Change in Educational Organizations.* Berkeley, Calif.: McCutchan, 1975.

Blum, A.'Collective Bargaining: Ritual or Reality.' *Harvard Business Review*, Nov–Dec. 1961, **39**, 63–69.

Cohen, E. G., Deal, T. E., Meyer, J. W., and Scott, W. R. 'Technology and Teaming in the Elementary School.' *Sociology of Education*, Jan. 1979, **52**, 20–33.

Cohen, M., and March, J. G. *Leadership and Ambiguity.* New York: McGraw-Hill, 1974.

Deal, T.E., and Nutt, S. C. *Promoting, Guiding, and Surviving Change in School Districts.* Cambridge, Mass.: Abt Associates, 1980.

Deal, T. E., and Ross, F. 'The Effects of an Externally Directed Organizational Change Intervention on the Structure of a Small Elementary School District' Paper presented at annual meeting of the American Educational Research Association, New York, 1977.

Dornbusch, S., and Scott, W. R. *Evaluation and the Exercise of Authority.* San Francisco: Jossey-Bass, 1975.

Edelfson, C., Johnson, R., and Stromquist, N. *Participatory Planning in a School District.* Washington, D. C.: National Institute of Education, 1977.

Edelman, M. J. *The Symbolic Uses of Politics.* Madison: University of Wisconsin Press, 1977.

Ellul, J. *Propaganda.* New York: Basic Books, 1965.

Enderud, H. G. 'The Perception of Power.' In J. G. March and J. Olsen (eds.), *Ambiguity and Choice in Organizations.* Bergen, Norway: Universitetsforlaget, 1976.

Floden, R. E., and Weiner, S. S. 'Rationality to Ritual.' *Policy Sciences*, 1978, **9**, 9–18.

Kamens, D. H. 'Legitimating Myths and Education Organizations – Relationship Between Organizational Ideology and Formal Structure.' *American Sociological Review*, 1977, **42**, 208–219.

Lawrence, P., and Lorsch, J. *Organization and Environment*. Boston : Division of Research, Harvard Business School, 1967.

Mangham, I. L., and Overington, M. A. *Organizations as Theatre: A Social Psychology of Dramatic Appearances*. New York: Wiley, 1987.

March, J. G., and Olsen, J. *Ambiguity and Choice in Organizations*. Bergen, Norway: Universitetsforlaget, 1976.

Meyer, J., and Rowan, B. 'The Structure of Educational Organizations.' In M. W. Meyer and Associates, *Environments and Organizations: Theoretical and Empirical Perspectives*. San Francisco: Jossey-Bass, 1978.

Olsen, J. 'The Process of Interpreting Organizational History.' In J. G. March and J. Olsen (eds.), *Ambiguity and Choice in Organizations*. Bergen, Norway: Universitetsforlaget, 1976a.

Olsen, J. 'Reorganization as a Garbage Can.' In J. G. March and J. Olsen (eds.), *Ambiguity and Choice in Organizations*. Bergen, Norway: Universitetsforlaget, 1976b.

Perrow, C. *Complex Organizations: A Critical Essay*. (2nd Ed.) Glenview, Ill.: Scott, Foresman, 1979.

Rallis, S. 'Different Views of Knowledge Use by Practitioners.' Unpublished qualifying paper, Graduate School of Education, Harvard University, 1980.

Sapolsky, H. *The Polaris System Development*. Cambridge, Mass.: Harvard University Press, 1972.

Soderlind, R. 'Polish Leader Calls for Unity.' *Boston Globe*, Sept. 10, 1980, p. 1.

Weick, K. E. 'Educational Organizations as Loosely Coupled Systems.' *Administrative Science Quarterly*, 1976a, **21**, 1–19.

Weiner, S. 'Participation, Deadlines, and Choice.' In J. G. March and J. Olsen (eds.), *Ambiguity and Choice in Organizations*. Bergen, Norway: Universitetsforlaget, 1976.

Weiss, C. H. *Social Science Research and Decision Making*. New York: Columbia University Press, 1980.

Woodward, J. (ed.). *Industrial Organizations: Behavior and Control*. Oxford, England: Oxford University Press, 1970.

Source: Bolman, Lee G. and Deal, Terrence E. (1991) The organization as theater. In L. Bolman and T. Deal, *Reframing Organizations*, Jossey-Bass, San Francisco, pp. 272–289.

6 Cultural change: an integration of three different views[1]

Debra Meyerson and Joanne Martin

Introduction

Organizational cultures are resistant to change, incrementally adaptive, and continually in flux. In this article we explain these seemingly contradictory statements about cultural change. Underlying our argument is the premise that cultures are socially constructed realities (Berger and Luckman, 1966) and, as such, the definition of what culture is and *how cultures change* depends on how one perceives and enacts culture. Stated differently, what we notice and experience as cultural change depends directly on how we conceptualize culture. In accord with our opening statement, we will offer three very different ways – we believe equally compelling – of thinking about and enacting culture and cultural change.

We take the position that organizations *are* cultures. That is, we will treat culture as a metaphor of organization, not just as a discrete variable to be manipulated at will (Smircich, 1983a). We view organizations, then, as patterns of meaning, values, and behaviour (e.g. Morgan, Frost and Pondy 1983; Weick, 1979).[2] By emphasizing different kinds of patterns, the three views of culture that we will describe shed light on different aspects of organizational change.

Because we see organizations as cultures, our approach to organizational change emphasizes changes in patterns of behaviour, values, and meanings. We do not mean to imply that these are the only facets of organizational change, however. While it is beyond the scope of this paper to discuss other critical approaches to organizational change – for example, changes in strategy, structure, and leadership – these other approaches are intimately connected to cultural change. We believe, for instance, that structure is both a manifestation of and constraint on organizational cognitions, values, and behaviour (e.g. Giddens, 1979; Goffman, 1967). Similarly, strategy can be viewed as an outcome as well as a determinant of interactions and ideas (e.g. Burgleman, 1983). Leadership at once shapes and is shaped by the organization of belief and meaning (e.g. Calder, 1977; Smircich and Morgan, 1982). We hope that, by presenting three different views of cultural change, with differing implications for managerial control, we will raise questions of relevance to researchers working on these approaches to the change process. Full exploration of the relationships among cultural and 'non-cultural' approaches to organizational change, however, must remain outside the scope of this article.

Because the three views of culture and cultural change are so different, we will refer to them as 'paradigms'. Paradigms, as we will use the term, are alternative points of view that members and researchers bring to their experience of culture. Paradigms serve as theoretical blinders for researchers and as perceptual and behavioural maps for cultural members. Paradigms determine the criteria and content of what we attend to, and as such, they determine what we notice and enact as cultural change. Below, these paradigms of culture and cultural change are described.

Paradigm 1: Integration

Culture is often defined as that which is shared by and/or unique to a given organization or group (e.g. Clark, 1970; Schein, 1985; Smircich, 1983b). Culture, according to this definition, is an integrating mechanism (Geertz, 1973; Schein, 1983), the social or normative glue that holds together a potentially diverse group of organizational members. Given this definition of culture, paradigm 1 researchers use 'shared' as a codebreaker for identifying relevant manifestations of a culture, seeking, for example, a common language, shared values, or an agreed-upon set of appropriate behaviours. Paradigm 1 culture researchers differ in the types of cultural manifestations they study. Some paradigm 1 researchers focus on the espoused values of top management (e.g. Deal and Kennedy, 1982; Peters and Waterman, 1982). Other paradigm 1 researchers focus primarily on formal or informal practices, such as communication or decision-making norms (e.g. Ouchi, 1981; Schall, 1983), or the more obviously symbolic aspects of cultural life, such as rituals (Pettigrew, 1979; Trice and Beyer, 1984) or stories (e.g. Martin, 1982; Wilkins, 1983). Still others attend to deeper products of culture: basic assumptions (Schein, 1983, 1985), codes of meaning (Barley, 1983), or shared understandings (Smircich, 1983b). Paradigm 1 portrayals of culture may emphasize different kinds and levels of cultural manifestations. Yet three characteristics are central in all these paradigm 1 portrayals of culture: consistency across cultural manifestations, consensus among cultural members, and – usually – focus on leaders as culture creators.

An impression of consistency emerges because paradigm 1 views of culture focus only on manifestations that are consistent with each other. For example, Pettigrew (1979) examined the values and goals of school headmasters and then recounted ways in which these values and goals were reinforced by rituals. The second defining characteristic of a paradigm 1 view of culture is an emphasis on consensus. It is tacitly assumed, asserted, or (more occasionally) empirically demonstrated that cultural members drawn from various levels and divisions of an organizational hierarchy share a similar viewpoint. For example, Schein (1983) examined a top executive's commitment to the value of confronting conflicts and then cited evidence from fiercely argumentative group decision-making meetings to demonstrate that the leader's values were shared and enacted by lower level employees. Often, the ideas, values, and behavioural norms that apparently generate consensus are highly abstract (see, for example, Martin, Sitkin and Boehm, 1985, on the interpretation of organizational histories or Schein, 1983, on shared assumptions).

The third characteristic is that many, but by no means all, paradigm 1 portrayals focus on a leader as the primary source of cultural content (e.g. Clark, 1970; Pettigrew, 1979; Schein, 1983, 1985). Cultural manifestations that reflect the leader's own personal value system are stressed, offering the possibility that the charisma of a particularly effective leader might be institutionalized, giving that leader an organizational form of immortality (e.g. Bennis, 1983; Hackman, 1984; Trice and Beyer, 1984).

As a final defining feature, paradigm 1 portrayals of culture deny ambiguity. Such portrayals recognize only those cultural manifestations that are consistent with each other, and only those interpretations and values that are shared, culture becomes that which is clear: 'an area of meaning cut out of a vast mass of meaninglessness, a small clearing of lucidity in a formless, dark, always ominous jungle' (Berger, 1967, p. 23, quoted in Wuthnow, Hunter, Bergesen and Kurzweil, 1984, p. 26). In its quest for lucidity, paradigm 1 defines culture in a way that excludes ambiguity.

Because ambiguity will become an increasingly important concept in this article, a brief digression about its meaning is appropriate. By ambiguity we mean that which is unclear, inexplicable, and perhaps capable of two or more meanings (Webster, 1985). Ambiguity is an internal state that may feel like confusion; individuals become confused when information that is expected is absent. This type of ambiguity is resolved when and if information becomes available. Another type of ambiguity from inherently irresolvable conflict or irreducible paradox may be inherently unsolvable. When individuals simultaneously embrace two or more irreconcilable meanings, they experience ambiguity.

To clarify the relationships between ambiguity and cultural change, we will rely on examples drawn from the same organization: The Peace Corps/Africa. We persist with a single organizational example throughout the paper in order to facilitate comparison and contrast across the cultural paradigms. We selected the Peace Corps/Africa as our case to demonstrate the generality of this argument (most previous cultural research has focused on private sector organizations), rather than to illustrate idiosyncratic relevance to unusual organizations. Case studies of other types of organizations have also been conducted using this three-paradigm approach (see, for example, Martin and Meyerson, 1986, for a study of a large electronics corporation and Johnsen, Weilbach and Williams, 1986 for an analysis of a submarine).

Figure 1 presents a paradigm 1 view of the culture of Peace Corps/Africa, during the Kennedy and Johnson administrations. The umbrella symbolizes the single dominant culture that is espoused by Kennedy and Johnson, reinforced by the top Peace Corps staff in Africa, and apparently shared by volunteers across the continent. Central themes in this dominant culture include: idealism, particularly about the value of this kind of voluntary work; altruism, including an obligation to help others; and open-mindedness, especially concerning the excitement of living in new environments. These themes were enthusiastically adopted by Peace Corps volunteers who thought that, through these ideals, they could literally change the world:

> an idea, to conquer, must fuse with the will of men and women who are prepared to dedicate their lives to its realization. We had a sense twenty-five years ago at the Peace Corps' conception that there were such men and women in America waiting to be called, impatient to carry the idea of service to mankind. As it turned out I think we underestimated their numbers and their dedication (Shriver, 1986, p. 18).

However, beneath this apparent cultural unity lurked sources of diversity and possible conflict. For example, volunteers were assigned to different countries and projects. As individuals, volunteers brought different backgrounds and perspectives to their work. These sources of difference are given little cultural significance in a paradigm 1 portrayal of the Peace Corps/Africa culture.

According to paradigm 1, then, culture is a monolith. Integrating aspects – consistency, consensus, and usually leader-centredness – are emphasized. Ambiguity is denied. A picture of harmony emerges. Because of this promise of clarity and organizational harmony, according to many paradigm 1 researchers, culture offers the key to managerial control, worker commitment, and organizational effectiveness (e.g. Deal and Kennedy, 1982; Ouchi, 1981; Pascale and Athos, 1981; Peters and Waterman, 1982). Thus, Peters and Waterman's 'excellently managed' companies and Ouchi's Theory Z organizations, to name a few, celebrate cultural harmony as the source of organizational effectiveness. Implicit or explicit in such arguments is the managerial imperative of 'engineering', or at least partially controlling culture.

Researchers and cultural members[3] who endorse this paradigm 1 view of cultural change usually restrict their conception of culture to relatively

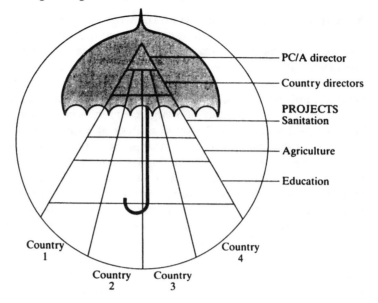

Key: Umbrella=dominant culture

Figure 1   *Paradigm 1 view of Peace Corps/Africa (PC/A)*

superficial manifestations, such as the espoused values of top management. Those aspects of culture are, almost by definition, easier to control. Moreover, these advocates of cultural engineering usually think of culture as one of many organizational variables to manipulate, another managerial lever, (in contrast to Smircich's view of culture as something an organization is).

Other paradigm 1 researchers focus on deeper manifestations of culture, such as taken-for-granted assumptions and understandings that underlie behavioural norms or artefacts, such as stories (e.g. Barley, 1983; Schein, 1983; 1985; Smircich, 1983b). Cultural persistence (Zucker, 1977) and habit (Berger and Luckmann, 1966) are implied in an approach that conceives of culture in terms of these deeper, taken-for-granted qualities. Thus, researchers who view culture in this institutionalized light accept persistence, inertia and thus resistance to change as part of their culture conception (e.g. Clark, 1970; Sathay, 1985; Selznick, 1957). Yet, regardless of the revolutionary nature of this process, even these researches do admit (and some even advocate) the possibility of cultural change.

A paradigm 1 view of cultural change

Both sets of paradigm 1 perspectives – those based on relatively superficial manifestations and those rooted in deep assumptions – view cultural change in terms of a monolithic process, as an organization-wide phenomenon. Paradigm 1 researchers usually define cultural change in attitudinal or cognitive terms, to distinguish it from other forms of organizational change. For example, Schein (1985) focuses on change in basic assumptions, while Brunsson (1985) studies change in organizational ideologies, and Barley (1983) defines change in terms of fluctuations in shared meanings. Green-wood and Hinings (1986) have proposed patterns of change in 'design archetypes': 'underlying ideas, values, and beliefs i.e. provinces of meaning or interpretive schemes . . .' (p. 3). Perhaps because of their attitudinal or cognitive focus, most paradigm 1 views of cultural change are similar to models of individual learning (e.g. Bandura, 1977; Rogers, 1961).

Schein, for example, describes individual and cultural change as a three-stage process (Schein, 1968, 1985), requiring a temporary lapse in denial of ambiguity. First, individuals (and organizations) experience an unfreezing stage. The ambiguity of the unknown is acknowledged and disconfirming evidence is recognized. Schein argues that a critical part of this unfreezing stage is the creation of psychological safety. Such safety is essential for disconfirming information, and the resulting ambiguity, to be allowed into consciousness. In stage two change takes place. New behaviours and their meanings are learned. In stage three, which Schein calls 'refreezing', ambiguity is again denied and the new ways of behaving and interpreting become internalized. In this model, the acknowledgement of ambiguity is strictly a temporary, albeit necessary, stage in the change process. Schein's change model assumes that leaders can and do affect cultural change in organizations.

> What great leaders and change agents do is to simultaneously create ambiguity and enough psychological safety to induce motivation to change. If either is missing there will be no incentive to change, and the art of changeagentry is to balance the two – enough disconfirmation to motivate change and enough psychological safety to feel that one can allow the disconfirming information into consciousness . . . (E. Schein, personal communication; June, 1985).

Other researchers agree that an essential (and possibly the only) function of leaders is the management of meaning in organizations (Clark, 1972; Pfeffer, 1981).

Jonsson and Lundin (1977) offer a strikingly similar description of the cultural change process. They discuss change as cycles of enthusiasm and discouragement, focused on key ideas or 'myths' about the meaning and necessity of certain organizational behaviours. Enthusiasm for a myth makes action possible. Internal conflict decays the enthusiasm around a given myth until a new 'ghost myth' formulates and crises begin to occur. Crises bring the acknowledgement of ambiguity and its concomitant, anxiety. Action paralysis is often the by-product (Latane and Darley, 1970). In order to decide how to act, cultural members seek a return to clarity; the new myth is thus substituted for the old. This process recurs. Schein, Jonsson and Lundin, and other paradigm 1 models of change (e.g. Brunsson, 1985; Pettigrew, 1985) offer a sequential portrayal of the organization-wide collapse and regeneration of a monolithic culture: clarity, the introduction of ambiguity, new clarity.

A paradigm 1 approach to change can be applied to the Peace Corps/Africa example. When Nixon became president, he dismantled many social service programmes, such as the War on Poverty. He was distressed with the overly idealistic and 'revolutionary' (out to change the world) tone of the Peace Corps culture described in Figure 1. He replaced the top staff of the Peace Corps in Washington and in Africa. Instead of seeking liberal arts majors as volunteers, the Peace Corps was ordered to recruit people (including non-students) with technical expertise. These changes in leadership and employee selection procedures were deeply disturbing to many members of the old Peace Corps/Africa culture whose early sentiments are reflected in this statement: 'Peace Corps volunteers must bring more than science and technology. They must touch the idealism of America and bring that to us, too' (Shriver, 1986: p. 21). Many staff and volunteers left as soon as they could, and the number of volunteers fell dramatically. After this period of ambiguity, turmoil, and considerable turnover, a new dominant culture for Peace Corps/Africa emerged. In place of idealism and revolutionary fervour, the new culture emphasized pragmatic and conservative values, geared primarily toward technical change in host countries.

In this example, one clarifying and unifying cultural umbrella has been replaced by another. Two aspects of this case are characteristic of paradigm 1 portrayals of cultural change. First, the description of the change process focuses on the actions of a leader. Second, considerable turnover and new selection criteria – or other internal incidences of turmoil – are essential precursors to cultural change.

Paradigm 1 descriptions of the cultural change process, such as the Peace Corps/Africa example above, focus attention on organization-wide changes in what is shared. A total world view is collapsed, to be replaced by an equally monolithic perspective. This is revolutionary change, similar in many ways to Kuhn's (1962) portrait of scientific revolutions. However, to varying extents, paradigm 1 researchers and practitioners assume that this process can (and several will argue *should*) be intentionally engineered or at least controlled by top management (Barnard, 1938; Golding, 1980; Selznick, 1957). While important differences exist among paradigm 1 researchers, they generally emphasize these characteristics and share a common set of blind spots. These blind spots, and their importance, become evident if we look at culture and cultural change from alternative lenses.

Paradigm 2: Differentiation

In contrast to paradigm 1's emphasis on integration and homogeneity, a paradigm 2 approach to culture is characterized by differentiation and diversity (see Martin and Meyerson, 1988, for a more detailed explanation of these attributes). Paradigm 1's view of culture as a master blueprint with uniform interpretations is incongruous with a paradigm 2 perspective. Paradigm 2 researchers pay attention to inconsistencies, lack of consensus, and non-leader-centred sources of cultural content. This approach emphasizes the importance of various subunits, including groups and individuals (Louis, 1983; Nord, 1985) who represent constituencies based within and outside the organization. In contrast to paradigm 1's relatively closed-system conception of culture, a paradigm 2 perspective is an open-system perspective; culture is formed by influences from inside and outside the organization.

According to paradigm 2, organizations are not simply a single, monolithic dominant culture. Instead, a culture is composed of a collection of values and manifestations, some of which may be contradictory. For example, espoused values may be inconsistent with actual practices (e.g. Christenson and Kreiner, 1984; Meyer and Rowan, 1977), or rituals and stories may reflect contradictions between formal rules and informal norms (e.g. Siehl, 1984; Smith and Simmons, 1983). Sometimes, the assumption of a common language must be suspended, as it becomes clear that the same words carry contrasting meanings in different contexts (e.g. Jamison, 1985).

In part because of this stress on inconsistency, paradigm 2 portrayals of culture often emphasize disagreement rather than consensus. Complex organizations reflect broader societal cultures and contain elements of occupational, hierarchical, class, racial, ethnic, and gender-based identifications (Beyer, 1981; Trice and Beyer, 1984; Van Maanen and Barley, 1984). These sources of diversity often create overlapping, nested subcultures.

Different types of subcultures can be distinguished (Louis, 1983). For example, subcultural differences may represent disagreements with an organization's dominant culture, as in a counter-culture (Martin and Siehl, 1983). Or, subcultural identifications may be orthogonal to a dominant culture, reflecting functional, national, occupational, ethnic, or project affiliations (e.g. Gregory, 1983; Van Maanen and Barley, 1984). Or still, a subculture might enhance a dominant culture. For example, members of one particular functional area may fanatically support the values espoused by top management (e.g. Martin, Sitkin and Boehm, 1985).

Paradigm 2 emphasizes multiple, rather than leader generated, sources of cultural content. Gregory (1983), representing an extreme paradigm 2 position, argues that organizations are reflections and amalgamations of surrounding cultures, including national, occupational, and ethnic cultures.

An organization, she argues, is simply an arbitrary boundary around a collection of subcultures. According to Gregory, there is little that is unique about an organization's culture. We argue that the usefulness of a cultural approach is severely constrained if organizational culture is defined as only that which is unique to a given organizational context. This is a relatively small, perhaps minor, part of cultural life in that context (see Martin et al., 1983 for evidence on this point). Instead, we believe it is more informative to define organizational culture as a nexus where broader, societal 'feeder' cultures come together. What is unique, then, is the specific combination of cultures that meet within an organization's boundary (Martin, 1986).

This version of the paradigm 2 viewpoint may be clarified by illustration. Figure 2 shows a depiction of the culture of Peace Corps/Africa consistent with Gregory's view: a set of volunteer projects nested within a set of nations under the auspices of the Peace Corps/Africa. This is a somewhat arbitrary choice of organizational boundary that could be replaced, leaving many projects and certainly the relevant nations intact. In this depiction, unlike that of Figure 1, no dominant cultural umbrella is salient.

Some researchers combine a paradigm 2 with a paradigm 1 appraoch. For example, Lawrence and Lorsch (1967) argue that an organization's proper mix of integrating and differentiating forces is based, in part, on the nature of its environment. In cultural terms this means that an organization would probably be composed of a diverse set of subcultures that share some integrating elements of a dominant culture (e.g. Martin, Sitkin and Boehm, 1985). As in formal structure, the mix of cultural integration and differentiation would depend in part on the nature of the organization and its environment. In the Peace Corps example, subcultural identifications associated with status within the Peace Corps hierarchy, country assignment, and project responsibility might co-exist with a shared identification with a dominant, Peace Corps/Africa culture. Rather than only focusing on the integrating dominant umbrella, as from a purely paradigm 1 perspective, this hybrid view of culture also draws attention to the differentiated subcultures beneath it.

Some complications, due to the conceptual relationship between paradigms 1 and 2, merit discussion. Even if a paradigm 2 portrayal of an organizational culture includes an acknowledgement of elements of a dominant culture, the primary focus of attention is on inconsistencies and subcultural differentiation. This focus is complicated by considerations of levels of analysis. Any subculture is a smaller version of paradigm 1 integration, characterized within its boundaries by consistency and consensus. Thus, the contradictions and disagreements, characteristic of paradigm 2, become visible only at higher, organization-wide levels of analysis. In addition, at the individual level of analysis, a single person may be a member of several overlapping, nested subcultures, some of which may hold opposing views. For example, an organizational member may be a divisional manager, an engineer, a Stanford

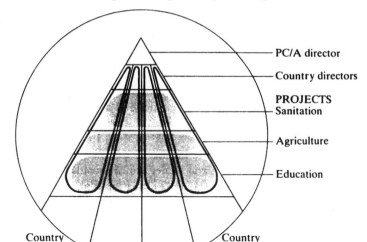

PC/A director

Country directors

PROJECTS
Sanitation

Agriculture

Education

Country
1

Country
4

Country
2

Country
3

Key:

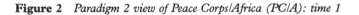

──── Subcultural boundaries due to country assignment

☐ Subcultural boundaries due to project assignment

Figure 2 *Paradigm 2 view of Peace Corps/Africa (PC/A): time 1*

MBA, a New England Yankee, and a female. Each of these individual characteristics may be associated with membership in an organizational subculture, creating psychological inconsistency and conflict at the individual level of analysis. Thus, paradigm 2 has implications for organizational subcultural, and individual levels of analysis.

Because of its awareness of these levels of analysis and its inclusion of sources of cultural content external to the organization, a paradigm 2 portrayal of cultural content is complicated. Yet these complications are still relatively clear, not ambiguous. Paradigm 2 reduces awareness of ambiguity by channelling it, and thereby limits its potentially bewildering and paralysing effects. In doing so, paradigm 2 does not completely deny ambiguity and restrict attention to that which is clear. However, paradigm 2 has limits to the amount of ambiguity acknowledged. Paradigm 2 examines inconsistencies as well as consistencies, but attention is restricted to cultural manifestations that either do, or do not, contradict each other. The potential complexities of the cultural domain are thereby reduced to dichotomies. Each subculture is an island of localized lucidity, so that ambiguity lies only in the interstices among the subcultures. Paradigm 2 channels ambiguity, as swift currents create

Name	Paradigm 1: integration	Paradigm 2: differentiation	Paradigm 3: ambiguity
Degree of consistency among cultural manifestations	Consistency	Inconsistency and consistency	Lack of clarity (neither clearly consistent nor clearly inconsistent), and irreconcilable inconsistencies
Degree of consensus among members of culture	Organization-wide	Within, not between, subcultures	Issue-specific consensus, dissensus, and confusion among individuals
Reaction to ambiguity	Denial	Channelling	Acceptance
Metaphor for paradigm	Hologram; Clearing in jungle	Islands of clarity in sea of ambiguity	Web; jungle

Figure 3   *Contrasting the paradigms*

channels around islands. This frees each subculture to perceive and respond to only a small part of the complexities and uncertainties of the organization's environment. Environmental complexity and uncertainty are therefore experienced as manageable, rather than as overwhelming ambiguity. Figure 3 summarizes these differences between paradigms 1 and 2.

Perhaps because of the complexity of even presenting a static view of a paradigm 2 culture, few if any paradigm 2 researchers have attempted to articulate a systematically dynamic view of culture. Below, we construct a picture of cultural change consistent with a paradigm 2 perspective. Not surprisingly, paradigm 2's version of cultural change is much more complex than the processes depicted by paradigm 1.

A paradigm 2 view of cultural change

A paradigm 1 perspective draws attention to cultural changes that are often controlled by top management and shared throughout an organization. With a paradigm 2 perspective, however, diffuse and unintentional sources of change are more salient. This is an open-system perspective that explicitly links cultural change to other sources and types of change. Due to the prevalence of subcultural differentiation, such cultural changes will be more localized, rather than organization-wide, and more incremental, rather than revolutionary. Thus, paradigm 2 discussions of cultural change emphasize fluctuations in the content and composition of subcultures, variations in the structural and interpersonal relations among subcultures, and changes in the connections between subcultures and the dominant culture. Such localized changes may be loosely coupled to changes occuring within a dominant culture (Weick, 1976).

For example, consider the relationships among the Peace Corps/Africa subcultures that are diagrammed in Figure 2. An unanticipated change in environmental conditions, such as a drought, could have technological consequences that would mandate changes in the composition of these subcultures. More volunteers would be assigned to countries where drought conditions were worst and new drought-stricken countries might be added. In each of these countries, the nature of projects would also change. Water-dependent sanitation plans will no longer be workable. Crop rotation systems, dependent on plentiful water supplies, will have to be revised, so that drought-resistant crops can be grown. Perhaps the volunteers previously assigned to water-dependent sanitation projects can be reassigned to irrigation projects that will utilize their pipe-laying skills, and volunteers assigned to education, who usually teach English to children, can help with the adult education component of the new crop rotation and irrigation projects.

These task assignment changes, and resulting changes in country assignments and volunteer recruitment policies, would eventually cause changes in the subcultural alignments in Peace Corps/Africa. For example, the subculture that arose among sanitation project volunteers would disappear, although it might be partially reconstituted among the staff on the irrigation projects. The educational subculture would change, as adults rather than children became a primary focus. The isolation of the educational subculture might be reduced as educational staff became more involved in irrigation and crop rotation education. Staff levels in the various countries might change, strengthening or weakening country-based subcultures. These changes in the subcultural composition of Peace Corps/Africa are outlined in Figure 4.

Paradigm 2 views of cultural change, like this example, emphasize environmental (or external) catalysts for change that have localized impact on many facets of organizational functioning. These local changes may be loosely coupled to each other and they frequently may be neither planned nor controlled by top management. These emphases on environmental sources of change and external control of organizational functioning are central to mainstream macro-level organizational theory. Thus, paradigm 2 offers a window, a place where cultural research can most obviously benefit from

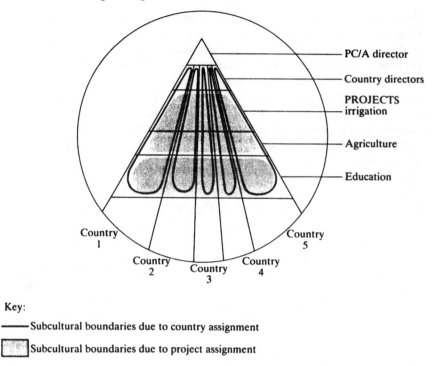

PC/A director

Country directors

PROJECTS
irrigation

Agriculture

Education

Country
1

Country
5

Country
2

Country
3

Country
4

Key:

──── Subcultural boundaries due to country assignment

▨ Subcultural boundaries due to project assignment

Figure 4   *Paradigm 2 view of Peace Corps/Africa (PC/A): time 2*

direct integration with work of non-cultural organizational theorists. The next section of this paper focuses on recent work in two traditional non-cultural domains, differentiation and loose coupling, and explores the relevance of these ideas for a paradigm 2 view of change.

Differentiation channels attention so that a single organizational subunit enacts and responds to a small portion of an organization's overall environment. Channelling attention in this manner links subunits more tightly to their immediate environments, yet perhaps more loosely to each other (March and Olsen, 1976; March and Simon, 1958). Thus, subcultures in differentiated organizations are often loosely coupled to each other. Loose coupling can buffer the effects of subunits' responses, encouraging localized adaptation and experimentation (Weick, 1976). Loose coupling dampens the flow of information within an organization across subunits. Subunits can experiment and respond to turbulent environments knowing the effects of actions and interpretations will be localized and the organization, as a whole, will be buffered from the repercussions of their actions. For example, subunits at an organization's periphery may be loosely coupled to subunits as its technical core (Meyer and Rowan, 1977; Scott, 1981; Thompson, 1967;

Weick, 1976). Or, subunits that reflect an organization's dominant ideology may be loosely coupled to subunits that reflect dissent or deviance.

By localizing subunit responses (including behaviours, beliefs, and interpretations), and allowing inconsistencies to persist, loose coupling provides local havens for deviance and change. Indeed, loose coupling may provide the psychological safety that, according to Schein, is necessary to induce change. A paradigm 1 view of cultural change is traumatic because it entails an organization-wide collapse of a world view. In contrast, a paradigm 2 model of cultural change is incremental and localized; abrupt jolts that are caused by subcultures' adaptive responses, experiments, and idiosyncratic actions are dampened by loose coupling. Although loose coupling has some beneficial effects, such as permitting deviance, providing safety for experimentation, and encouraging localized responses, it may also cause problems. For example, loose coupling may inhibit organization-wide changes. Top down organization-wide planned change efforts would have to cope with loosely coupled information channels and subunits' differential responses to information. Localized responses to environmental contingencies, and lessons from such responses, may not ripple beyond an acting subunit. A loosely coupled organization may not be equipped with the structures or processes which would enable it to transmit and retain the lessons from incremental, localized responses (Weick, 1979).

Change from a paradigm 2 perspective, then, is localized, incremental, and often environmentally stimulated (if not controlled). Those studying or enacting change from a paradigm 2 perspective, but desiring an organization-wide impact, would therefore face a difficult predicament. Because locally based changes are often diffuse and loosely coupled to each other, their organization-wide repercussions are difficult to predict and problematic to control.

Paradigm 2's focus on locally based change is quite different from paradigm 1's concern with global patterns of change. When viewing an organization through a paradigm 2 lens, cultural members and researchers may not even be able to recognize changes in organization-wide patterns of consistency and consensus. A shared, integrating vision or common language is often unrecognized from this perspective. Moreover, paradigm 2 channels ambiguity. So, in addition to missing these paradigm 1 sources of clarity and integration, members and researchers with a paradigm 2 perspective also miss some evidence of people's perceptions of ambiguity.

Paradigm 3: Ambiguity

Paradigm 3 differs from the other two paradigms primarily in its treatment of ambiguity. Paradigms 1 and 2 both minimize the experience of ambiguity.

Paradigm 1 denies it by attending to that which is clear, consistent, and shared. When change comes to a paradigm 1 view of culture, that change is revolutionary. A temporary and traumatic acknowledgement of ambiguity is required before retreat into a new, shared, and unambiguous ideological haven becomes possible. Ambiguity is strictly a temporary, albeit necessary, state of transition in this view of cultural change.

Change, from a paradigm 2 perspective, is not revolutionary, and a traumatic dose of ambiguity awareness is not necessary to catalyse change. Instead, differentiation channels ambiguity so that it is perceived as manageable. Subcultures therefore can avoid the action paralysis that can accompany an overwhelming awareness of ambiguity, and multiple localized changes can occur simultaneously.

There is a third reaction to ambiguity that results in such a different concept of culture (and cultural change) that we have called it paradigm 3. Rather than denying or channelling it, ambiguity could be accepted. Complexity and lack of clarity could be legitimated and even made the focus of attention; from a paradigm 3 perspective, irreconcilable interpretations are simultaneously entertained; paradoxes are embraced. A culture viewed from a paradigm 3 vantage point would have no shared, integrated set of values, save one: an awareness of ambiguity itself.

Unlike paradigm 1, in paradigm 3 awareness of ambiguity is not experienced as a temporary stage in the process of attaining a new vision of clarity. From a paradigm 3 perspective, ambiguity is thought of as the way things are, as the 'truth', not as a temporary state awaiting the discovery of 'truth'. From this perspective, the clarity of paradigm 1 is viewed as over-simplification. Consistency and consensus are considered abstract illusions created by management (Siehl, 1984) for the purposes of control.

In paradigm 3, cultural manifestations are not clearly consistent or inconsistent with each other. Instead, the relationships among manifestations are characterized by a lack of clarity from ignorance or complexity. Differences in meaning, values, and behavioural norms are seen as incommensurable and irreconcilable. Paradigm 2's attempts to achieve reconciliation by channelling attention (and thus differences) to discrete subunits (March and Simon, 1958), or even attempts to resolve differences through sequential attention (Cyert and March, 1963), would be seen as inevitably unsuccessful efforts to mask enduring difficulties. Similarly, organizational processes designed to resolve irreconcilable conflict are seen as temporary and superficial smoke screens. From a paradigm 3 perspective, researchers and cultural members see (and even look for) confusion, paradox, and perhaps even hypocrisy – that which is not clear. Rather than being 'a small clearing of lucidity in a formless, dark, always ominous jungle', a paradigm 3 enacted culture is the jungle itself.

A paradigm 3 portrayal of culture cannot be characterized as generally harmonious or full of conflict. Instead, individuals share some viewpoints, disagree about some, and are ignorant of or indifferent to others. Consensus, dissensus, and confusion coexist, making it difficult to draw cultural and subcultural boundaries. Certainly those boundaries would not coincide with structural divisions or permanent linking roles, as an absence of stability and clarity would weaken the impact of these integrating and differentiating mechanisms. Even the boundary around the organization would be amorphous and permeable, as various 'feeder' cultures from the surrounding environment fade in and out of attention. These attributes of paradigm 3 are summarized, in contrast to the other two paradigms, in Figure 5.

Paradigm 3 accepts ambiguity as an inevitable part of organizational life. Although to date no cultural researchers have used a paradigm 3 perspective in their research, this perspective resembles some non-cultural streams of organizational research. The first stream is exemplified by the work of March and his colleagues in their characterization of some organizations – particularly large public sector bureaucracies and educational institutions – as 'organized anarchies' (e.g. Brunsson, 1985; March and Cohen, 1986; March and Olsen, 1976; Sproull, Weiner and Wolf, 1978; Starbuck, 1983). New or unusually innovative organizations are often viewed from a paradigm 3 perspective. Subcultures may also be havens from a paradigm 3 perspective. For example, members of research and development laboratories, 'skunk

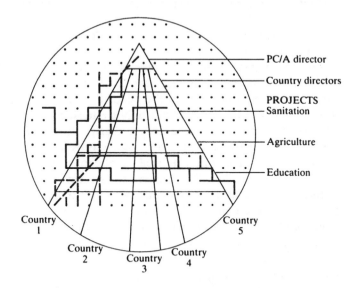

Key
- • Individuals
- —— Concern with educational issues
- – – – Concern with Nigeria (country 1)

Figure 5 *Paradigm 3 view of Peace Corps/Africa (PC/A)*

works', and independent business units working within a larger corporate framework often seem to retain an unusual degree of comfort with ambiguity, and may even thrive on it. That kind of comfort is also evident among members of some occupational subcultures, such as academic research, book publishing, social work, and international business development. Finally, personality research indicates that some individuals develop unusually high tolerances for ambiguity (e.g. Kahn et al., 1964; Rokeach, 1960; Van Sell, Brief and Schuler, 1981). Thus, the acceptance of ambiguity, characteristic of paradigm 3, can surface at various levels of analysis.

One metaphor for a paradigm 3 enacted culture is a web. Individuals are nodes in the web, temporarily connected by shared concerns to some but not all the surrounding nodes. When a particular issue becomes salient, one pattern of connections becomes relevant. That pattern would include a unique array of agreements, disagreements, pockets of ignorance, and hypocrisy. A different issue would draw attention to a different pattern of connections. But from a paradigm 3 perspective, patterns of attention are transient and several issues and interpretations – some of which are irreconcilable – may become salient simultaneously. Thus, at the risk of mixing metaphors, the web itself is a momentary and blurred image, merely a single frame in a high speed motion picture: 'from this standpoint, culture is as much a dynamic, evolving way of thinking and doing as it is a stable set of thoughts and actions' (Van Maanen and Barley, 1984, p. 307).

Figure 5 is a depiction of such a web. Peace Corps/Africa is viewed as a loosely linked set of individuals with patterns of connections within and outside the organization. A concern with educational issues, coupled with disagreements about teaching methods, links volunteers in the educational projects, teachers from outside the Peace Corps, volunteers in the irrigation projects who are concerned about public education, and potential 'students' from the surrounding community. Similarly, an involvement with Nigerian concerns links past and present Peace Corps employees who have been involved with that country, as well as Nigerians themselves. Other shared concerns that could elicit a pattern of connections include concerns with farming or left wing politics. Thus, an individual's momentary 'place' (or 'places') in a paradigm 3 cultural web depends on which issues are currently salient and how patterns of connection are drawn.

A paradigm 3 view of cultural change

What does change mean within this context? If culture is enacted or perceived in terms of a 'web' culture, in terms of transient patterns of attention that loosely link an amorphous set of individuals, then culture must be continually changing. Any change among and between individuals, among the patterns of connections and interpretations, *is* cultural change (at the organizational or sub-organizational level). Whereas paradigm 2 focuses our attention on environmental sources of subcultural change, paradigm 3 stresses individual adjustment to environmental fluctuations, including patterns of attention and interpretation.

> Culture . . . does not itself adapt to environments but is the means through which *individuals* adapt to their environment . . . Culture develops, elaborates, or stagnates in a process of individual cultural innovation (Salisbury, 1975, p. 145, quoted in Keesing, 1981, p. 167).

The Peace Corps/Africa example can be used to illustrate this form of change. Suppose we notice that several of the volunteers in Senegal are becoming politically active in trying to change the educational opportunities in that country. Also, a disproportionally small amount of volunteer time is spent in the villages educating. A group of new volunteers is trying to become accustomed to village life. The culture of Peace Corps/Africa is continually changing, because the culture is, at any given time, the 'web' of the constantly fluctuating concerns of these individuals. If such changes are considered cultural change, and at the same time culture is the means through which individuals change, then culture, like individuals' attention patterns must be continually changing (cf. March, 1981).

Although cultural change is continual in a paradigm 3 enacted culture, it may go unnoticed. To be salient, change requires a backdrop of clarity. For a change in organizational patterns to be recognized, relatively stable patterns must have been acknowledged. For a subculture to be considered different in some way, members must be aware of their past subcultural connections. For a change in role relationships to be acknowledged, roles had to have been understood. A paradigm 3 portrayal of cultural change is paradoxical: it is continual and obscure. Whereas ambiguity tends to be invisible from the perspectives of paradigms 1 and 2, changes, as well as patterns of stability, become invisible from a paradigm 3 viewpoint. Not surprisingly, cultural change, conceived from such a dynamic and open-system perspective is virtually uncontrollable. Figure 6 summarizes the three paradigms' views of cultural change.

Paradigm 3 offers an approach to psychological safety that is radically different from that of the other two paradigms. That approach to safety has important implications for cultural change. In paradigm 1 psychological safety is provided by a solid foundation of clarity. In paradigm 2 psychological safety is provided by loose coupling between the locus of change – the subculture – and the rest of the organization. In paradigm 3 psychological safety is provided by a heightened awareness and acceptance of ambiguity. Expectations and evaluation criteria are not clear. Means and ends are perceived as connected loosely, if at all. Because it is difficult to connect actions to outcomes, individuals are less at risk when they experiment. Negative consequences of

Characteristics of cultural change	Paradigm 1	Paradigm 2	Paradigm 3
Nature of process	Revolutionary	Incremental	Continual
Scope	Organization-wide	Localized and loosely coupled	Issue-specific changes among individuals
Source	Often leader-centred	External and internal catalysts	Individual adjustments attention interpretation
Implications for managing process	If superficial, then controllable; if deeper, then difficult but possible, to control	Predictable and unpredictable sources and consequences of change	Relatively uncontrollable due to continual change

Figure 6   *Contrasting the approaches to cultural change*

their actions are hard to detect. To the extent that a locus of control exists, it lies within the individual. Thus, a paradigm 3 perspective gives individuals a heightened sense of autonomy, and that autonomy brings safety.

Acceptance of ambiguity allows individuals greater freedom to act, to play, and to experiment (March and Olsen, 1976; Rogers, 1961; Weick, 1979). With this freedom, preferences and interpretations can be allowed to emerge from actions, rather than prospectively guide behaviours (Brunsson, 1985; March, 1981; March and Olsen, 1976; Starbuck, 1983; Weick, 1979, 1985). For these reasons, a paradigm 3 perspective should be most likely to be adopted in settings where creativity and constant experimentation are valued (classrooms, research laboratories, innovative industries, etc.); in contexts where ambiguity is unavoidably salient (large public bureaucracies and political organizations); in occupations where technology is unclear (social work and book publishing); and in work where ideological and cognitive openness is required (such as cross-cultural business and inter-organizational negotiations). In these situations, change is constant; indeed, change is the business of many of these kinds of organizations and occupations. Ironically then, paradigm 3's acceptance of ambiguity simultaneously fosters and obscures continual change – the very prevalence of that change makes it difficult to control.

Conclusion

Each cultural paradigm draws attention to a distinct set of organizational processes and simultaneously blinds others. With each set of processes comes a distinct view of how cultures change. Each of these views has implications about inter-related facets of organizational change; we have only hinted at these. For example, a paradigm 1 perspective draws attention to monolithic and revolutionary changes in what is shared. Such changes often are attributed to the actions of a leader, frequently as concomitants (or consequences) of changes in leadership or organizational strategy. Whether such revolutionary change can actually be controlled by the actions of a leader is a separate question, as yet unresolved. The response to this question would largely depend on how culture is viewed. Is culture seen strictly in terms of surface level manifestations and espoused values, managerial levers to be manipulated at will? Or, does culture include those deeper-level assumptions that make behaviours and understandings taken-for-granted or habitualized, inertial forces that resist change?

A paradigm 2 perspective draws attention to localized, incremental changes – deviances, adaptations, and experiments – among and within subunits. Change may be catalysed from inside and/or outside the organization. Thus, paradigm 2 focuses our attention on how an organization enacts, responds to, and ultimately reflects its environment.

From a paradigm 3 perspective, it is difficult to notice discrete fluctuations. Ironically, the ambiguity and continual change that characterize this perspective obscure change. A paradigm 3 enacted culture *is* dynamic, paradoxical, confusing. This perspective draws attention to irreconcilable meanings. Pockets of ignorance and confusion, and actions that precede preferences are made salient. Paradigm 3 makes possible play, serendipitous outcomes (Miner, 1985), and ambiguity in decision-making procedures – the importance of temporal patterns of attention and decision opportunities (Cohen, March and Olsen, 1972). Janus-faced thinking – the ability to see and interpret in opposite directions – which has been associated with creativity (Rothenberg, 1976) also becomes possible with a paradigm 3 view. Thus, paradigm 3 draws attention to those changes, by definition uncontrollable, that may underlie processes of innovation.

These three paradigmatic views have quite different implications for those who wish to manage the cultural change process. Paradigm 1 carries the hope, and often the promise, that organization-wide cultural changes can be successfully initiated and controlled by those who hold leadership positions. It is of little surprise, then, that researchers and practitioners who write about the possibility and pragmatics of managing cultural change, usually do so from a paradigm 1 view (e.g. Kilmann, Saxton and Serpa, 1985; Pascale and Athos, 1981; Pettigrew, 1985; Schein, 1985; Tichy, 1983; Wilkins, 1983). Paradigm

2 offers a more constricted view, suggesting that efforts to manage cultural change have localized impact – both intentional and unintentional – but that predictable, organization-wide control will be unlikely. Paradigm 3 suggests that all cultural members, not just leaders, inevitably and constantly change and are changed by the cultures they live in. Thus, beliefs about cultural control are determined and reflected by a person's choice or paradigmatic viewpoints.

The predicament of would-be 'value engineers' is further complicated if we are correct in our belief that, at any given time, a culture can be described and enacted from any and all three paradigms. To varying degrees, the processes of change suggested by each paradigm may be simultaneously occuring within a single organization. Thus, it is crucially important, for full understanding, to view any one organizational setting from all three paradigmatic viewpoints. This three-paradigm perspective draws attention to those aspects of cultural change that are, and more importantly perhaps, are not amenable to managerial control.

However, since paradigms serve as blinders for researchers and organizational members, it is likely that any one individual will find it easiest to view culture from only one paradigmatic perspective. This causes blind spots. If cultural change is perceived and enacted from only one paradigmatic perspective, then other sources and types of change may not be considered. If researchers and members focus on 'top-down' organizational-level processes, they will miss 'bottom-up' sources of change. If they attend only to locally based changes, they will miss global patterns and masked ambiguities. And, if ambiguities are ignored or hidden, experimentation and 'playfulness' may be inhibited. But by maintaining a constant awareness of ambiguity, individuals may not be able to notice change. Or, if their acknowledgement of ambiguity is sudden, they risk trauma and action paralysis.

An awareness of all three paradigms simultaneously would avoid the usual blind spots associated with any single perspective. However, a paradigm comprises a set of assumptions about culture, and thus, about organization. It determines the cultural 'reality' that members and researchers socially construct. As such, holding all three paradigms simultaneously – enacting multiple realities (and understanding their dynamic inter-relationships) – is extremely difficult. Yet to develop a better understanding of how organizations change, we must consider the complex dynamics of culture as well as those inter-related change processes from such a multi-paradigm approach.

Notes

1 The authors wish to thank Dan Denison, David Jemison, Peter Robertson, Edgar Schein, and Sim Sitkin for their helpful comments on an earlier draft. Portions of this article were presented at the meetings of the International

Conference on Organizational Culture and Symbolism, Montreal, Canada, 1986, and the Annual meeting of the Academy of Management, Chicago, 1986.

2 Unlike many researchers who take a cognitive approach to culture (e.g. Geertz, 1973), we believe behaviours, as reflected in informal and formal organizational practices, must be included as part of culture. Because practices reflect specific, material conditions of existence that often are not reflected in the world of beliefs or ideas, it is essential that the study of culture includes these structural, economic, and social realities. (Martin and Meyerson, forthcoming, p. 29).

3 Paradigms are viewpoints, not objective attributes of a culture. Thus, both researchers and cultural members may or may not adopt the same paradigmatic perspective on a specific cultural context.

References

Bandura, A. (1977). *Social Learning Theory*. Englewood Cliffs, NJ: Prentice-Hall.
Barley, S. (1983). 'Semiotics and the study of occupational and organizational cultures'. *Administrative Science Quarterly*, **28**, 393–413.
Barnard, C. (1938). *Functions of the Executive*, Cambridge: Harvard University Press.
Bennis, W. (1983). 'The artform of leadership'. In Srivastrva, S. and Assoc. (Eds.), *The Executive Mind*. San Francisco: Jossey-Bass.
Berger, P. (1967). *The Sacred Canopy*. Garden City: Doubleday.
Berger, P. and Luckmann, T. (1966). *The Social Construction of Reality*. New York: Doubleday.
Beyer, J. B. (1981). 'Ideologies, values, and decision-making in organizations'. In Nystrom, P. and Starbuck, W. (Eds.), *Handbook of Organizational Design*: 166–201. New York: Oxford University Press.
Brunnson, N. (1985). *The Irrational Organization*. New York: Wiley.
Burgleman, R. (1983). 'A process model of internal corporate venturing in the diversified major firm'. *Administrative Science Quarterly*, **28**, 223–44.
Calder, B. (1977). 'An attribution theory of leadership'. In Staw, B. M. and Cummings, L. L. (Eds.), *New Directions in Organizational Behavior*, **3**, 283–302. Greenwich, CT: JAI Press.
Christensen, S. and Kreiner, K. (1984). *On the Origin of Organizational Cultures*. Paper prepared for the First International Conference on Organizational Symbolism and Corporate Culture, Lund, Sweden.
Clark, B. (1970). *The Distinctive College: Antioch, Reed and Swarthmore*. Chicago: Aldine.
Clark, B. (1972). 'The organizational saga in higher education'. *Administrative Science Quarterly*, **17**, 178–84.
Cohen, M., March, J. and Olsen, J. (1972). 'A garbage can model of organizational choice'. *Administrative Science Quarterly*, **17**, 1–25.
Cyert, R. and March, J. (1963). *A Behavioral Theory of the Firm*. Englewood Cliffs, NJ: Prentice-Hall.

Deal, T. and Kennedy, A. (1982). *Corporate Cultures: The Rites and Rituals of Corporate Life*. Reading, Mass.: Addison-Wesley.

Geertz, C. (1973). *The Interpretation of Culture*. New York: Basic Books.

Giddens, A. (1979). *Central Problems in Social Theory*. Berkeley: University of California Press.

Goffman, E. (1967). *Interaction Ritual*. New York: Anchor Books.

Golding, D. (1980). 'Establishing blissful clarity in organizational life: Managers'. *Sociological Review*, **28**, 763–82.

Greenwood, R. and Hinings, C. R. (1986). *Organizational Design Types, Tracks and the Dynamics of Change*. Research Report, Faculty of Business, University of Alberta, Alberta.

Gregory, K. (1983). 'Native view paradigms: multiple cultures and culture conflicts in organizations'. *Administrative Sciences Quarterly*, **28**, 359–76.

Hackman, R. (1984). 'The Transition that Hasn't Happened'. Unpublished manuscript, Yale University, New Haven.

Jamison, M. (1985). 'The joys of gardening: collectivist and bureaucratic cultures in conflict'. *The Sociological Quarterly*, **26**, 473–90.

Johnsen, K., Weilbach, S. and Williams, S. (1986). 'Organizational cultures: a look at life on a submarine'. Unpublished manuscript, Graduate School of Business, Stanford University, Stanford.

Jonsson, S. and Lundin, R. (1977). 'Myths and wishful thinking as management tools'. In Nystrom, P. and Starbuck, W. (Eds.), *Studies in the Management Sciences*, **5**, 157–70. New York: North-Holland.

Kahn, R., Wolfe, D., Quinn, R. and Snoek, J. D. (1964). *Organizational Stress: Studies in the Role Conflict and Ambiguity*. New York: Wiley.

Keessing, R. (1981). *Cultural Anthropology: A Contemporary Perspective* (2nd Ed.). New York: Holt, Rinehart and Winston.

Kilmann, R., Saxton, M. and Serpa, R. (1985). *Gaining Control of the Corporate Culture*. San Francisco: Jossey-Bass.

Kuhn, T. (1962). *The Structure of Scientific Revolutions*. Chicago: University of Chicago Press.

Latane, B. and Darley, J. (1970). *The Unresponsive Bystander*. New York: Appleton.

Lawrence, P. and Lorsch, J. (1967). 'Differentiation and integration in complex organizations'. *Administrative Science Quarterly*, **12**, 1–47.

Louis, M. (1983). 'Organizations as culture bearing milieux'. In Pondy, L., Frost, P. Morgan, G. and Dandridge, T. (Eds.), *Organizational Symbolism*, 39–54. Greenwich, CT: JAI Press.

March, J. G. (1981). 'Footnotes to organizational change'. *Administrative Science Quarterly*, **26**, 563–77.

March, J. G. and Cohen, M. D. (1986). *Leadership and Ambiguity* (2nd Ed.). Boston: Harvard Business School Press.

March, J. G. and Olsen, J. P. (1976). 'Organizational choice under ambiguity'. In March, J. G. and Olsen, J. P. (Eds.) *Ambiguity and Choice in Organizations*, 10–23. Bergen, Norway: Universitetsforlaget.

March, J. G. and Simon, H. A. (1958). *Organizations*. New York: Wiley.

Martin, J. (1982). 'Stories and scripts in organizational settings'. In Hastorf, A. and Isen, A. (Eds.), *Cognitive Social Psychology*: 255–305. New York: Elsevier-North Holland.

Martin, J. (1986). 'Homogeneity, diversity, and ambiguity in organizational cultures'. Invited address presented to Division 8 at the American Psychological Association, Washington DC.

Martin, J., Feldman, M., Hatch, M. J. and Sitkin, S. (1983). 'The uniqueness paradox in organizational stories'. *Administrative Science Quarterly*, **28**, 438–53.

Martin, J. and Meyerson, D. (1986). 'Organizational Culture at the OZ Company'. Unpublished manuscript, Graduate School of Business, Stanford University, Standford.

Martin, J. and Meyerson, D. (1988). 'Organizational cultures and the denial, channeling and acceptance of ambiguity'. In McCaskey, M., Pondy, L. and Thomas, H. (Eds.), *Managing Ambiguity and Changes*. New York: Wiley.

Martin, J. and Siehl, C. (1983). 'Organizational cultures and counter-culture: an uneasy symbiosis'. *Organizational Dynamics*, 52–64.

Martin, J., Sitkin, S. and Boehm, M. (1985). 'Founders and the elusiveness of a cultural legacy'. In Frost, P., Moore, L., Louis, M., Lundberg, C. and Martin J. (Eds.), *Organizational Culture: the Meaning of Life in the Workplace*. Beverly Hills: Sage.

Meyer, J. and Rowan, B. (1977). 'Institutionalized organizations: formal structure as myth and ceremony'. *American Journal of Sociology*, **83**, 340–63.

Miner, A. (1985). 'The Strategy of Serendipity: Ambiguity, Uncertainty, and Idiosyncratic Jobs'. Unpublished doctoral dissertation, Stanford University, Stanford.

Morgan, G., Frost, J. and Pondy, L. (1983). 'Organizational symbolism'. In Pondy, L., Frost, P., Morgan, G. and Dandridge, T. (Eds.), *Organizational Symbolism*, 55–65. Greenwich, CT: JAI Press.

Nord, W. (1985). 'Can organizational culture be managed?', In Frost, P., Moore, L., Louis, M., Lundberg, C. and Martin, J. (Eds.), *Organizational Culture: The Meaning of Life in the Workplace*. Beverly Hills: Sage.

Ouchi, W. (1981). *Theory Z*. Reading, Mass.: Addison-Wesley.

Pascale, R. and Athos, A. (1981). *The Art of Japanese Management*. New York: Warner.

Peters, T. and Waterman, B. (1982). *In Search of Excellence*. New York: Harper and Row.

Pettigrew, A. (1979). 'On studying organizational cultures'. *Administrative Science Quarterly*, **24**, 570–81.

Pettigrew, A. (1985). *The Awakening Giant: Continuity and Change in ICI*. Oxford: Blackwell.

Pfeffer, J. (1981). 'Management as symbolic action: the creation and maintenance of organizational paradigms'. In Staw, B. and Cummings, L. (Eds.), *Research in Organizational Behavior*, **3**, 1–52. Greenwich, CT: JAI Press.

Rogers, C. (1961). *On Becoming a Person: a Therapists View of Psychotherapy*. Boston: Houghton Mifflin.

Rokeach, M. (1960). *The Open and Closed Mind*. New York: Basic Books.

Rothenberg, A. (1976). 'Janusian thinking and creativity'. *Psychoanalytic Study of Society*, **7**, 1–30.

Sathay, V. (1985). *Culture or Related Corporate Realities*. New York: Irwin.

Schall, M. (1983). 'A communication-rules approach to organizational culture'. *Administrative Science Quarterly*, **28**, 557–81.

Schein, E. (1968). 'Organizational socialization and the profession of management'. *Industrial Management Review*, 191–201.

Schein, E. (1983). 'The role of the founder in creating organizational culture'. *Organizational Dynamics*. Summer, 13–28.

Schein, E. (1985). *Organizational Culture and Leadership*. San Francisco: Jossey-Bass.

Scott, W. R. (1981). *Organizations: Rational, Natural and Open Systems*. Englewood Cliffs, NJ: Prentice-Hall.

Selznick, P. (1957). *Leadership in Administration*. Evanston: Row Peterson.

Shriver, S. (1986). 'The vision'. In Viorst, M. (Ed.), *Making a Difference: the Peace*

Corps at Twenty Five, 15–29. New York: Weidenfeld & Nicolson.

Siehl, C. (1984). 'Cultural Sleight-of-Hand: the Illusion of Consistency'. Unpublished doctoral dissertation, Stanford University, Stanford.

Smircich, L. (1983a). 'Concepts of culture and organizational analysis'. *Administrative Science Quarterly*, **28**, 339–59.

Smircich, L. (1983b). 'Organizations as shared meanings'. In Pondy, L., Frost, P., Morgan, G. and Dandridge, T. (Eds.), *Organizational Symbolism*, 55–65. Greenwich, CT: JAI Press.

Smircich, L. and Morgan, G. (1982). 'Leadership: the management of meaning.' *Journal of Applied Behavioral Science*, **18**, 257–73.

Smith, K. and Simmons, V. (1983). 'A Rumpelstiltskin organization: metaphors on metaphors in field research'. *Administrative Science Quarterly*, **28**, 377–92.

Sproull, L., Weiner, S. and Wolf, D. (1978). *Organizing an Anarchy*. Chicago: University of Chicago Press.

Starbuck, W. (1983). 'Organizations as action generators'. *American Sociological Review*, **48**, 91–102.

Thompson, J. (1967). *Organizations in Action*. New York: McGraw-Hill.

Tichy, N. (1983). *Managing Strategic Change: Technical, Political, and Cultural Dynamics*. New York: Wiley.

Trice, H. and Beyer, J. (1984). 'Studying organizational cultures through rites and ceremonials'. *Academy of Management Review*, **9**, 653–69.

Van Maanen, J. and Barley, S. (1984). 'Occupational communities: culture and conrol in organizations'. In Staw, B. and Cummings, L. (Eds.), *Research on Organizational Behaviour*, **6**. Greenwich, CT: JAI Press.

Van Sell, M., Brief, A. and Schuler, R. (1981). 'Role conflict and role ambiguity: integration of the literature and directions for future research'. *Human Relations*, **34**, 43–71.

Webster(1985). *The American Heritage Dictionary*, New York: Dell Publishing.

Weick, K. (1976). 'Educational organizations as loosely coupled systems'. *Administrative Science Quarterly*, **21**, 1–19.

Weick, K. (1979). *The Social Psychology of Organizing* (2nd Ed.). Reading, Mass.: Addison-Wesley.

Weick, K. (1985). 'Sources of order in underorganized systems: themes in recent organizational theory'. In Lincoln, Y. (Ed.), *Organizational Theory and Inquiry: the Paradigm Revolution*, 106–36. Beverly Hills: Sage.

Wilkins, A. (1983). 'Organizational stories as symbols which control the organization'. In Pondy, L., Frost, P., Morgan, G. and Dandridge, T. (Eds.), *Organizational Symbolism*. Greenwich, CT: JAI Press.

Wuthnow, R., Hunter, J., Bergesen, A. and Kurzweil, E. (1984). *Cultural Analysis*. Boston: Routledge and Kegan Paul.

Zucker, L. (1977). 'The role of institutionalization in cultural persistence'. *American Sociological Review*, **42**, 726–43.

Source: Meyerson, Debra and Martin, Joanne (1987) Cultural change: an integration of three different views, *Journal of Management Studies*, **24**, 623–647.

Part Four

The Organization is in the Mind: Enacting Organizational Reality

---

We have to remember that what we observe is not nature in itself, but nature exposed to our method of questioning.

Werner Heisenberg (Physics and Philosophy)

Organizations talk in order to discover what they are saying, act in order to discover what they are doing.

Karl Weick (Re-punctuating the Problem)

7 Organization as flux and transformation

Gareth Morgan

Autopoiesis: the logic of self-producing systems

Traditional approaches to organization theory have been dominated by the idea that change originates in the environment. The organization is typically viewed as an open system in constant interaction with its context, transforming inputs into outputs as a means of creating the conditions necessary for survival. Changes in the environment are viewed as presenting challenges to which the organization must respond. While there is great debate as to whether adaptation or selection is the primary factor influencing survival, both contingency theorists and population ecologists are at one in believing that the major problems facing modern organizations stem from changes in the environment.

This basic idea is challenged by the implications of a new approach to systems theory developed by two Chilean scientists, Humberto Maturana and Francisco Varela. They argue that all living systems are organizationally closed, autonomous systems of interaction that make reference only to themselves. The idea that living systems are open to an environment is, in their view, the product of an attempt to make sense of such systems from the standpoint of an external observer. Their theory challenges the validity of distinctions drawn between a system and its environment, and offers a new perspective for understanding the logic through which living systems change.

Maturana and Varela base their argument on the idea that living systems are characterized by three principal features: autonomy, circularity, and self-reference. These lend them the ability to self-create or self-renew. Maturana and Varela have coined the term *autopoiesis* to refer to this capacity for self-production through a closed system of relations. They contend that the aim of such systems is ultimately to produce themselves: their own organization and identity is their most important product.

How is it possible to say that living systems such as organisms are autonomous, closed systems? Maturana and Varela argue that this is the case because living systems strive to maintain an identity by subordinating all changes to the maintenance of their own organization as a given set of relations. They do so by engaging in circular patterns of interaction whereby change in one element of the system is coupled with changes elsewhere, setting up continuous patterns of interaction that are always self-referential. They are self-referential because a system cannot enter into interactions that are not specified in the pattern of relations that define its organization. Thus a system's interaction with its 'environment' is really a reflection and part of its own organization. It interacts with its environment in a way that facilitates its own self-production, and in this sense we can see that its environment is really a part of itself.

In saying that living systems are closed and autonomous Maturana and Varela are not saying that systems are completely isolated. The closure and autonomy to which they refer is organizational. They are saying that living systems close in on themselves to maintain stable patterns of relations, and that it is this process of closure or self-reference that ultimately distinguishes a system as a system. In order to discover the nature of the total system it is necessary to interact with it and trace the circular pattern of interaction through which it is defined. In doing so we encounter the problematic question of where the system begins and ends. Maturana and Varela recognize that in any systems analysis one will usually have to stop unwinding the pattern of circular relations at some point, because systems, like Chinese boxes, can be seen as being made up of wholes within wholes. However they believe that this kind of self-referential paradox is fundamental. There is no beginning and no end to the system because it is a closed loop of interaction.

Thus, to take an example, in the organization of a biological organism, such as the honeybee we find self-referring systems within self-referring systems. The bee as an organism comprises a chain of self-referring biological systems with their own circular organization, and lives within a society of bees where relations are also circular. In turn, the relationship between the society of bees and the wider ecology is also circular. Eliminate the bees and the whole ecology will change, for the bee system is linked with the botanical system, which is linked with insect, animal, agricultural, human, and social systems. All these systems are self-referential and turn back on each other. A change in any one system, e.g., a decision to use an insecticide which eliminates bees as a side effect, can transform all the others.

We could attempt to understand such systems by drawing an artificial boundary between system and environment, e.g., around the individual bee, or the society of bees, or the bee-flora-fauna system, but in doing so we would break the circular chain of interaction. An understanding of the autopoietic nature of systems requires that we understand how each element simultaneously combines the maintenance of itself with the maintenance of the others.

It is simply not good enough to dismiss a large part of the circular chain of interaction as 'the environment.' The environment is part of the bee system, and the different levels are in effect coproduced.

To provide a further illustration of these ideas it is useful to consider how Maturana and Varela reinterpret the way the human brain and nervous system operate. One of the most familiar images of the brain is that of an information-processing system, importing information from the environment and initiating appropriate responses. The brain is viewed as making representations of the environment, recording these in memory, and modifying the information thus stored through experience and learning. In contrast, Maturana and Varela argue that the brain is closed, autonomous, circular, and self-referential. They argue that the brain does not process information from an environment, and does not represent the environment in memory. Rather, it establishes and assigns patterns of variation and points of reference as expressions of its own mode of organization. The system thus organizes its environment as part of itself. If one thinks about it, the idea that the brain can make representations of its environment presumes some external point of reference from which it is possible to judge the degree of correspondence between the representation and the reality. This implicitly presumes that the brain must have a capacity to see and understand its world from a point of reference outside itself. Clearly this cannot be so, thus the idea that the brain represents reality is open to serious question. Maturana and Varela's work identifies this paradox and suggests that the brain creates images of reality as expressions or descriptions of its own organization and interacts with these images, modifying them in the light of actual experience.

To those of us who have become used to thinking about organisms and organizations as open systems this kind of circular reasoning may seem very strange indeed. We have learned to see living systems as distinct entities characterized by numerous patterns of interdependence, both internally and in relation to their environment. As noted earlier, Maturana and Varela argue that this is because we insist on understanding these systems from *our* point of view as observers, rather than attempting to understand their inner logic. As my colleague Peter Harries-Jones has put it, in doing this we tend to confuse and mix the domain of organization with that of explanation. If we put ourselves 'inside' such systems we come to realize that we are within a closed system of interaction and that the environment is *part of* the system's organization because it is part of its domain of essential interaction.

The theory of autopoiesis thus recognizes that systems can be recognized as having 'environments,' but insists that relations with any environment are *internally* determined. While there may be countless chains of interaction within and between systems, A being linked to B, to C, D, E, and so forth, there is no independent pattern of causation. Changes in A do not cause changes in B, C, D, or E, since the whole chain of relations is part of the same self-determining pattern. Gregory Bateson and other theorists who have interested themselves in the ecological aspects of systems have made a similar point in emphasizing that 'wholes' evolve as complete fields of relations that are mutually determining and determined. The system's pattern has to be understood as a whole, and as possessing a logic of its own. It cannot be understood as a network of separate parts. This is ultimately why it makes no sense to say that a system interacts with an external environment. For a system's transactions with an environment are really transactions within itself.

These theoretical insights have important implications. For if systems are geared to maintaining their own identity, and if relations with the environment are internally determined, then systems can evolve and change only along with self-generated changes in identity. How then does this occur?

When we recognize that identity involves the maintenance of a recurring set of relations, we quickly see that the problem of change hinges on the way systems deal with variations that influence their current mode of operation. Our attention is thus drawn to system processes that try to maintain identity by ignoring or counteracting threatening fluctuations, and to the way variations can lead to the emergence of new modes of organization. These issues have received considerable attention from cyberneticians. Their work emphasizes that systems can maintain stable identities by sustaining processes of negative feedback that allow them to detect and correct deviations from operating norms, and can evolve by developing capacities for double-loop learning that allow them to modify these norms to take account of new circumstances.

But where do the variations in system operation come from? What is the source of potential change? The theory of autopoiesis locates the source of change in random variations occurring *within* the total system. These may stem from random modifications introduced through processes of reproduction, or through the combination of chance interactions and connections that give rise to the development of new system relations.

In this insight the theory of autopoiesis has much in common with recent developments in a variety of scientific disciplines. For example, in 1978 Illya Prigogine of Brussels received a Nobel prize for his work on 'dissipative structures' in chemical reaction systems, which shows that random changes in a system can lead to new patterns of order and stability. The same insights have been found to apply in other living systems. Termites and bees engage in random behaviors that increase the variety of the systems to which they belong. If these random behaviors attract a critical level of support, they then often become incorporated in the ongoing organization of the system. For example, termites build elaborate arches and tunnels by making random deposits of earth, which, after they attain a certain size, become a focus of attention for other termites, and thereafter a focus of deliberate activity. Random piles of dirt thus become transformed into coherent structures. In these and numerous other living systems order and self-organization emerge from randomness, large fluctuations triggering instabilities and quantum jumps capable of transforming the whole system of activity. Human ideas and practices seem to develop in a similar manner, exerting a major transformational effect once they acquire a critical level of support.

From an autopoietic standpoint random variation provides the seed of possibility that allows the emergence and evolution of new system identities. Random changes can trigger interactions that reverberate throughout the system, the final consequences being determined by whether or not the current identity of the system will dampen the effects of the new disturbance through compensatory changes elsewhere, or whether a new configuration of relations will be allowed to emerge.

The theory of autopoiesis thus encourages us to understand the transformation or evolution of living systems as the result of internally generated change. Rather than suggesting that the system adapts to an environment or that the environment selects the system configuration that survives, autopoiesis places principal emphasis on the way the total system of interactions shapes its own future. It is the pattern, or whole, that evolves. In providing this kind of explanation, autopoiesis presents an alternative to Darwinian theory. While recognizing the importance of system variation and the retention of 'selected' features in the process of evolution, the theory offers different explanations as to how this occurs.

Organizations as self-producing systems

Maturana and Varela developed their theory primarily as a new interpretation of biological phenomena, and they have strong reservations about applying it to the social world. However, used as metaphor, the theory of autopoiesis has intriguing implications for our understanding of organizations.

First, a creative interpretation of the theory helps us to see that organizations are always attempting to achieve a form of self-referential closure in relation to their environments, enacting their environments as projections of their own identity or self-image. Second, it helps us to understand that many of the problems that organizations encounter in dealing with their environments are intimately connected with the kind of identity that they try to maintain. And third, it helps us to see that explanations of the evolution, change, and development of organizations must give primary attention to the factors that shape an organization's self-identity, and hence its relations with the wider world.

Enactment as a form of narcissism: organizations interact with projections of themselves

Organizations enact their environments: they assign patterns of variation and significance to the world in which they operate. The ideas on autopoiesis add to our understanding of this enactment, in that they encourage us to view organizational enactments as part of the self-referential process through which an organization attempts to tie down and reproduce its identity. For in enacting an environment an organization is attempting to achieve the kind of closure that is necessary for it to reproduce itself in its own image.

Consider, for example, the cartoon in Figure 1. We find here a typical process of organizational self-reference. An organization has convened a meeting to discuss certain policy issues and to take a general look at its environment.

Where do we stand?
What's happening in the environment?
Why are our sales people having so much trouble this month?
What scope is there for penetration of new markets?
What business are we in?
Are we in the right business?

Questions such as these allow those asking them to make representations of themselves, their organization, and the environment, in a way that helps orient action to create or maintain a desirable identity. The charts that decorate the walls of the meeting room are really mirrors. Like the reflecting globe in Escher's lithograph they allow members of the organization to see themselves within the context of their ongoing activity. The figures and pictures that an organization produces on market trends, competitive position, sales forecasts, raw-material availability, and so forth are really projections of the organization's own interests and concerns. They reflect the organization's understanding of itself. It is through this process of self-reference that organizational members can intervene in their own functioning, and thus participate in creating and maintaining their identity.

When we view the enactment process as an attempt to achieve a form of closure in relation to the environment, the whole idea of enactment assumes new significance. For we come to realize that enactment is not just a mode of perception whereby we see or emphasize certain things while ignoring or downplaying others, but is a much more active process. By projecting itself onto its environment and thereby organizing its environment, and organization sets the basis for acting in relation to that environment in a way that actually allows it to produce itself.

Autopoietic systems are closed loops: self-referential systems that strive to shape themselves in their own image.

Hand with reflecting globe. Self-portrait by M. C. Escher (lithograph, 1935).

Figure 1 *Systems that look at themselves. Source: Escher self-portrait reprinted by permission of Haags Gemeentemuseum, The Hague, and courtesy of Vorpal Gallery, San Francisco and New York City, by permission of the heirs of M. C. Escher, © W M. C. Escher heirs c/o Cordon Arts-Baarn-Holland.*

Well Jack, where do we stand ?

Figure 1 continued　*Boardroom cartoon reproduced by permission of the artist*

Identity and closure: egocentricism versus systemic wisdom

Nowadays many organizations are preoccupied with understanding their environment as a kind of 'world out there' that has an existence of its own. The ideas discussed above show the dangers in this kind of thinking, and suggest that if one really wants to understand one's environment, one must begin by understanding oneself, for one's understanding of the environment is always a projection of oneself. As an organization 'looks at' its environment, or makes exploratory probes to test its nature, it should thus appreciate that it is really creating an opportunity to understand itself and its relation with the wider world.

Many organizations encounter great problems in dealing with the wider world, because they do not recognize how they are a part of their environment. They see themselves as discrete entities that are faced with the problem of surviving *against* the vagaries of the outside world, which is often constructed as a domain of threat and opportunity. This is most evident in the practices of what I call *egocentric organizations*, which have a rather fixed notion of who they are, or what they can be, and are determined to impose or sustain that identity at all costs.

This kind of egocentricism leads organizations to become preoccupied with and to overemphasize the importance of themselves, while underplaying the significance of the wider system of relations in which they exist. When we look at ourselves in a mirror we create a relation between 'figure,' the face that we see, and 'ground,' the context in which our face is located. When we focus on our face, our context is pretty well eliminated from view. The egocentric enactments through which organizations attempt to structure and understand their environments often manifest a similar imbalance. In their quest to see and promote their own self-interest against that of the wider context, they create an overassertive relation between figure and ground. Just as a face in a mirror is dependent on a host of conditions for its existence, such as the biological processes that create and sustain the face and the physical and cultural conditions required for the existence of the mirror, the defining features of organizations are dependent on a host of less obvious contextual relations that must be maintained if the organization is to continue to exist. The figure and its ground are part of the same system of relations, and exist only in relation with each other. In enacting and dealing with their environment in a egocentric way, organizations often do not understand their own complexity and the numerous recursive loops on which they depend for their very existence.

As a result of this kind of egocentricism, many organizations end up trying to sustain unrealistic identities, or to produce identities that ultimately destroy the contexts of which they are part.

A good example of the former is found in those firms making watches and typewriters that failed to take account of developments in digital and microprocessing technology. Seeing themselves as 'watchmakers' or 'type-writer firms,' they continued in the production of traditional products with traditional technologies, failing to understand that these identities were no longer relevant or realistic. As a result, many were obliterated by new forms of competition. We can correctly say in retrospect that all firms serving the traditional markets *should have* seen and included the new developments as part of their environment. But this misses the important point: that their understanding of the environment was a product of their identity as watchmakers or typewriter manufacturers. To be successful they needed very different conceptions of themselves and of what their future might entail.

Good examples of how egocentricism can destroy the context on which an organization depends are found in many modern industries. For example, producers of toxic chemicals create all kinds of environmental and social hazards as a side effect of their interest in making profits. They implicitly treat the physical and social environment as a kind of external dumping ground, setting the basis for long-run problems that challenge their future viability. The pollution and health problems created by toxins are likely to eliminate or severely constrain the operations of this industry in the long term. Similarly, in agriculture the use of fertilizers, pesticides, fungicides, and other chemicals, and mechanized methods of farming, are bringing short-term profits while destroying the soil and other aspects of the ecology on which farming ultimately depends.

Egocentric organizations draw boundaries around a narrow definition of themselves, and attempt to advance the self-interest of this narrow domain. In the process, they truncate and distort their understanding of the wider context in which they operate, and surrender their future to the way the context evolves. Because of their truncated and distorted understanding, they cannot be proactive in a systemic sense. Their fate thus often rests in 'seeing what happens' rather than in attempting to shape what happens. For example, the future of many firms in agriculture or the chemical business will depend on how government, consumers, and citizens will react to and punish their activities, rather than on systematic attempts to change themselves.

One of the strengths of the theory of autopoiesis is that it shows us that while the preservation of an identity is fundamental for all living systems, there are different ways in which closure in relation to the environment can be achieved. When we recognize that the environment is not an independent domain, and that we don't necessarily have to compete or struggle against the environment, a completely new relationship becomes possible. For example, an organization can explore possible identities and the conditions under which they can be realized. Organizations committed to this kind of self-discovery are able to develop a kind of systemic wisdom. They become more aware of their role and significance within the whole, and of their ability to facilitate patterns of change and development that will allow their identity to evolve *along with* that of the wider system.

Toward a new view of organizational evolution and change

These ideas have important implications for how we understand the process of organizational evolution. For we see organizations as playing an active role in constructing their environment along with their own identities. All organizations are successful in creating identities of one kind or another, for in many respects the whole process of organizing is the realization of an identity. But some identities are likely to be more robust and enduring than others.

As organizations assert their identities they can initiate major trans-formations in the social ecology to which they belong. They can set the basis for their own destruction. Or they can create the conditions that will allow them to evolve along with the environment. For example, a chemical industry that has a systemic sense of identity could attempt to transform itself to eliminate the threat of toxics to the environment. As it is, however, many organizations eat away their future livelihood, creating the opportunity for new patterns of relations to emerge, but at the expense of their own future existence. Egocentric organizations see survival as hinging on the preservation of their own fixed and narrowly defined identity rather than on the evolution of the more fluid and open identity of the system to which they belong. It is often difficult for them to relinquish identities and strategies that have brought them into being or provided the basis for past success, yet this is what survival and evolution often require. As in nature, many lines of organizational development can prove to be dead ends. While viable and considerably successful for a while, particular organizations or industries may experience a change in fortune as a result of who they are, and as a result of the actions and inactions this sense of identity encourages. In the long run, survival can only be survival *with*, never survival against the environment or context in which one is operating. Less egocentric conceptions of identity facilitate this process by requiring organizations to appreciate that they are always more than themselves. In seeing how one's suppliers, one's market, one's labor force, one's local, national, and worldwide community, and even one's competition are really parts of the same system of organization, it becomes possible to move towards an appreciation of systemic interdependence.

The challenge presented by the theory of autopoiesis is to understand how organizations change and transform themselves along with their environment, and to develop approaches to organization that can foster the kind of open-ended evolution discussed above.

If one wished to summarize the implications of the above argument in a kind of motto it might read, 'Think and act systemically: more self-reflection, less self-centredness.' An organization's self-image is critical in shaping almost every aspect of its functioning and in particular its impact on the context of which it is part, and thus organizations should give considerable attention to discovering and developing an appropriate sense of identity.

Recent interest in corporate culture has begun to grasp this. However, our discussion shows that the kind of self-image that an organization develops is crucial. While an egocentric image may lend an organization a clear and strong identity, and even considerable short-run success, in the long run it is likely to have many unfortunate effects. Indeed, it is important to put the issue more strongly than this. Egocentric corporate cultures that are strong and successful in the short run often achieve their success at the expense of their wider context, and in advancing themselves they are capable of destroying the whole. Our development of corporate culture should always be approached with this important point in mind.

The ideas discussed above highlight the key role of corporate strategy. However, it is in certain respects a more modest role than that advocated in much conventional theory. The corporate strategist is usually seen as someone in command, directing the path of corporate development. But the ideas presented here suggest that successful strategic development can never be unilateral. An individual or organization can influence or shape change, but the process is always dependent on complex patterns of reciprocal connectivity that can never be predicted or controlled. As in nature, significant combinations of chance circumstances can transform social systems in ways that were never dreamed possible. Robotization introduced to reduce costs of manufacturing can reverberate in its effects in completely unpredictable ways; a strategy for achieving one competitive advantage or competence can generate repercussions that eventually transform the system in other ways as well. The theory of autopoiesis suggests that the pattern of organization that unfolds over time does so in an open-ended and evolving way. Some forms disappear and others survive through transformations controlled by the self-referential processes that define the total system. Individuals and organizations have an ability to influence this process by choosing the kind of self-image that is to guide their actions and thus to help shape their future.

Bibliography

Maturana, H. and Varela, F., *Autopoiesis and Cognition,* London: Reidl, 1980
Maturana, H. and Varela, F. *The Tree of Knowledge,* Boston: Shambhala, 1988
Varela, F. *Principles of Biological Autonomy,* Amsterdam: Elsevier, 1979
Prigogine, I. and Stengers, I., *Order out of Chaos,* London: Flamingo, 1984

Source: Morgan, Gareth (1986) Organization as flux and transformation. In G. Morgan, *Images of Organization*, Sage, London, pp. 235–247.

8 Organizational culture as a source of high reliability

Karl E. Weick

As organizations and their technologies have become more complex, they have also become susceptible to accidents that result from unforeseen consequences of misunderstood interventions.[1] Recent examples include Bhopal, the Challenger, and Three Mile Island.

What is interesting about these examples is that they involve issues of reliability, not the conventional organizational issues of efficiency. Organizations in which reliability is a more pressing issue than efficiency often have unique problems in learning and understanding, which, if unresolved, affect their performance adversely.

One unique problem is that a major learning strategy, trial and error, is not available to them because errors cannot be contained. The more likely an error is to propagate, the less willing a system is to use trial and error to understand that source of error firsthand. Because of this limitation, systems potentially know least about those very events that can be most damaging because they can propagate widely and rapidly. This article will explore an unconventional means by which organizations achieve error-free performance despite limited use of trial and error.

The point is that accidents occur because the humans who operate and manage complex systems are themselves not sufficiently complex to sense and anticipate the problems generated by those systems. This is a problem of 'requisite variety,'[2] because the variety that exists in the system to be managed exceeds the variety in the people who must regulate it. When people have less variety than is requisite to cope with the system, they miss important information, their diagnoses are incomplete, and their remedies are short-sighted and can magnify rather than reduce a problem.

If the issue of accidents is posed this way, then there should be fewer accidents when there is a better match between system complexity and human complexity. A better match can occur basically in one of two ways: either the system becomes less complex or the human more complex. This article has more to say about the latter alternative than about the former.

Since learning and reliable performance are difficult when trial and error are precluded, this means that reliable performance depends on the development of substitutes for trial and error. Substitutes for trial and error come in the form of imagination, vicarious experiences, stories, simulations, and other symbolic representations of technology and its effects. The accuracy and reasonableness of these representations, as well as the value people place on constructing them, should have a significant effect on the reliability of performance.

The basic idea is that a system which values stories, storytellers, and storytelling will be more reliable than a system that derogates these substitutes for trial and error. A system that values stories and storytelling is potentially more reliable because people know more about their system, know more of the potential errors that might occur, and they are more confident that they can handle those errors that do occur because they know that other people have already handled similar errors.

Training as a source of accidents

Training is often used to prevent errors, but in fact can create them.

Training for the operation of high reliability systems if often tough and demanding so that the faint of heart and the incompetent are weeded out. People training to be air traffic controllers, for example, are targets of frequent verbal abuse in the belief that this will better prepare them to deal with pilots who are hostile, stubborn, and unresponsive. As one trainer said, 'When you are training to be an air traffic controller, you only walk away from your screen once in anger and you're out.' The trainer assumes that people who walk away from training screens under instructor abuse would walk away from real screens under pilot abuse. The problem with that assumption is that its validity never gets tested.

Furthermore, trainees who are unable to handle trainer hostility may be good controllers because they are more likely to sense emotions conveyed by pilots and be better able to predict impending problems. Thus, a person who walks away from a training screen may be better able to deal with the more frequent problem of emotional communications than with the less frequent problem of pilot abuse. The other side of the argument, however, is that in situations where there is the possibility of catastrophic failure, the marginal gain made by keeping controllers who are more sensitive to emotions is less important than the possibility that the price of this sensitivity is occasional inadequate response.

Training settings themselves often have modest validity, as is shown by the widespread agreement that much that is learned during training for air traffic control has to be unlearned once the controller starts to work traffic. For example, simulators used in training do not accurately simulate change of speed in an airplane. When a plane on the simulator changes speed, the new speed takes effect immediately, whereas in real life the change in speed is gradual. That discrepancy could become consequential because people under pressure revert to their first-learned ways of behaving.[3] Under pressure, controllers who first learned to control planes that changed speed swiftly might systematically underestimate the time it actually takes for planes to execute the speed changes that are ordered. Thus, a controller will assume that developing problems can be resolved more quickly than in fact is the case.

When people are trained for high reliability, the first tendencies they learn are crucial because those may be the ones that reappear when pressure increases. If trainers are more concerned with weeding out than with the adequacy of initial responses, then training could again become the source of a breakdown in reliability which it was designed to prevent.

Even when training works, there are problems. If training is successful, there is usually no pattern to the errors trainees make once they actually operate the system. But if operational errors are randomly distributed because the training is good, then it is not clear how operators can reduce those errors that still occur, since there is no way to predict them.

In each of these examples, the benefits of training are either diluted or reversed due to unanticipated effects of emotional, social, and interpretive processes. Closer attention to these processes may uncover new ways to cope with conditions that set accidents in motion. To illustrate this possibility, following is an examination of three ways in which variations in the social construction of reality can affect the likelihood of error-free operations.

Reliability and requisite variety

As noted, to regulate variety, sensors must be as complex as the system which they intend to regulate. An interesting example of less complicated humans who try to manage more complicated systems is found in the repeated observation that the first action of many senior airline captains, when they enter the cockpit and sit down, is to turn up the volume control on the radio equipment to a level which the junior officers regard as unnecessarily high.[4] Data show that the number of aircraft system errors are inversely related to pilots acknowledging the information they receive from controllers. More errors are associated with fewer acknowledgements.[5] When pilots acknowledge a message, they are supposed to repeat the message to verify that they have received it correctly, but busy pilots often acknowledge a transmission by saying simply 'Roger,' and at other times, they make no acknowledgement at all.

While aircraft errors are often attributed to communication deficiencies, the observation that senior officers turn up the volume on the radio suggest that one source of error may be a hearing deficiency. Older commercial pilots often learned to fly in older, noisier aircraft; and chronic exposure to these conditions may cause current messages to be missed or heard incorrectly. (The hypothesis of a hearing deficiency was not ruled out in the Tenerife disaster on March 27, 1977, and is consistent with all the data assembled about that accident.)

Problems with hearing deficiency are not confined to the airways. Before people are licensed to operate the reactor at Diablo Canyon, they spend up to 5 years as Auxiliary Operators, which means they work on the floor servicing pipes and valves before they ever set foot inside a control room. As is true with most power generation plants, Diablo Canyon is noisy. This creates the same possible history for reactor operators as is created for senior pilots: they develop less sensory variety than is present in the systems of signals, alarms, voices, and strange noises that are symptoms of changes in the system they are trying to control.

Humans gain as well as lose the variety that is requisite for reliability in several ways. Daft and Lengel, for example, propose that the ways in which people receive information provide varying amounts of requisite variety.[6] Information richness is highest when people work face-to-face, and informational richness declines steadily as people move from face-to-face interaction to interaction by telephone, written personal communiques (letters and memos), written formal communiques (bulletins, documents), and numeric formal communiques (computer printouts). Effectiveness is postulated to vary as a function of the degree to which informational richness matches the complexity of organizational phenomena. Rich media provide multiple cues and quick feedback which are essential for complex issues but less essential for routine problems. Too much richness introduces the inefficiencies of overcomplication, too little media richness introduces the inaccuracy of oversimplification.

In the context of the Daft and Lengel argument, it becomes potentially important that communication between Morton Thiokol and NASA about the wisdom of launching Challenger in unusually cold temperatures was made by a conference telephone call,[7] a medium with less variety than a face-to-face conversation. With only voice cues, NASA did not have visual data of facial expressions and body cues which might have given them more vivid information about the intensity of Thiokol's concerns.

Face-to-face communication in high reliability systems is interesting in the context of the large number of engineers typically found in such systems. One way to describe (and admittedly stereotype) engineers is as smart people who don't talk. Since we know that people tend to devalue what they don't do well, if high reliability systems need rich, dense talk to maintain complexity, then they may find it hard to generate this richness if talk is devalued or if people are unable to find substitutes for talk (e.g., electronic mail may be a substitute).

Up to this point, we have been talking largely about the development of requisite variety in individuals, but in high reliability organizations, requisite variety is often gained or lost by larger groups. When technical systems have more variety than a single individual can comprehend, one of the few ways humans can match this variety is by networks and teams of divergent individuals. A team of divergent individuals has more requisite variety than a team of homogeneous individuals. In problems of high reliability, the fact of divergence may be more crucial than the substance of divergence. Whether team members differ in occupational specialities, past experience, gender, conceptual skills, or personality may be less crucial than the fact that they do differ and look for different things when they size up a problem. If people look for different things, when their observations are pooled they collectively see more than any one of them alone would see. However, as team members become more alike, their pooled observations cannot be distinguished from their individual observations, which means collectively they know little more about a problem than they know individually. And since individuals have severe limits on what they can comprehend, a homogeneous team does little to offset these limits. This line of argument, which suggests that collective diversity increases requisite variety which in turn improves reliability, may conflict with the common prescription that redundancy and parallel systems are an important source of reliability. That prescription is certainly true. But a redundant system is also a homogeneous system and homogeneous systems often have less variety than the environments they are trying to manage and less variety than heterogeneous systems that try to manage those same environments.

The issues with collective requisite variety are fascinating as well as complex.

As an example of collective requisite variety, the operating team in the control room at Diablo Canyon has five people who stay together as a team when they change shifts. The lead person on the team is the Shift Foreman whose responsibility is to maintain the 'big picture' and not to get into details. There is a Shift Technical Advisor who has engineering expertise and a Senior Control Room Operator who is the most senior union person in the control room. Under the Senior Operator are the Control Room Operator and the Assistant Control Room Operator, the latter being the person who has the newest operating license and who most recently has worked outside the control room. What is striking about this team is the spread of attention among several issues induced by diverse roles.[8]

The issue of effective delegation of responsibility is crucial in high reliability systems. The most effective means for airline pilots to handle crisis, for example, is for the captain to delegate the task of flying the plane and then make decisions about how to handle the crisis without worrying about the details of flying. Obvious as this solution may seem, a failure to delegate positive responsibility for flying the plane has often meant that a crisis absorbed everyone's attention, no one flew the plane, and it crashed.[9]

The importance of collective requisite variety as a means to enhance reliability is one reason people are increasingly concerned about the reduction of flight crews from three to two people, and are especially concerned when that two-person crew is mixed gender. A female co-pilot adds considerable requisite variety, but if it is hard for a male to trust a woman communicating in an environment that has culturally always been a 'man's world,' then the two-person crew quickly loses variety and errors become more likely.

Collective requisite variety is higher when people both trust others, which enlarges the pool of inputs that are considered before action occurs, and themselves act as trustworthy reporters of their own observations to enlarge that same pool of inputs. Trust, however, is often difficult when diversity increases, because as people become more diverse they also become harder to trust and it is harder to be trusted by them.

Social psychologists have studied these issues in the context of the Asch conformity experiments. Collective requisite variety 'is maximized when each person so behaves as to be in his turn a valid dependable model for the others. Each acts as both model and observer.'[10] Translated to the Asch situation, this means that the best response for the sake of requisite variety is for the naive subject exposed to discrepant reports to say, ' "You fellows are probably right, but I definitely see line B as longer," i.e., both rationally respecting others as a source of information about the world, and so reporting that others can rationally depend on his report in turn. It is failure in this latter respect that instigates our moral indignation at the conformant chameleon character who parasitically depends upon the competence of others but adds no valid information, no clarifying triangulation, to the social pool.'[11]

Requisite variety is enhanced by face-to-face communications for two reasons. First, face-to-face contact makes it easier to assess and build trust and trustworthiness. Second, face-to-face contact makes it easier to get more complete data once trust and trustworthiness have been established. Since people are the medium through which reliability is accomplished, signals relevant to reliability flow through them. When those people are both trusted and dealt with face to face, more information is conveyed, which should produce earlier detection of potential errors.

Building trust in high reliability systems is difficult because so much is at stake. People want to delegate responsibility, but not too soon and not without continued surveillance to see that continued delegation is warranted. A neat resolution of this dilemma is found in the comment of a Navy nuclear propulsion expert who parries a complaint from a second-class petty officer. The complaint goes, 'Sir, I'm not stupid or incompetent. I've had over a year of specialized training and two years of experience, but no one trusts me. Everything I do is checked and double-checked.' The engineer replies, 'It's not a matter of trust. Your ability, training, and experience allow me to trust completely that in an emergency you will do the right thing – or at least a survivable thing. In a non-emergency situation, however, . . . we all make mistakes . . . . That is why your work is checked.'[12]

This particular system builds reliability by institutionalizing an important bit of evolutionary wisdom: 'Ambivalence is the optimal compromise.'[13] The answer to the question 'Don't you trust me?' is both yes and no: 'Yes, I trust you if it's an emergency; no, I don't trust you if it's practice.' Application of this rule presumably builds confidence, competence, and trustworthiness so that trust takes care of itself when the stakes rise dramatically.

Reliability is a dynamic non-event

Reliability is both dynamic and invisible, and this creates problems. Reliability is dynamic in the sense that it is an ongoing condition in which problems are momentarily under control due to compensating changes in components. Reliability is invisible in at least two ways. First, people often don't know how many mistakes they could have made but didn't, which means they have at best only a crude idea of what produces reliability and how reliable they are. For example, if a telephone switching unit normally loses dial tone for 12 minutes out of 72 hours, but could have potentially lost it for 15 minutes, that suggests very different information about its reliability than if it could have lost dial tone for 120 minutes during that same period. Reliability is also invisible in the sense that reliable outcomes are constant, which means there is nothing to pay attention to. Operators see nothing and seeing nothing, presume that nothing is happening. If nothing is happening and if they continue to act the way they have been, nothing will continue to happen. This diagnosis is deceptive and misleading because dynamic inputs create stable outcomes.

A nuclear power plant operator: 'I'll tell you what dull is. Dull is operating the power plant.' Another operator describing his plight: 'I have total concentration, for five hours, on nothing happening.' A senior officer on a nuclear carrier: 'When planes are missing the arresting wire, and can't find the tanker where they are to refuel, and the wind is at 40 knots and the ship is turning, there are no errors.' This latter experience is confirmed in studies of air-traffic controllers. There tend to be more errors in air traffic control under light traffic load than under heavy load because, under high load, controllers visually sweep the entire radar screen whereas in low load they don't. When they fail to sweep the screen, problems can build to more extreme levels at the edges.

When there are non-events, attention not only flags, it is often discouraged. Consider the homespun advice: if it ain't broke, don't fix it. The danger in that advice is that something that isn't broken today, may be tomorrow. Just because a two-engine Boeing 767 airplane hasn't crashed yet while crossing the Atlantic Ocean doesn't mean that a system with two rather than three pilots having two rather than three engines is a reliable system. What it means is that there hasn't been any trial and error on two-engine transatlantic flights, which means people don't yet have any idea of what they know about such flying. That uncertainty can give way to an illusion that since there have been no errors, there must be nothing to learn, which must mean we know what there is to know.

More attentiveness and more reliability might be induced if we were able to shift the homespun advice from its static form to a more dynamic form: if it isn't breaking, don't fix it. Such a modification might alert observers to the dynamic properties of reliable situations, to the fact that small errors can enlarge, to the possibility that complacency is dangerous, to the more active search for incipient errors rather than the more passive wait for developed errors. Both the early explosions of the de Haviland Comet jet airliners as well as the capsizing of the newly designed Alexander L. Keilland oil rig were traced to small cracks that enlarged gradually and then catastrophically under high stress.[14] The Comet aircraft exploded when a crack, which started at the edge of one cabin window after repeated pressurization and depressurization, suddenly enlarged and ripped open the skin of the aircraft.[15] The oil rig collapsed when a 3-inch crack in the frame, which was painted over rather than re-welded, enlarged during a North Sea gale.[16]

Part of the mindset for reliability requires chronic suspicion that small deviations may enlarge, a sensitivity that may be encouraged by a more dynamic view of reliability. People need to see that inertia is a complex state, that forcefield diagrams have multiple forces operating in opposed directions, and that reliability is an ongoing accomplishment. Once situations are made reliable, they will unravel if they are left unattended.

While it is a subtle point, most situations that have constant outcomes – situations such as a marriage, or social drinking, or an alcohol rehabilitation program – collapse when people stop doing whatever produced the stable outcome. And often what produced the stable outcome was continuous change, not continuous repetition. We all smile when we hear the phrase, 'the more things change, the more they stay the same.' The lesson in that truism for problems of reliability is that sameness is a function of change. For a relationship to stay constant, a change of one element must be compensated for by a change in other elements.

When people think they have a problem solved, they often let up, which means they stop making continuous adjustments. When the shuttle flights continued to depart and return successfully, the criterion for a launch – 'Convince me that I should send the Challenger' – was dropped. Under-estimating the dynamic nature of reliability, managers inserted a new criterion – 'Convince me that I shouldn't send the Challenger.'

Reward structures need to be changed so that when a controller says, 'My God, I did it again . . . not a single plane collided in my sector today,' that is not treated as a silly remark. If a controller can produce a dull, normal day, that should earn recognition and praise because the controller had to change to achieve that outcome.

People aren't used to giving praise for reliability. Since they see nothing when reliability is accomplished, they assume that it is easier to achieve reliability than in fact is true. As a result, the public ignores those who are most successful at achieving reliability and gives them few incentives to continue in their uneventful ways.

Reliability as enactment

A peculiar problem of systems is that people in them do not do what the system says they are doing. John Gall illustrates this problem with the example of shipbuilding. 'If you go down to Hampton Roads or any other shipyard and look around for a shipbuilder, you will be disappointed. You will find – in abundance – welders, carpenters, foremen, engineers, and many other specialists, but no shipbuilders. True, the company executives may call themselves shipbuilders, but if you observe them at their work, you will see that it really consists of writing contracts, planning budgets, and other administrative activities. Clearly, they are not in any concrete sense building ships. In cold fact, a *system* is building ships, and the *system* is the shipbuilder.'[17]

If people are not doing what the system says they are doing, then they know less about what is dangerous and how their own activities might create or undermine reliability. Just as nurses commit medical errors when they forget that the chart is not the patient, operators commit reactor errors when they forget that the dial is not the technology.

These misunderstandings, however, are not inevitable. There are systems which achieve high reliability because, for them, the chart is the patient. They provide one model of ways to restructure other systems which have reliability problems.

The system that will illustrate the argument is the air traffic control system. One striking property of air traffic control is that controllers are the technology, they don't watch the technology. Controllers build their own system in the sense that they build the pattern of aircraft they manage by interacting with pilots, using standard phraseology, and allocating space. The instructions that controllers issue are the system and hold the system together. Controllers do not suffer the same isolation from the world they work with as do people in other systems. For example, air traffic controllers on the carrier Carl Vinson make an effort to learn more about the quirks of their carrier pilots. As a result, they are able to separate quick responders from slow responders. This knowledge enables controllers to build a more stable environment when they line up pilots to land on a carrier under conditions where high reliability performance is threatened. Because controllers also use voice cues, they often are able to build a more complete picture of the environment they 'face' because they are able to detect fear in voices and give a fearful pilot more airspace than is given to a confident pilot.

The ability of controllers to enact their environments can be interpreted as the use of slack as a means of increasing reliability. Controllers can add slack to the system by standardizing their customers so that they expect more delays. Overload comes not so much from the number of planes that a controller is working as from the complexity of the interactions with the pilot that occur. A complicated reroute can monopolize so much time that a nearly empty sky can become dangerous when the few remaining planes are totally neglected. If controllers can reduce the number of times they talk to a pilot and the length of time they talk to a pilot, they can add slack to their system.

Controllers can also hold planes on the ground, slow them, accelerate them, turn them sooner, line them up sooner, stack them, or refuse to accept them, to build an environment in which reliability is higher. Airplanes stacked into holding patterns provide a perfect example of an enacted environment. Space which had previously been formless and empty now is structured to have layers 1000 feet apart, a shape, and a pattern in which planes enter at the top and exit from the bottom. An environment has been created by the controller which then constrains what he or she does.

While a stack is a good example of an enacted environment, it also illustrates that when people construct their own environments, they create problems as well as solutions. When a controller creates slack by stacking airplanes, this solution creates at least two problems. First, stacks 'get loose,' which means that planes drift outside the circular pattern as well as up or down from their assigned altitude. Second, a stack, when viewed on a radar screen, creates lots of clutter in a small space so it is harder for the controller to keep track of all the players.

As if discretion and looseness were not enough heresy to introduce into a discussion of high reliability, it is also important to make the point that the air traffic control system works partly because it is an exercise in faith. Unless pilots and controllers each anticipate what the other is going to say, the clipped phraseology they use would never work. Their communiques usually ratify expectations rather than inform, which means that if an unexpected remark is made, then people begin to listen to one another.

For example, foreign national pilots (e.g., China Air) who fly into San Francisco International Airport, and for whom English is a distant second language, are hard to understand. Controllers are unsure what those pilots have heard or what their intentions are. In cluttered skies, this uncertainty increases the probability of error. The system around San Francisco is held together by faith in the sense that the pilots and controllers each anticipate what they will be told to do and each tries to meet these anticipations as much as possible. The elegant solution adopted when the language problem is especially severe is that the foreign pilot is directed to fly straight to the airport and land, and all other aircraft, piloted by people who have better command of English, are routed around the straight-in flight.

The importance of faith in holding a system together in ways that reduce errors has been discussed for some time as 'The Right Stuff.' The right stuff often creates reliability, and the way it does so is important to identify, partly

No system can completely avoid errors. Any discussion of reliability must start with that as axiomatic. Actors frequently underestimate the number of errors that can occur. But if these same actors are dedicated people who work hard, live by their wits, take risks, and improvise, then their intense efforts to make things work can prevent some errors. Because they are able to make do and improvise, they essentially create the error-free situation they expected to find. What they fail to see is that their own committed efforts, driven by faith in the system, knit that system together and create the reliability which up to that point existed only in their imaginations.

While this mechanism is sometimes interpreted as macho bravado,[18] it is important to remember that confidence is just as important in the production of reliability as is doubt. The mutually exclusive character of these two determinants can be seen in the growing doubt among astronauts that they have been flying the safe system they thought they were. Notice that the system itself has not suddenly changed character. What has changed is the faith that may have brought forth a level of commitment that created some of the safety that was anticipated. Obviously, there are limits to faith. The Challenger did explode. But whatever increments to safety the process of faith may have added are no longer there as astronauts see more clearly the shortcuts, problems, and uncertainties which their committed efforts had previously transformed into a temporarily functioning system.

While the activity of air traffic control can be viewed in many ways, I have chosen to emphasize that qualities such as discretion, latitude, looseness, enactment, slack, improvisation, and faith work through human beings to increase reliability. The air traffic control system seem to keep the human more actively in the loop of technology than is true for other systems in which reliability is a bigger problem. It is not immediately clear what the lesson in design is for a nuclear power generation facility, but neither is it self-evident that such a design question is nonsensical. The air traffic control system, because it has not been taken over by technology, accommodates to human limitations rather than automates them away.

But there are threats to the enacted quality of air traffic control and they come from plans to automate more control functions so that the system can be speeded up. Any automated system that controls traffic can go down without warning, which forces controllers to intervene and pick up the pieces.[19] If automated control allows planes to fly closer together (e.g., separated by 10 seconds), the problem is that when the control fails, humans will not be able to pick up the pieces because they are not smart enough or fast enough. A system in which looseness, discretion, enactment, and slack once made reliability possible will have become a system in which reliability is uncontrollable.

Automation, however, is not at fault. Automation makes a 10-second separation possible. But just because such separation is possible, doesn't mean it has to be implemented. That remains a human decision. The heightened capacity isn't dumb, but the decision to heighten capacity may be.

Cultures of reliability

In many of the problems we've looked at, the recurring question is, 'What's going on here?' That's not so much a question of what decision to make as it is a question of what meaning is appropriate so we can then figure out what decision we need to make. It is important to underscore that difference because more attention is paid to organizations as decision makers than to organizations as interpretation systems that generate meaning. That's one reason why the recent interest in organizational culture is important, because it has redistributed the amount of attention that is given to issues of meaning and deciding. That shift in emphasis is summarized in Cohen, March, and Olsen's observation that 'an organization is a set of procedures for argumentation and interpretations as well as for solving problems and making decisions.'[20]

One reason organizational theorists have had trouble trying to think clearly about issues of reliability is that they have made a fundamental error when they think about meaning and decisions. A discussion by Tushman and Romanelli illustrates the problem.[21] In their presentation of an evolutionary model of organization, they argue that managers are concerned both with making decisions and with managing meaning. They accommodate these two rather different activities by arguing that managers make decisions when environments are turbulent and make meanings when environments are stable. I think they've got it backwards, and that's symptomatic of the problems people have when they think about reliability and how to achieve it.

To make decisions, you need a stable environment where prediction is possible, so that the value of different options can be estimated. The rational model works best in a stable environment. When environments become unstable, then people need first to make meaning in order to see what, if anything, there is to decide. When there is swift change, you either label the change to see what you should be paying attention to, or you take action in an effort to slow the change so that you can then make a rational decision.

Stabilization and enactment make meaning possible, which means they necessarily precede decision making.

Making meaning is an issue of culture, which is one reason culture is important in high reliability systems. But culture is important for another reason. Throughout the preceding analysis, I have highlighted the importance of discretion and have played down the necessity for centralization. But the real trick in high reliability systems is somehow to achieve simultaneous centralization and decentralization. People need to benefit from the lessons of previous operators and to profit from whatever trials and errors they have been able to accumulate. And when errors happen, people need a clear chain of command to deal with the situation. These are requirements of centralization. There has to be enough centralization that no one objects when the airline captain delegates authority for flying the plane while he tries to focus his full attention on the crisis. A control room full of people all shouting contradictory diagnoses and directions, as was the case at Three Mile Island, does little to clarify thinking.

But a system in which both centralization and decentralization occur simultaneously is difficult to design. And this is where culture comes in. Either culture or standard operating procedures can impose order and serve as substitutes for centralization. But only culture also adds in latitude for interpretation, improvisation, and unique action.

Before you can decentralize, you first have to centralize so that people are socialized to use similar decision premises and assumptions so that when they operate their own units, those decentralized operations are equivalent and coordinated.[22] This is precisely what culture does. It creates a homogeneous set of assumptions and decision premises which, when they are invoked on a local and decentralized basis, preserve coordination and centralization. Most important, when centralization occurs via decision premises and assumptions, compliance occurs without surveillance. This is in sharp contrast to centralization by rules and regulations or centralization by standardization and hierarchy, both of which require high surveillance. Furthermore, neither rules nor standardization are well equipped to deal with emergencies for which there is no precedent.

The best example of simultaneous centralization and decentralization remains Herbert Kaufmann's marvelous study of the Forest Ranger[23] which shows, as do many of Philip Selznick's analyses,[24] that whenever you have what appears to be successful decentralization, if you look more closely, you will discover that it was always preceded by a period of intense centralization where a set of core values were hammered out and socialized into people before the people were turned loose to go their own 'independent,' 'autonomous' ways.

It is potentially relevant that operators and managers in many nuclear power reactors (those with fewest errors?) have had prior Navy nuclear experiences and that many FAA controllers are former military controllers. In both cases, there are previously shared values concerning reliability which then allows for coordinated, decentralized action. The magnitude of shared values varies among power stations as does the content of the values which are shared. A research question that may predict the likelihood of errors is the extent of sharing and the content that is shared on operating teams.

Culture coordinates action at a distance by several symbolic means, and one that seems of particular importance is the use of stories. Stories remind people of key values on which they are centralized. When people share the same stories, those stories provide general guidelines within which they can customize diagnosis and solutions to local problems.

Stories are important, not just because they coordinate, but also because they register, summarize, and allow reconstruction of scenarios that are too complex for logical linear summaries to preserve. Stories hold the potential to enhance requisite variety among human actors, and that's why high reliability systems may handicap themselves when they become preoccupied with traditional rationality and fail to recognize the power of narrative rationality.[25]

Daft and Wiginton have argued that natural language, metaphors, and patterns that connect have more requisite variety than do notation, argumentative rationality, or models.[26] Models are unable to connect as many facts as stories, they preserve fewer interactions, and they are unable to put these interactions in motion so that outcomes can be anticipated.

Richard Feynman tells a story about the Challenger disaster when he dips O-ring material from the booster into a glass of ice water and discovers that it becomes brittle. Rudolph Pick, a chemical engineer writing to the *New York Times* on January 14, 1986, observed that the only way he could impress people with the danger of overfilling vessels with chemicals was to use what he called the psychological approach. 'After I immersed a piece of chicken meat for several minutes in the toxic and corrosive liquid, only the bone remained. Nobody took any short cuts to established procedures after this demonstration and there were no injuries.' Pick tells this story about hydrofluoric acid and the message remains with people once they scatter to their various assignments. Thus, the story coordinates them by instilling a similar set of decision premises. But the story also works because, from this small incident, people are able to remember and reconstruct a complicated set of chemical interactions that would be forgotten were some other medium, such as a set of regulations, used.

When people do troubleshooting, they try to tell stories that might have, as their punch lines, the particular problem that now confronts them.[27] When stories cannot be invented, troubleshooting and reliability become more difficult. For example, Diablo Canyon has a poor memory for some past decisions and relatively few stories. This creates trouble when people find that a problem can be traced to an odd configuration of pipes. When this happens, they face the disturbing possibility that the odd configuration may solve some larger, more serious problem that no one can remember. Rerouting may solve the immediate problem, but it might also set in motion an unexpected set of interactions that were once anticipated and blocked, though no one now can recall them. Stories about infrastructure are not trivial.

What all of this leads to is an unusual reconstruction of the events of the night of January 27, 1986, when NASA was arguing with Morton Thiokol about whether freezing weather would disable the booster rocket. That conversation apparently took the traditional course of people arguing in linear, sequential fashion about the pros and cons of a launch. If, somewhere in those discussions, someone had said, 'That reminds me of a story,'[28] a different rationality might have been applied and a different set of implications might have been drawn. Those, in turn, might well have led to a different outcome. There are precedents in history. The solution of the Cuban Missile crisis by a surgical airstrike was dropped when Robert Kennedy recalled the story of Pearl Harbor, and portrayed a U.S. attack on Cuba as Pearl Harbor in reverse.[29]

We have thought about reliability in conventional ways using ideas of structure, training, and redundancy, and seem to be up against some limits in where those ideas can take us. Re-examination of the issue of reliability using a less traditional set of categories associated with an interpretive point of view seems to suggest some new places to attack the problem.

References

1 C. Perrow, *Normal Accidents* (New York, NY: Basic Books, 1984).

2 See, for example, W. Buckley, 'Society as a Complex Adaptive System,' in W. Buckley, ed., *Modern Systems Research for the Behavioral Scientist* (Chicago, IL: Aldine, 1968), pp. 490–513.

3 K. E. Weick, 'A Stress Analysis of Future Battlefields,' in J. G. Hunt and J. D. Blair, eds., *Leadership on the Future Battlefield* (Washington, D.C.: Pergamon, 1985), pp. 32–46.

4 R. Hurst, 'Portents and Challenges,' in R. Hurst and L. R. Hurst, eds., *Pilot Error: The Human Factors*, 2nd Ed. (New York, NY: Aronson, 1982), p. 175.

5 Ibid., p. 176.

6 R. L. Daft and R. H. Lengel, 'Information Richness: A New Approach to Manager Information Processing and Organization Design,' in B. Staw and L. L. Cummings, eds., *Research in Organizational Behavior: Vol. 6* (Greenwich, CT: JAI Press, 1984), pp. 191–233.

7 R. J. Smith, 'Shuttle Inquiry Focuses on Weather, Rubber Seals, and Unheeded Advice,' *Science*, 231 (1986): 909.

8 N. W. Biggart and G. G. Hamilton, 'The Power of Obedience,' *Administrative Science Quarterly*, 28 (1984): 540–549.

9 See, for example, E. L. Wiener, 'Mid-Air Collisions: The Accidents, the Systems, and the Realpolitik,' in R. Hurst and L. R. Hurst, eds., *Pilot Error: The Human Factors*, 2nd Ed. (New York, NY: Aronson, 1982), pp. 101–117.

10 D. T. Campbell, 'Conformity in Psychology's Theories of Acquired Behavioral Dispositions,' in I. A. Berg and B. M. Bass, eds., *Conformity and Deviation* (New York, NY: Harper, 1961), p. 123.

11 Ibid.

12 J. D. Jones, 'Nobody Asked Me, But . . .,' *United States Naval Institute Proceedings*, November 1977, p. 87.

13 D. T. Campbell, 'Ethnocentric and Other Altruistic Motives,' in D. Levine, ed., *Nebraska Symposium on Motivation, 1965* (Lincoln, NE: University of Nebraska), pp. 2283–2311.

14 H. Petroski, *To Engineer Is Human* (New York, NY: St. Martin's Press, 1985).

15 Ibid., p. 178.

16 Ibid., p. 174.

17 J. Gall, *Systematics: How Systems Work and Especially How They Fail* (New York, NY: New York Times Book Co., 1977), pp. 32–33.

18 M. Allnutt, 'Human Factors: Basic Principles,' In R. Hurst and L. R. Hurst, eds., *Pilot Errors: The Human Factors*, 2nd Ed. (New York, NY: Aronson, 1982), pp. 14–15.

19 J. M. Finkelman and C. Kirschner, 'An Information-Processing Interpretation of Air Traffic Control Stress,' *Human Factors*, 22 (1980): 561.

20 M. D. Cohen, J. G. March, and J. P. Olsen, 'People, Problems, Solutions, and the Ambiguity of Relevance,' in J. G. March and J. P. Olsen, eds., *Ambiguity and Choice in Organizations* (Bergen, Norway: Universitetsforlaget, 1976), p. 25.

21 M. L. Tushman and E. Romanelli, 'Organizational Evolution: A Metamorphosis Model of Convergence and Reorientation,' in L. L. Cummings and B. M. Staw, eds., *Research in Organizational Behavior:* Vol. 7 (Greenwich, CT: JAI Press, 1985), pp. 196, 209–212.

22 C. Perrow, 'The Bureaucratic Paradox: The Efficient Organization Centralizes in Order to Decentralize.' *Organizational Dynamics*, 5/4 (1977): 3–14.

23 H. Kaufman, *The Forest Ranger* (Baltimore, MD: Johns Hopkins, 1967).

24 P. Selznick, *Leadership in Administration* (New York, NY: Harper & Row, 1957).

25 K. E. Weick and L. B. Browning, 'Argument and Narration in Organizational Communication,' *Journal of Management*, 12 (1986): 243–259.

26 R. L. Daft and J. Wiginton, 'Language and Organizations,' *Academy of Management Review*, 4 (1979): 179–191.

27 N. M. Morris and W. B. Rouse, 'Review and Evaluation of Empirical Research in Troubleshooting,' *Human Factors*, 27 (1985): 503–530.

28 M. H. Brown, 'That Reminds Me of a Story: Speech Action in Organizational Socialization,' *Western Journal of Speech Communication*, 49 (1985): 27–42.

29 P. A. Anderson, 'Decision Making by Objection and the Cuban Missile Crisis,' *Administrative Science Quarterly*, 28 (1983): 211–212.

Source: Weich, Karl E. (1987) Organizational culture as a source of high reliability. *California Management Review*, **XXIX**, 112–127.

Part Five

Order Without Design: Self-organization

The criterion of understanding is clearly not in the order's actual words, nor in the mind of the person giving the order, but solely in the understanding of the situation and in the responsible behavior of the person who obeys. Even when an order is written down so one can be sure it will be correctly understood and executed, no one assumes that it makes everything explicit. The comic situation in which orders are carried out literally but not according to their meaning is well known. Thus there is no doubt that the recipient of an order must perform a definite creative act in understanding its meaning.

Hans-Georg Gadamer (Truth and Method)

9 Organizational learning and communities-of-practice: toward a unified view of working, learning and innovation

John Seely Brown and Paul Duguid

Introduction

Working, learning, and innovating are closely related forms of human activity that are conventionally thought to conflict with each other. Work practice is generally viewed as conservative and resistant to change; learning is generally viewed as distinct from working and problematic in the face of change; and innovation is generally viewed as the disruptive but necessary imposition of change on the other two. To see that working, learning, and innovating are interrelated and compatible and thus potentially complementary, not conflicting forces requires a distinct conceptual shift. By bringing together recent research into working, learning, and innovating, we attempt to indicate the nature and explore the significance of such a shift.

The source of the oppositions perceived between working, learning, and innovating lies primarily in the gulf between precepts and practice. Formal descriptions of work (e.g., 'office procedures') and of learning (e.g., 'subject matter') are abstracted from actual practice. They inevitably and intentionally omit the details. In a society that attaches particular value to 'abstract knowledge,' the details of practice have come to be seen as nonessential, unimportant, and easily developed once the relevant abstractions have been grasped. Thus education, training, and technology design generally focus on abstract representations to the detriment, if not exclusion of actual practice. We, by contrast, suggest that practice is central to understanding work. Abstractions *detached from practice* distort or obscure intricacies of that practice. Without a clear understanding of those intricacies and the role they play, the practice itself cannot be well understood, engendered (through training), or enhanced (through innovation).

We begin by looking at the variance between a major organization's formal descriptions of work both in its training programs and manuals and the actual work practices performed by its members. Orr's (1990a, 1990b, 1987a, 1987b) detailed ethnographic studies of service technicians illustrate how an organization's view of work can overlook and even oppose what and who it takes to get a job done. Based on Orr's specific insights, we make the more general claim that reliance on espoused practice (which we refer to as *canonical practice*) can blind an organization's core to the actual, and usually valuable practices of its members (including *noncanonical practices*, such as 'work arounds'). It is the actual practices, however, that determine the success or failure of organizations.

Next, we turn to learning and, in particular, to Lave and Wenger's (1990) practice-based theory of learning as 'legitimate peripheral participation' in 'communities-of-practice.' Much conventional learning theory, including that implicit in most training courses, tends to endorse the valuation of abstract knowledge over actual practice and as a result to separate learning from working and, more significantly, learners from workers. Together Lave and Wenger's analysis and Orr's empirical investigation indicate that this knowledge-practice separation is unsound, both in theory and in practice. We argue that the composite concept of 'learning-in-working' best represents the fluid evolution of learning through practice.

From this practice-based standpoint, we view learning as the bridge between working and innovating. We use Daft and Weick's (1984) interpretive account of 'enacting' organizations to place innovation in the context of changes in a community's 'way of seeing' or interpretive view. Both Orr's and Lave and Wenger's research emphasize that to understand working and learning, it is necessary to focus on the formation and change of the communities in which work takes place. Taking all three theories together, we argue that, through their constant adapting to changing membership and changing circumstances, evolving communities-of-practice are significant sites of innovating.

1 Working

(a) Canonical practice

Orr's (1990a, 1990b, 1987a, 1987b) ethnography of service technicians (reps) in training and at work in a large corporation paints a clear picture of the divergence between espoused practice and actual practice, of the ways this divergence develops, and of the trouble it can cause. His work provides a 'thick' (see Geertz 1973), detailed description of the way work actually progresses. Orr contrasts his findings with the way the same work is thinly described in the corporation's manuals, training courses, and job descriptions.[1]

The importance of such an approach to work in progress is emphasized by Bourdieu (1973), who distinguishes the *modus operandi* from the *opus operatum* – that is, the way a task, as it unfolds over time, looks to someone at work on it, while many of the options and dilemmas remain unresolved, as opposed to the way it looks with hindsight as a finished task. (Ryle (1954) makes a similar point.) The *opus operatum*, the finished view, tends to see the action in terms of the task alone and cannot see the way in which the process of doing the task is actually structured by the constantly changing conditions of work and the world. Bourdieu makes a useful analogy with reference to a journey as actually carried out on the ground and as seen on a map ('an abstract space, devoid of any landmarks or any privileged centre' (p. 2)). The latter, like the *opus operatum*, inevitably smooths over the myriad decisions made with regard to changing conditions: road works, diversions, Memorial Day parades, earthquakes, personal fatigue, conflicting opinions, wrong-headed instructions, relations of authority, inaccuracies on the map, and the like. The map, though potentially useful, by *itself* provides little insight into how *ad hoc* decisions presented by changing conditions can be resolved (and, of course, each resolved decision changes the conditions once more). As a journey becomes more complex, the map increasingly conceals what is actually needed to make the journey. Thick description, by contrast, ascends from the abstraction to the concrete circumstances of actual practice, reconnecting the map and the mapped.

Orr's study shows how an organization's maps can dramatically distort its view of the routes its members take. This 'misrecognition,' as Bourdieu calls it, can be traced to many places, including pedagogic theory and practice. Often it has its more immediate cause in the strategy to downskill positions. Many organizations are willing to assume that complex tasks can be successfully mapped onto a set of simple, Tayloristic, canonical steps that can be followed without need of significant understanding or insight (and thus without need of significant investment in training or skilled technicians). But as Bourdieu, Suchman (1987a), and Orr show, actual practice inevitably involves tricky interpolations between abstract accounts and situated demands. Orr's reps' skills, for instance, are most evident in the improvised strategies they deploy to cope with the clash between prescriptive documentation and the sophisticated, yet unpredictable machines they work with. Nonetheless, in the corporation's eyes practices that deviate from the canonical are, by definition, deviant practices. Through a reliance on

---

[1] For a historical overview of anthropology of the workplace, see Burawoy (1979).

canonical descriptions (to the extent of overlooking even their own non-canonical improvisations), managers develop a conceptual outlook that cannot comprehend the importance of noncanonical practices. People are typically viewed as performing their jobs according to formal job descriptions, despite the fact that daily evidence points to the contrary (Suchman 1987b). They are held accountable to the map, not to road conditions.[2]

In Orr's case, the canonical map comes in the form of 'directive' documentation aimed at 'single point failures' of machines. Indeed, the documentation is less like a map than a single predetermined route with no alternatives: it provides a decision tree for diagnosis and repair that assumes both predictable machines and an unproblematic process of making diagnoses and repairs through blindly following diagnostic instructions. Both assumptions are mistaken. Abstractions of repair work fall short of the complexity of the actual practices from which they were abstracted. The account of actual practice we describe below is anything but the blind following of instructions.

The inadequacies of this corporation's directive approach actually make a rep's work more difficult to accomplish and thus perversely demands more, not fewer, improvisational skills. An ostensible downskilling and actual upskilling therefore proceed simultaneously. Although the documentation becomes more prescriptive and ostensibly more simple, in actuality the task becomes more improvisational and more complex. The reps develop sophisticated noncanonical practices to bridge the gulf between their corporation's canonical approach and successful work practices, laden with the dilemmas, inconsistencies, and unpredictability of everyday life. The directive documentation does not 'deprive the workers of the skills they have;' rather, 'it merely reduces the amount of information given them' (Orr 1990a, 26). The burden of making up the difference between what is provided and what is needed then rests with the reps, who in bridging the gap actually protect the organization from its own shortsightedness. If the reps adhered to the canonical approach, their corporation's services would be in chaos.

Because this corporation's training programs follow a similar downskilling approach, the reps regard them as generally unhelpful. As a result, a wedge is driven between the corporation and its reps: the corporation assumes the reps are untrainable, uncooperative, and unskilled; whereas the reps view the overly simplistic training programs as a reflection of the corporation's low estimation of their worth and skills. In fact, their valuation is a testament to the depth of the rep's insight. They recognize the superficiality of the training because they are conscious of the full complexity of the technology and what it takes to keep

---

[2] Not all the blame should be laid on the managers' desk. As several anthropologists, including Suchman (1987a) and Bourdieu (1977) point out, 'informants' often describe their jobs in canonical terms though they carry them out in noncanonical ways. Lave (1988) argues that informants, like most people in our society, tend to privilege abstract knowledge. Thus they describe their actions in its terms.

it running. The corporation, on the other hand, blinkered by its implicit faith in formal training and canonical practice and its misinterpretation of the rep's behavior, is unable to appreciate either aspect of their insight.

In essence, Orr shows that in order to do their job the reps must – and do – learn to make better sense of the machines they work with than their employer either expects or allows. Thus they develop their understanding of the machine not in the training programs, but in the very conditions from which the programs separate them – the authentic activity of their daily work. For the reps (and for the corporation, though it is unaware of it), learning-in-working is an occupational necessity.

(b) Noncanonical practice

Orr's analyses of actual practice provide various examples of how the reps diverge from canonical descriptions. For example, on one service call (Orr 1990b, 1987b) a rep confronted a machine that produced copious raw information in the form of error codes and obligingly crashed when tested. But the error codes and the nature of the crashes did not tally. Such a case immediately fell outside the directive training and documentation provided by the organization, which tie errors to error codes. Unfortunately, the problem also fell outside the rep's accumulated, improvised experience. He summoned his technical specialist, whose job combines 'trouble-shooting consultant, supervisor, and occasional instructor.' The specialist was equally baffled. Yet, though the canonical approach to repair was exhausted, with their combined range of noncanonical practices, the rep and technical specialist still had options to pursue.

One option – indeed the only option left by canonical practice now that its strategies for repair had been quickly exhausted – was to abandon repair altogether and to replace the malfunctioning machine. But both the rep and the specialist realized that the resulting loss of face for the company, loss of the customer's faith in the reps, loss of their own credit within their organization, and loss of money to the corporation made this their last resort. Loss of face or faith has considerable ramifications beyond mere embarrassment. A rep's ability to enlist the future support of customers and colleagues is jeopardized. There is evidently strong social pressure from a variety of sources to solve problems without exchanging machines. The reps' work is not simply about maintaining machines; it is also and equally importantly, about maintaining social relations: 'A large part of service work might better be described as repair and maintenance of the social setting' (Orr 1990b, 169). The training and documentation, of course, are about maintaining machines.

Solving the problem *in situ* required constructing a coherent account of the malfunction out of the incoherence of the data and documentation. To do this, the rep and the specialist embarked on a long story-telling procedure. The machine, with its erratic behavior, mixed with information from the user and memories from the technicians, provided essential ingredients that the two aimed to account for in a composite story. The process of forming a story was, centrally, one of diagnosis. The process, it should be noted, *begins* as well as ends in a communal understanding of the machine that is wholly unavailable from the canonical documents.

While they explored the machine or waited for it to crash, the rep and specialist (with contributions from the ethnographer) recalled and discussed other occasions on which they had encountered some of the present symptoms. Each story presented an exchangeable account that could be examined and reflected upon to provoke old memories and new insights. Yet more tests and more stories were thereby generated.

> The key element of diagnosis is the situated production of understanding through narration, in that the integration of the various facts of the situation is accomplished through a verbal consideration of those facts with a primary criterion of coherence. The process is situated, in Suchman's terms, in that both the damaged machine and the social context of the user site are essential resources for both the definition of the problem and its resolution . . . . They are faced with a failing machine displaying diagnostic information which has previously proved worthless and in which no one has any particular confidence this time. They do not know where they are going to find the information they need to understand and solve this problem. In their search for inspiration, they tell stories (Orr 1990b, 178–179).

The story-telling process continued throughout the morning, over lunch, and back in front of the machine, throughout the afternoon, forming a long but purposeful progression from incoherence to coherence: 'The final trouble-shooting session was a five hour effort . . . . This session yielded a dozen anecdotes told during the trouble shooting, taking a variety of forms and serving a variety of purposes' (Orr 1990b, 10).

Ultimately, these stories generated sufficient interplay among memories, tests, the machine's responses, and the ensuing insights to lead to diagnosis and repair. The final diagnosis developed from what Orr calls an 'antiphonal recitation' in which the two told different versions of the same story: 'They are talking about personal encounters with the same problem, but the two versions are significantly different' (Orr 1987b, 177). Through story-telling, these separate experiences converged, leading to a shared diagnosis of certain previously encountered but unresolved symptoms. The two (and the ethnographer) had constructed a communal interpretation of hitherto uninterpretable data and individual experience. Rep and specialist were now in a position to modify previous stories and build a more insightful one. They both increased their own understanding and added to their community's collective knowledge. Such stories are passed around, becoming part of the repertoire available to all reps. Orr reports hearing a concise, assimilated version of this particular false error code passed among reps over a game of cribbage in the lunch room three months later (Orr 1990b, 181ff.). A story, once in the possession of the community, can then be used – and further modified – in similar diagnostic sessions.

(c) Central features of work practice

In this section, we analyze Orr's thick description of the rep's practice through the overlapping categories, 'narration,' 'collaboration,' and 'social construction' – categories that get to the heart of what the reps do and yet which, significantly, have no place in the organization's abstracted, canonical accounts of their work.

Narration. The first aspect of the reps' practice worth highlighting is the extensive narration used. This way of working is quite distinct from following the branches of decision tree. Stories and their telling can reflect the complex social web within which work takes place and the relationship of the narrative, narrator, and audience to the specific events of practice. The stories have a flexible generality that makes them both adaptable and particular. They function, rather like the common law, as a usefully underconstrained means to interpret each new situation in the light of accumulated wisdom and constantly changing circumstances.

The practice of creating and exchanging of stories has two important aspects. First of all, telling stories helps to diagnose the state of a troublesome machine. Reps begin by extracting a history from the users of the machine, the user's story, and with this and the machine as their starting point, they construct their own account. If they cannot tell an adequate story on their own, then they seek help – either by summoning a specialist, as in the case above, or by discussing the problem with colleagues over coffee or lunch. If necessary, they work together at the machine, articulating hunches, insights, misconceptions, and the like, to dissect and augment their developing understanding. Story telling allows them to keep track of the sequences of behavior and of their theories, and thereby to work towards a coherent account of the current state of the machine. The reps try to impose coherence on an apparently random sequence of events in order that they can decide what to do next. Unlike the documentation, which tells reps *what* to do but not *why*, the reps' stories help them develop causal accounts of machines, which are essential when documentation breaks down. (As we have suggested, documentation, like machines, will always break down, however well it is designed.) What the reps do in their story telling is develop a causal map out of their experience to replace the impoverished directive route that they have been furnished by the corporation. In the absence of such support, the reps Orr studied cater to their own needs as well as they can. Their narratives yield a story of the machine fundamentally different from the prescriptive account provided by the documentation, a story that is built in response to the particulars of breakdown.

Despite the assumptions behind the downskilling process, to do their job in any significant sense, reps need these complex causal stories and they produce and circulate them as part of their regular noncanonical work practice. An important part of the reps' skill, though not recognized by the corporation, comprises the ability to create, to trade, and to understand highly elliptical, highly referential, and to the initiated, highly informative war stories. Zuboff (1988) in her analysis of the skills people develop working on complex systems describes similar cases of story telling and argues that it is a necessary practice for dealing with 'smart' but unpredictable machines. The irony, as Orr points out, is that for purposes of diagnosis the reps have no smart machines, just inadequate documentation and 'their own very traditional skills.'

It is worth stressing at this point that we are not arguing that communities simply can and thus should work without assistance from trainers and the corporation in general. Indeed, we suggest in our conclusion that situations inevitably occur when group improvisation simply cannot bridge the gap between what the corporation supplies and what a particular community actually needs. What we are claiming is that corporations must provide support that corresponds to the real needs of the community rather than just to the abstract expectations of the corporation. And what those needs are can only be understood by understanding the details and sophistications of actual practice. In Orr's account, what the reps needed was the means to understand the machine causally and to relate this causal map to the inevitable intricacies of practice. To discern such needs, however, will require that corporations develop a less formal and more practice-based approach to communities and their work.

The second characteristic of story telling is that the stories also act as repositories of accumulated wisdom. In particular, community narratives protect the reps' ability to work from the ravages of modern idealizations of work and related downskilling practices. In Orr's example, the canonical decision trees, privileging the decontextualized over the situated, effectively sweep away the clutter of practice. But it is in the face of just this clutter that the reps' skills are needed. Improvisational skills that allow the reps to circumvent the inadequacies of both the machines and the documentation are not only developed but also preserved in community story telling.

Jordan's (1989) work similarly draws attention to the central, dual role of informal stories. She studied the clash between midwifery as it is prescribed by officials from Mexico City and as it is practiced in rural Yucatan. The officials ignore important details and realities of practice. For instance, the officials instruct the midwives in practices that demand sterile instruments though the midwives work in villages that lack adequate means for sterilization. The midwives' noncanonical practices, however, circumvent the possibility of surgical operations being carried out with unsterile instruments. These effective practices survive, despite the government's worryingly decontextualized attempts to replace them with canonical practices, through story telling. Jordan notes that the two aspects of story telling, diagnosis and preservation, are inseparable. Orr also suggests that 'The use of story-telling both to preserve knowledge and to consider it in subsequent diagnoses coincides with the narrative character of diagnosis' (Orr 1990b, 178). We have pulled them apart for the purpose of analysis only.

Collaboration. Based as it is on shared narratives, a second important aspect of the reps' work is that it is obviously communal and thereby *collaborative*. In Orr's example, the rep and specialist went through a collective, not individual process. Not only is the learning in this case inseparable from working, but also individual learning is inseparable from collective learning. The insight accumulated is not a private substance, but socially constructed and distributed. Thus, faced with a difficult problem reps like to work together and to discuss problems in groups. In the case of this particular problem, the individual rep tried what he knew, failed, and there met his limits. With the specialist he was able to trade stories, develop insights, and construct new options. Each had a story about the condition of the machine, but it was in telling it antiphonally that the significance emerged.

While it might seem trivial, it is important to emphasize the collaborative work within the reps' community, for in the corporation's eyes their work is viewed individually. Their documentation and training implicitly maintain that the work is individual and the central relationship of the rep is that between an individual and the corporation:

> The activities defined by management are those which one worker will do, and work as the relationship of employment is discussed in terms of a single worker's relationship to the corporation. I suspect the incidence of workers alone in relations of employment is quite low, and the existence of coworkers must contribute to those activities done in the name of work . . . . The fact that work is commonly done by a group of workers together is only sometimes acknowledged in the literature, and the usual presence of such a community has not entered into the definition of work (Orr 1990a, 15).

In fact, as Orr's studies show, not only do reps work with specialists, as in the example given here, but throughout the day they meet for coffee or for meals and trade stories back and forth.

Social Construction. A third important aspect of Orr's account of practice, and one which is interfused with the previous two and separated here only to help in clarification, involves *social construction*. This has two parts. First and most evident in Orr's example, the reps constructed a shared understanding out of bountiful conflicting and confusing data. This constructed understanding reflects the reps' view of the world. They developed a *rep's* model of the machine, not a trainer's, which had already proved unsatisfactory, nor even an engineer's, which was not available to them (and might well have been unhelpful, though Orr interestingly points out that reps cultivate connections throughout the corporation to help them circumvent the barriers to understanding built by their documentation and training). The reps' view, evident in their stories, interweaves generalities about 'this model' with particularities about 'this site' and 'this machine.'

Such an approach is highly situated and highly improvisational. Reps respond to whatever the situation itself – both social and physical – throws at them, a process very similar to Levi-Strauss's (1966) concept of *bricolage*: the ability to 'make do with"whatever is to hand"' (p. 17). What reps need for *bricolage* are not the partial, rigid models of the sort directive documentation provides, but help to build, *ad hoc* and collaboratively, robust models that do justice to particular difficulties in which they find themselves. Hutchins, in his analysis of navigation teams in the US Navy (in press, 1991), similarly notes the way in which understanding is constructed within and distributed throughout teams.

The second feature of social construction, as important but less evident than the first, is that in telling these stories an individual rep contributes to the construction and development of his or her own identity as a rep and reciprocally to the construction and development of the community of reps in which he or she works. Individually, in telling stories the rep is becoming a member. Orr notes, 'this construction of their identity as technicians occurs both in doing the work and in their stories, and their stories of themselves fixing machines show their world in what they consider the appropriate perspective' (Orr 1990b, 187). Simultaneously and interdependently, the reps are contributing to the construction and evolution of the community that they are joining – what we might call a 'community of interpretation,' for it is through the continual development of these communities that the shared means for interpreting complex activity get formed, transformed, and transmitted.

The significance of both these points should become apparent in the following sections, first, as we turn to a theory of learning (Lave and Wenger's) that, like Orr's analysis of work, takes formation of identity and community membership as central units of analysis; and second as we argue that innovation can be seen as at base a function of changes in community values and views.

2 Learning

The theories of learning implicated in the documentation and training view learning from the abstract stance of pedagogy. Training is thought of as the *transmission* of explicit, abstract knowledge from the head of someone who knows to the head of someone who does not in surroundings that specifically exclude the complexities of practice and the communities of practitioners. The setting for learning is simply assumed not to matter.

Concepts of knowledge or information transfer, however, have been under increasing attack in recent years from a variety of sources (e.g., Reddy 1979). In particular, learning theorists (e.g. Lave 1988; Lave and Wenger 1990) have rejected transfer models, which isolate knowledge from practice, and developed a view of learning as social construction, putting knowledge back into the contexts in which it has meaning (see also Brown, Collins, and Duguid 1989; Brown and Duguid, in press; Pea 1990). From this perspective, learners can in one way or another be seen to construct their understanding out of a wide range of materials that include ambient social and physical circumstances and the histories and social relations of the people involved. Like a magpie with a nest, learning is built out of the materials to hand and in relation to the structuring resources of local conditions. (For the importance of including the structuring resources in any account of learning, see Lave 1988.) What is learned is profoundly connected to the conditions in which it is learned.

Lave and Wenger (1990), with their concept of *legitimate peripheral participation* (LPP), provide one of the most versatile accounts of this constructive view of learning. LPP, it must quickly be asserted, is *not* a method of education. It is an analytical category or tool for understanding learning across different methods, different historical periods, and different social and physical environments. It attempts to account for learning, not teaching or instruction. Thus this approach escapes problems that arise through examinations of learning from pedagogy's viewpoint. It makes the conditions of learning, rather than just abstract subject matter, central to understanding what is learned.

Learning, from the viewpoint of LPP, essentially involves becoming an 'insider.' Learners do not receive or even construct abstract, 'objective,' individual knowledge; rather, they learn to function in a community – be it a community of nuclear physicists, cabinet makers, high school classmates, street-corner society, or, as in the case under study, service technicians. They acquire that particular community's subjective viewpoint and learn to speak its language. In short, they are enculturated (Brown, Collins, and Duguid 1989). Learners are acquiring not explicit, formal 'expert knowledge,' but the embodied ability to behave as community members. For example, learners learn to tell and appreciate community-appropriate stories, discovering in doing so, all the narrative-based resources we outlined above. As Jordan (1989) argues in her analysis of midwifery, 'To acquire a store of appropriate stories and, even more importantly, to know what are appropriate occasions for telling them, is then part of what it means to become a midwife' (p. 935).

Workplace learning is best understood, then, in terms of the communities being formed or joined and personal identities being changed. The central issue in learning is *becoming* a practitioner not learning *about* practice. This approach draws attention away from abstract knowledge and cranial processes and situates it in the practices and communities in which knowledge takes on significance. Learning about new devices such as the machines Orr's technicians worked with, is best understood (and best achieved) in the context of the community in which the devices are used and that community's particular interpretive conventions. Lave and Wenger argue that learning, understanding, and interpretation involve a great deal that is not explicit or explicable, developed and framed in a crucially *communal* context.

Orr's study reveals this sort of learning going on in the process of and inseparable from work. The rep was not just an observer of the technical specialist. He was also an important participant in this process of diagnosis and story telling, whose participation could legitimately grow in from the periphery as a function of his developing understanding not of some extrinsically structured training. His legitimacy here is an important function of the social relations between the different levels of service technician, which are surprisingly egalitarian, perhaps as a result of the inherent incoherence of the problems this sort of technology presents: a specialist cannot hope to exert hierarchical control over knowledge that he or she must first construct cooperatively. 'Occupational communities . . . have little hierarchy; the only real status is that of member' (Orr 1990a, 33).

(a) Groups and communities

Having characterized both working and learning in terms of communities, it is worth pausing to establish relations between our own account and recent work on groups in the workplace. Much important work has been done in this area (see, for example, the collections by Hackman (1990) and Goodman and Associates (1988)) and many of the findings support our own view of work activity. There is, however, a significant distinction between our views and this work. Group theory in general focuses on groups as canonical, bounded entities that lie within an organization and that are organized or at least sanctioned by that organization and its view of tasks. (See Hackman 1990, pp. 4–5.). The communities that we discern are, by contrast, often noncanonical and not recognized by the organization. They are more fluid and inter-penetrative than bounded, often crossing the restrictive boundaries of the organization to incorporate people from outside. (Orr's reps can in an important sense be said to work in a community that includes both suppliers and customers.) Indeed, the canonical organization becomes a questionable unit of analysis from this perspective. And significantly, communities are emergent. That is to say their shape and membership emerges in the process of activity, as opposed to being created to carry out a task. (Note, by contrast, how much of the literature refers to the *design* or *creation* of new groups (e.g. Goodman and Associates 1988). From our viewpoint, the central questions more involve the *detection* and *support* of emergent or existing communities.)

If this distinction is correct then it has two particularly important corollaries. First, work practice and learning need to be understood not in terms of the groups that are ordained (e.g. 'task forces' or 'trainees'), but in terms of the communities that emerge. The latter are likely to be noncanonical (though not necessarily so) while the former are likely to be canonical. Looking only at canonical groups, whose configuration often conceals extremely influential interstitial communities, will not provide a clear picture of how work or learning is actually organized and accomplished. It will only reflect the dominant assumptions of the organizational core.

Second, attempts to introduce 'teams' and 'work groups' into the workplace to enhance learning or work practice are often based on an assumption that without impetus from above, an organization's members configure themselves as individuals. In fact, as we suggest, people work and learn collaboratively and vital interstitial communities are continually being formed and reformed. The reorganization of the workplace into canonical groups can wittingly or unwittingly disrupt these highly functional noncanonical – and therefore often invisible – communities. Orr argues:

> The process of working and learning together creates a work situation which the workers value, and they resist having it disrupted by their employers through events such as a reorganization of the work. This resistance can surprise employers who think of labor as a commodity to arrange to suit their ends. The problem for the workers is that this community which they have created was not part of the series of discrete employment agreements by which the employer populated the work place, nor is the role of the community in doing the work acknowledged. *The work can only continue free of disruption if the employer can be persuaded to see the community as necessary to accomplishing work* (Orr 1990, 48, emphasis added).

(b) Fostering learning

Given a community-based analysis of learning so congruent with Orr's analysis of working, the question arises, how is it possible to foster learning-in-working? The answer is inevitably complex, not least because all the intricacies of context, which the pedagogic approach has always assumed could be stripped away, now have to be taken back into consideration. On the other hand, the ability of people to learn *in situ*, suggests that as a fundamental principle for supporting learning, attempts to strip away context should be examined with caution. If learners need access to practitioners at work, it is essential to question didactic approaches, with their tendency to separate learners from the target community and the authentic work practices. Learning is fostered by fostering access to and membership of the target community-of-practice, not by explicating abstractions of individual practice. Thus central to the process are the recognition and legitimation of community practices.

Reliance on formal descriptions of work, explicit syllabuses for learning about it, and canonical groups to carry it out immediately set organizations at a disadvantage. This approach, as we have noted, can simply blind management to the practices and communities that actually make things happen. In particular, it can lead to the isolation of learners, who will then be unable to acquire the implicit practices required for work. Marshall (in Lave and Wenger 1990) describes a case of apprenticeship for butchers in which learning was extremely restricted because, among other things, 'apprentices . . . could not watch journeymen cut and saw meat' (p. 19). Formal training in cutting and sawing is quite different from the understanding of practice gleaned through informal observation that copresence makes possible and absence obviously excludes. These trainees were simply denied the chance to become legitimate peripheral participants. If training is designed so that learners cannot observe the activity of practitioners, learning is inevitably impoverished.

Legitimacy and peripherality are intertwined in a complex way. Occasionally, learners (like the apprentice butchers) are granted legitimacy but are denied peripherality. Conversely, they can be granted peripherality but denied legitimacy. Martin (1982) gives examples of organizations in which legitimacy is explicitly denied in instances of 'open door' management, where members come to realize that, though the door is open, it is wiser not to cross the threshold. If either legitimacy or peripherality is denied, learning will be significantly more difficult.

For learners, then, a position on the periphery of practice is important. It is also easily overlooked and increasingly risks being 'designed out,' leaving people physically or socially isolated and justifiably uncertain whether, for instance, their errors are inevitable or the result of personal inadequacies. It is a significant challenge for design to ensure that new collaborative technologies, designed as they so often are around formal descriptions of work, do not exclude this sort of implicit, extendable, informal periphery. Learners need legitimate access to the periphery of communication – to computer mail, to formal and informal meetings, to telephone conversations, etc., and, of course, to war stories. They pick up invaluable 'know how' – not just information but also manner and technique – from being on the periphery of competent practitioners going about their business. Furthermore, it is important to consider the periphery not only because it is an important site of learning, but also because, as the next section proposes, it can be an important site for innovation.

3 Innovating

One of the central benefits of these small, self-constituting communities we have been describing is that they evade the ossifying tendencies of large organizations. Canonical accounts of work are not only hard to apply and hard to learn. They are also hard to change. Yet the actual behaviors of communities-of-practice are constantly changing both as newcomers replace old timers and as the demands of practice force the community to revise its relationship to its environment. Communities-of-practice like the reps' continue to develop a rich, fluid, noncanonical world view to bridge the gap between their organization's static canonical view and the challenge of changing practice. This process of development is inherently innovative. 'Maverick' communities of this sort offer the core of a large organization a means and a model to examine the potential of alternative views of organizational activity through spontaneously occurring experiments that are simultaneously informed and checked by experience. These, it has been argued (Hedberg, Nystrom and Starbuck 1976; Schein 1990), drive innovation by allowing the parts of an organization to step outside the organization's inevitably limited core world view and simply try something new. Unfortunately, people in the core of large organizations too often regard these noncanonical practices (if they see them at all) as counterproductive.

For a theoretical account of this sort of innovation, we turn to Daft and Weick's (1984) discussion of interpretive innovation. They propose a matrix of four different kinds of organization, each characterized by its relationship to its environment. They name these relationships 'undirected viewing,' 'conditioned viewing,' 'discovering,' and 'enacting.' Only the last two concern us here. It is important to note that Daft and Weick too see the community and not the individual 'inventor' as the central unit of analysis in understanding innovating practice.

The *discovering organization* is the archetype of the conventional innovative organization, one which responds – often with great efficiency – to changes it detects in its environment. The organization presupposes an essentially prestructured environment and implicitly assumes that there is a correct response to any condition it discovers there. By contrast, the *enacting organization* is proactive and highly interpretive. Not only does it respond to its environment, but also, in a fundamental way, it creates many of the conditions to which it must respond. Daft and Weick describe enacting organizations as follows:

These organizations construct their own environments. They gather information by trying new behaviors and seeing what happens. They experiment, test, and stimulate, and they ignore precedent, rules, and traditional expectations (Daft and Weick 1984, p. 288).

Innovation, in this view, is not simply a response to empirical observations of the environment. The source of innovation lies on the interface between an organization and its environment. And the process of innovating involves actively constructing a conceptual framework, imposing it on the environment, and reflecting on their interaction. With few changes, this could be a description of the activity of inventive, noncanonical groups, such as Orr's reps, who similarly 'ignore precedent, rules, and traditional expectations' and break conventional boundaries. Like story telling, enacting is a process of interpretive sense making and controlled change.

A brief example of enacting can be seen in the introduction of the IBM Mag-I memory typewriter 'as a new way of organizing office work' (Pava cited in Barley 1988). In order to make sense and full use of the power of this typewriter, the conditions in which it was to be used had to be reconceived. In the old conception of office work, the potential of the machine could not be realized. In a newly conceived understanding of office practice, however, the machine could prove highly innovative. Though this new conception could not be achieved without the new machine, the new machine could not be fully realized without the conception. The two changes went along together. Neither is wholly either cause or effect. Enacting organizations differ from discovering ones in that in this reciprocal way, instead of waiting for changed practices to emerge and responding, they enable them to emerge and anticipate their effects.

Reregistering the environment is widely recognized as a powerful source of innovation that moves organizations beyond the paradigms in which they begin their analysis and within which, without such a reformation, they must inevitably end it. This is the problem which Deetz and Kersten (1983) describe as closure: 'Many organizations fail because . . . closure prohibits adaptation to current social conditions' (p. 166). Putnam (1983) argues that closure-generating structures appear to be 'fixtures that exist independent of the processes that create and transform them' (p. 36). Interpretive or enacting organizations, aware as they are that their environment is not a given, can potentially adopt new viewpoints that allow them to see beyond the closure-imposing boundary of a single world view.

The question remains, however, how is this reregistering brought about by organizations that seem inescapably trapped within their own world view? We are claiming that the actual noncanonical practices of interstitial communities are continually developing new interpretations of the world because they have a practical rather than formal connection to that world. (For a theoretical account of the way practice drives change in world view, see Bloch 1977.) To pursue our connection with the work of the reps, closure is the likely result of rigid adherence to the reps' training and documentation and the formal account of work that they encompass. In order to get on with their work, reps overcome closure by reregistering their interpretation of the machine and its ever changing milieu. Rejection of a canonical, predetermined view and the construction through narration of an alternative view, such as Orr describes, involve, at heart, the complex intuitive process of bringing the communicative, community schema into harmony with the environment by reformulating both. The potential of such innovation is, however, lost to an organization that remains blind to noncanonical practice.

An enacting organization must also be capable of reconceiving not only its environment but also its own identity, for in a significant sense the two are mutually constitutive. Again, this reconceptualization is something that people who develop noncanonical practices are continuously doing, forging their own and their community's identity in their own terms so that they can break out of the restrictive hold of the formal descriptions of practice. Enacting organizations similarly regard both their environment and themselves as in some sense unanalyzed and therefore malleable. They do not assume that there is an ineluctable structure, a 'right' answer, or a universal view to be discovered; rather, they continually look for innovative ways to impose new structure, asked new questions, develop a new view, become a new organization. By asking different questions, by seeking different *sorts* of explanations, and by looking from different points of view, different answers emerge – indeed different environments and different organizations mutually reconstitute each other dialectically or reciprocally. Daft and Weick (1984) argue, the interpretation can 'shape the environment more than the environment shapes the interpretation' (p. 287).

Carlson's attempts to interest people in the idea of dry photocopying – xerography – provide an example of organizational tendencies to resist enacting innovation. Carlson and the Batelle Institute, which backed his research, approached most of the major innovative corporations of the time – RCA, IBM, A. B. Dick, Kodak. All turned down the idea of a dry copier. They did not reject a flawed machine. Indeed, they all agreed that it worked. But they rejected the *concept* of an office copier. They could see no use for it. Even when Haloid bought the patent, the marketing firms they hired consistently reported that the new device had no role in office practice (Dessauer 1971). In some sense it was necessary both for Haloid to reconceive itself (as Xerox) and for Xerox's machine to help bring about a reconceptualization of an area of office practice for the new machine to be put into manufacture and use.

What the evaluations saw was that an expensive machine was not needed to make a record copy of original documents. For the most part, carbon paper already did that admirably and cheaply. What they failed to see was that a copier allowed the proliferation of copies and of copies of copies. The quantitative leap in copies and their importance independent of the original then produced a qualitative leap in the way they were used. They no longer served merely as records of an original. Instead, they participated in the productive interactions of organizations' members in a unprecedented way. (See Latour's (1986) description of the organizational role of 'immutable mobiles.') Only in use in the office, enabling and enhancing new forms of work, did the copier forge the conceptual lenses under which its value became inescapable.

It is this process of seeing the world anew that allows organizations reciprocally to see themselves anew and to overcome discontinuities in their environment and their structure. As von Hippel (1988), Barley (1988), and others point out, innovating is not always radical. Incremental improvements occur throughout an innovative organization. Enacting and innovating can be conceived of as at root sense-making, congruence-seeking, identity-building activities of the sort engaged in by the reps. Innovating and learning in daily activity lie at one end of a continuum of innovating practices that stretches to radical innovation cultivated in research laboratories at the far end.

Alternative world views, then, do not lie in the laboratory or strategic planning office alone, condemning everyone else in the organization to submit to a unitary culture. Alternatives are inevitably distributed throughout all the different communities that make up the organization. For it is the organiza-tion's communities, at all levels, who are in contact with the environment and involved in interpretive sense making, congruence finding, and adapting. It is from any site of such interactions that new insights can be coproduced. If an organizational core overlooks or curtails the enacting in its midst by ignoring or disrupting its communities-of-practice, it threatens its own survival in two ways. It will not only threaten to destroy the very working and learning practices by which it, knowingly or unknowingly, survives. It will also cut itself off from a major source of potential innovation that inevitably arises in the course of that working and learning.

4 Conclusion: organizations as communities-of-communities

The complex of contradictory forces that put an organization's assumptions and core beliefs in direct conflict with members' working, learning, and innovating arises from a thorough misunderstanding of what working, learning, and innovating are. As a result of such misunderstandings, many modern processes and technologies, particularly those designed to downskill, threaten the robust working, learning, and innovating communities and practice of the workplace. Between Braverman's (1974) pessimistic view and Adler's (1987) optimistic one, lies Barley's (1988) complex argument, pointing out that the intent to downskill does not *necessarily* lead to downskilling (as Orr's reps show). But the intent to downskill may first drive noncanonical practice and communities yet further underground so that the insights gained through work are more completely hidden from the organiza-tion as a whole. Then later changes or reorganizations, whether or not intended to downskill, may disrupt what they do not notice. The gap between espoused and actual practice may become too large for noncanonical practices to bridge.

To foster working, learning, and innovating, an organization must close that gap. To do so, it needs to reconceive of itself as a community-of-communities, acknowledging in the process the many noncanonical communities in its midst. It must see beyond its canonical abstractions of practice to the rich, full-blooded activities themselves. And it must legitimize and support the myriad enacting activities perpetrated by its different members. This support cannot be intrusive, or it risks merely bringing potential innovators under the restrictive influence of the existing canonical view. Rather, as others have argued (Nystrom and Starbuck 1984; Hedberg 1981; Schein 1990) communities-of-practice must be allowed some latitude to shake themselves free of received wisdom.

A major entailment of this argument may be quite surprising. Conventional wisdom tends to hold that large organizations are particularly poor at innovating and adapting. Tushman and Anderson (1988), for example, argue justifiably that the *typical*, large organization is unlikely to produce discontinuous innovation. But size may not be the single determining feature here. Large, *atypical*, enacting organizations have the potential to be highly innovative and adaptive. Within an organization perceived as a collective of communities, not simply of individuals, in which enacting experiments are legitimate, separate community perspectives can be amplified by interchanges among communities. Out of this friction of competing ideas can come the sort of improvisational sparks necessary for igniting organizational innovation. Thus large organizations, *reflectively structured*, are perhaps particularly well positioned to be highly innovative and to deal with discontinuities. If their internal communities have a reasonable degree of autonomy and independence from the dominant world view, large organizations might actually accelerate innovation. Such organizations are uniquely positioned to generate innovative discontinuities incrementally, thereby diminishing the disruptiveness of the periodic radical reorganization that Nadler calls 'frame breaking' (Nadler 1988). This occurs when conventional organizations swing wholesale from one paradigm to another (see also Bartunek 1984). An organization whose core is aware that it is the synergistic aggregate of agile, semiautonomous, self-constituting communities and not a brittle monolith is likely to be capable of extensible 'frame bending' well beyond conventional breaking point.

The important interplay of separate communities with independent (though interrelated) world views may in part account for von Hippel's (1988) account of the sources of innovation and other descriptions of the innovative nature of business alliances. Von Hippel argues that sources of innovation can lie outside an organization among its customers and suppliers. Emergent communities of the sort we have outlined that span the boundaries of an organization would then seem a likely conduit of external and innovative views into an organization. Similarly, the alliances Powell describes bring together different organizations with different interpretive schemes so that the composite group they make up has several enacting options to choose from. Because the separate communities enter as independent members of an alliance rather than as members of a rigid hierarchy, the alternative conceptual viewpoints are presumably legitimate and do not get hidden from the core. There is no concealed noncanonical practice where there is no concealing canonical practice.

The means to harness innovative energy in any enacting organization or alliance must ultimately be considered in the design of organizational architecture and the ways communities are linked to each other. This architecture should preserve and enhance the healthy autonomy of communities, while simultaneously building an interconnectedness through which to disseminate the results of separate communities' experiments. In some form or another the stories that support learning-in-working and innovation should be allowed to circulate. The technological potential to support this distribution – e-mail, bulletin boards, and other devices that are capable of supporting narrative exchanges – is available. But narratives, as we have argued, are embedded in the social system in which they arise and are used. They cannot simply be uprooted and repackaged for circulation without becoming prey to exactly those problems that beset the old abstracted canonical accounts. Moreover, information cannot be assumed to circulate freely just because technology to support circulation is available (Feldman and March 1981). Eckert (1989), for instance, argues that information travels differently within different socio-economic groups. Organizational assumptions that given the 'right' medium people will exchange information freely overlook the way in which certain socio-economic groups, organizations, and in particular, corporations, implicitly treat information as a commodity to be hoarded and exchanged. Working-class groups, Eckert contends, do pass information freely and Orr (1990a) notes that the reps are remarkably open with each other about what they know. *Within* these communities, news travels fast; community knowledge is readily available to community members. But these communities must function within corporations that treat information as a commodity and that have superior bargaining power in negotiating the terms of exchange. In such unequal conditions, internal communities cannot reasonably be expected to surrender their knowledge freely.

As we have been arguing throughout, to understand the way information is constructed and travels within an organization, it is first necessary to understand the different communities that are formed within it and the distribution of power among them. Conceptual reorganization to accommodate learning-in-working and innovation, then, must stretch from the level of individual communities-of-practice and the technology and practices used there to the level of the overarching organizational architecture, the community-of-communities.

It has been our unstated assumption that a unified understanding of working, learning, and innovating is potentially highly beneficial, allowing, it seems likely, a synergistic collaboration rather than a conflicting separation among workers, learners, and innovators. But similarly, we have left unstated the companion assumption that attempts to foster such synergy through a conceptual reorganization will produce enormous difficulties from the perspective of the conventional workplace. Work and learning are set out in formal descriptions so that people (and organizations) can be held accountable; groups are organized to define responsibility; organizations are bounded to enhance concepts of competition; peripheries are closed off to maintain secrecy and privacy. Changing the way these things are arranged will produce problems as well as benefits. An examination of both problems and benefits has been left out of this paper, whose single purpose has been to show where constraints and resources lie, rather than the rewards and costs of deploying them. Our argument is simply that for working, learning, and innovating to thrive collectively depends on linking these three, in theory and in practice, more closely, more realistically, and more reflectively than is generally the case at present.

References

Adler, P. S. (1987), 'Automation and Skill: New Directions,' *International Journal of Technology Management* 2 [5/6,], 761–771.

Barley, S. R. (1988), 'Technology, Power, and the Social Organization of Work: Towards a Pragmatic Theory of Skilling and Deskilling,' *Research in the Sociology of Organizations* **6**, 33–80.

Bartunek, J. M. (1984), 'Changing Interpretive Schemes and Organizational Restructuring: The Example of a Religious Order,' *Administrative Science Quarterly*, **29**, 355–372.

Bourdieu, P. (1977), *Outline of a Theory of Practice*, trans R. Nice. Cambridge: Cambridge University Press. (First published in French, 1973.)

Bloch, M. (1977), 'The Past and the Present in the Present,' *Man*[NS], **12**, 278–292.

Braverman, H. (1974), *Labor and Monopoly Capitalism: The Degradation of Work in the Twentieth Century*, New York: Monthly Review Press.

Brown, J. S. and P. Duguid, (in press), 'Enacting Design' in P. Adler (Ed.), *Designing Automation for Usability*, New York: Oxford University Press.

Brown, J. S., A. Collins and P. Duguid (1989), 'Situated Cognition and the Culture of Learning,' *Education Researcher*, **18**, 1, 32–42. (Also available in a fuller version as IRL Report 88–0008, Palo Alto, CA: Institute for Research on Learning.)

Burawoy, M. (1979), 'The Anthropology of Industrial Work,' *Annual Review of Anthropology*, **8**, 231–266.

Daft, R. L. and K. E. Weick (1984), 'Toward a Model of Organizations as Interpretation Systems,' *Academy of Management Review*, **9**, 2, 284–295.

Deetz, S. A. and A. Kersten (1983), 'Critical Models of Interpretive Research,' in L. L. Putnam and M. E. Pacanowsky (Eds.), *Communication and Organizations: An Interpretive Approach*, Beverly Hills, CA: Sage Publications.

Dessauer, J. H. (1971), *My Years with Xerox: The Billions Nobody Wanted*, Garden City, Doubleday.

Eckert, P. (1989), *Jocks and Burnouts*, New York: Teachers College Press.

Feldman, M. S. and J. G. March (1981), 'Information in Organizations as Signal and Symbol,' *Administrative Science Quarterly*, **26**, 171–186.

Geertz, C. (1973), *Interpretation of Cultures: Selected Essays*, New York: Basic Books.

Goodman, P. and associates (1988), *Designing Effective Work Groups*, San Francisco: Jossey-Bass.

Hackman, J. R. (Ed.) (1990), *Groups that Work (and Those that Don't)*, San Francisco: Jossey-Bass.

Hedberg, B. (1981), 'How Organizations Learn and Unlearn,' in P. C. Nystrom and W. H. Starbuck, *Handbook of Organizational Design, Vol. 1: Adapting Organizations to their Environments*, New York: Oxford University Press.

Hedberg, B., P. C. Nystrom and W. H. Starbuck (1976), 'Designing Organizations to Match Tomorrow,' in P. C. Nystrom and W. H. Starbuck (Eds.), *Prescriptive Models of Organizations*, Amsterdam, Netherlands: North-Holland Publishing Company.

Hutchins, E. (1991), 'Organizing Work by Adaptation,' *Organization Science*, **2, 1**, 14–39.

Hutchins, E. (in press), 'Learning to Navigate,' in S. Chalkin and J. Lave (Eds.), *Situated Learning*, Cambridge: Cambridge University Press.

Jordan, B. (1989), 'Cosmopolitical Obstetrics: Some Insights from the Training of Traditional Midwives,' *Social Science and Medicine*, **28, 9**, 925–944. (Also available in slightly different form as *Modes of Teaching and Learning: Questions Raised by the Training of Traditional Birth Attendants*, IRL report 88–0004, Palo Alto, CA: Institute for Research on Learning.)

Latour, B. (1986), 'Visualization and Cognition: Thinking with Eyes and Hands,' *Knowledge and Society*, **6**, 1–40.

Lave, J. (1988), *Cognition in Practice: Mind, Mathematics, and Culture in Everyday Life*, New York: Cambridge University Press.

Lave, J. C. and E. Wenger (1990), *Situated Learning: Legitimate Peripheral Participation*, IRL report 90–0013, Palo Alto, CA.: Institute for Research on Learning. (Also forthcoming (1990) in a revised version, from Cambridge University Press.)

Levi-Strauss, C. 1966), *The Savage Mind*, Chicago: Chicago University Press.

Martin, J. (1982), 'Stories and Scripts in Organizational Settings,' in A. H. Hastorf and A. M. Isen (Eds.), *Cognitive and Social Psychology*, Amsterdam: Elsevier.

Nadler, D. (1988), 'Organizational Frame Bending: Types of Change in the Complex Organization,' in R. H. Kilman, T. J. Covin, and associates (Eds.), *Corporate Transformation: Revitalizing Organizations for a Competitive World*, San Francisco: Jossey-Bass.

Nystrom, P. C. and W. H. Starbuck (1984), 'To Avoid Organizational Crises, Unlearn,' *Organizational Dynamics*, Spring, 53–65.

Orr, J. (1990a), 'Talking about Machines: An Ethnography of a Modern Job,' Ph.D. Thesis, Cornell University.

Orr, J. (1990b), 'Sharing Knowledge, Celebrating Identity: War Stories and Community Memory in a Service Culture,' in D. S. Middleton and D. Edwards (Eds.), *Collective Remembering: Memory in Society*, Beverley Hills, CA: Sage Publications.

Orr, J. (1987a), 'Narratives at Work: Story Telling as Cooperative Diagnostic Activity,' *Field Service Manager*, June, 47–60.

Orr, J. (1987b), *Talking about Machines: Social Aspects of Expertise*, Report for the Intelligent Systems Laboratory, Xerox Palo Alto Research Center, Palo Alto, CA.

Pea, R. D. (1990), *Distributed Cognition*, IRL Report 90–0015, Palo Alto, CA: Institute for Research on Learning.

Putnam, L. L. (1983), 'The Interpretive Perspective: An Alternative to Functionalism,' in L. L. Putnam and M. E. Pacanowsky (Eds), *Communication and Organizations: An Interpretive Approach*, Beverley Hills, CA: Sage Publications.

Reddy, M. J. (1979), 'The Conduit Metaphor,' in Andrew Ortony (Ed.), *Metaphor and Thought*, Cambridge: Cambridge University Press, 284–324.

Ryle, G. (1954), *Dilemmas: The Tarner Lectures*, Cambridge: Cambridge University Press.

Schein, R. H. (1990), 'Organizational Culture,' *American Psychologist*, **45**, 2, 109–119.

Schön, D. A. (1987). *Educating the Reflective Practitioner*, San Francisco: Jossey-Bass.

Schön, D A. (1984). *The Reflective Practitioner*. New York: Basic Books.

Schön, D. A. (1971), *Beyond the Stable State*, New York: Norton.

Scribner, S. (1984), 'Studying Working Intelligence,' in B. Rogoff and J. Lave (Eds). *Everyday Cognition: Its Development in Social Context*, Cambridge, MA: Harvard University Press.

Suchman, L. (1987a), *Plans and Situated Actions: The Problem of Human-Machine Communication*, New York: Cambridge University Press.

Suchman, L. (1987b), 'Common Sense in Interface Design,' *Techné*, **1**, 1, 38–40.

Tushman, M, L. and P. Anderson (1988), 'Technological Discontinuities and Organization Environments,' in A. M. Pettigrew (Ed.), *The Management of Strategic Change*, Oxford: Basil Blackwell.

van Maanen, J. and S. Barley (1984), 'Occupational Communities: Culture and Control in Organizations,' in B. Straw and L. Cummings (Eds), *Research in Organizational Behaviour*, London: JAI Press.

von Hippel, E. (1988), *The Sources of Innovation*, New York: Oxford University Press.

Zuboff, S. (1988), *In the Age of the Smart Machine: The Future of Work and Power*, New York: Basic Books.

Source: Brown, John Seely and Duguid, Paul (1991) Organizational learning and communities-of-practice: toward a unified view of working, learning and innovation. *Organization Science*, **2**, 40–57.

10 Of strategies, deliberate and emergent

Henry Mintzberg and James A. Waters

How do strategies form in organizations? Research into the question is necessarily shaped by the underlying conception of the term. Since strategy has almost inevitably been conceived in terms of what the leaders of an organization 'plan' to do in the future, strategy formation has, not surprisingly, tended to be treated as an analytic process for establishing long-range goals and action plans for an organization; that is, as one of formulation followed by implementation. As important as this emphasis may be, we would argue that it is seriously limited, that the process needs to be viewed from a wider perspective so that the variety of ways in which strategies actually take shape can be considered.

For over 10 years now, we have been researching the process of strategy formation based on the definition of strategy as 'a pattern in a stream of decisions' (Mintzberg, 1972, 1978; Mintzberg and Waters, 1982, 1984; Mintzberg et al., 1986, Mintzberg and McHugh, 1985; Brunet, Mintzberg and Waters, 1986). This definition was developed to 'operationalize' the concept of strategy, namely to provide a tangible basis on which to conduct research into how it forms in organizations. Streams of behaviour could be isolated and strategies identified as patterns or consistencies in such streams. The origins of these strategies could then be investigated, with particular attention paid to exploring the relationship between leadership plans and intentions and what the organizations actually did. Using the label strategy for both of these phenomena – one called *intended*, the other *realized* – encouraged that exploration. (Indeed, by this same logic, and because of practical necessity, we have been drawn into studying strategies as patterns in streams of actions, not decisions, since the latter represent intentions, too. A paper explaining this shift more fully is available from the authors.)

Comparing intended strategy with realized strategy, as shown in Figure 1, has allowed us to distinguish *deliberate* strategies – realized as intended – from *emergent* strategies – patterns or consistencies realized despite, or in the absence of, intentions. These two concepts, and especially their interplay, have

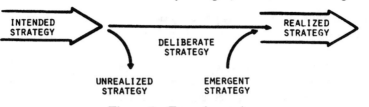

Figure 1 *Types of strategies*

become the central themes in our research, which has involved 11 intensive studies (as well as a larger number of smaller ones), including a food retailer, a manufacturer of women's undergarments, a magazine, a newspaper, an airline, an automobile firm, a mining company, a university, an architectural firm, a public film agency and a government fighting a foreign war.

This paper sets out to explore the complexity and variety of strategy formation processes by refining and elaborating the concepts of deliberate and emergent strategy. We begin by specifying more precisely what pure deliberate and pure emergent strategies might mean in the context of organization, describing the conditions under which each can be said to exist. What does it mean for an 'organization' – a collection of people joined together to pursue some mission in common – to act deliberately? What does it mean for a strategy to emerge in an organization, not guided by intentions? We then identify various types of strategies that have appeared in our empirical studies, each embodying differing degrees of what might be called deliberateness or emergentness. The paper concludes with a discussion of the implications of this perspective on strategy formation for research and practice.

Pure deliberate and pure emergent strategies

For a strategy to be perfectly deliberate – that is, for the realized strategy (pattern in actions) to form exactly as intended – at least three conditions would seem to have to be satisfied. First, there must have existed precise intentions in the organization, articulated in a relatively concrete level of detail, so that there can be no doubt about what was desired before any actions were taken. Secondly, because organization means collective action, to dispel any possible doubt about whether or not the intentions were organizational, they must have been common to virtually all the actors: either shared as their own or else accepted from leaders, probably in response to some sort of controls. Thirdly, these collective intentions must have been realized exactly as intended, which means that no external force (market, technological, political, etc.) could have interfered with them. The environment, in other words, must have been either perfectly predictable, totally benign, or else under the full control of the organization. These three conditions constitute a tall order, so that we are unlikely to find any perfectly deliberate strategies in organizations. Nevertheless, some strategies do come rather close, in some dimensions if not all.

For a strategy to be perfectly emergent, there must be order – consistency in action over time – in the absence of intention about it. (No consistency means no strategy or at least unrealized strategy – intentions not met.) It is difficult to imagine action in the *total* absence of intention – in some pocket of the organization if not from the leadership itself – such that we would expect the purely emergent strategy to be as rare as the purely deliberate one. But again, our research suggests that some patterns come rather close, as when an environment directly imposes a pattern of action on an organization.

Thus, we would expect to find tendencies in the directions of deliberate and emergent strategies rather than perfect forms of either. In effect, these two form the poles of a continuum along which we would expect real-world strategies to fall. Such strategies would combine various states of the dimensions we have discussed above: leadership intentions would be more or less precise, concrete and explicit, and more or less shared, as would intentions existing elsewhere in the organization; central control over organizational actions would be more or less firm and more or less pervasive; and the environment would be more or less benign, more or less controllable and more or less predictable.

Below we introduce a variety of types of strategies that fall along this continuum, beginning with those closest to the deliberate pole and ending with those most reflective of the characteristics of emergent strategy. We present these types, not as any firm or exhaustive typology (although one may eventually emerge), but simply to explore this continuum of emergentness of strategy and to try to gain some insights into the notions of intention, choice and pattern formation in the collective context we call organization.

The planned strategy

Planning suggests clear and articulated intentions, backed up by formal controls to ensure their pursuit, in an environment that is acquiescent. In other words, here (and only here) does the classic distinction between 'formulation' and 'implementation' hold up.

In this first type, called *planned strategy*, leaders at the centre of authority formulate their intentions as precisely as possible and then strive for their implementation – their translation into collective action – with a minimum of distortion, 'surprise-free'. To ensure this, the leaders must first articulate their intentions in the form of a plan, to minimize confusion, and then elaborate this plan in as much detail as possible, in the form of budgets, schedules and so on, to pre-empt discretion that might impede its realization. Those outside the planning process may act, but to the extent possible they are not allowed to decide. Programmes that guide their behaviour are built into the plan, and formal controls are instituted to ensure pursuit of the plan and the programmes.

But the plan is of no use if it cannot be applied as formulated in the environment surrounding the organization so the planned strategy is found in an environment that is, if not benign or controllable, then at least rather predictable. Some organizations, as Galbraith (1967) describes the 'new industrial states', are powerful enough to impose their plans on their environments. Others are able to predict their environments with enough accuracy to pursue rather deliberate, planned strategies. We suspect, however, that many planned strategies are found in organizations that simply extrapolate established patterns in environments that they assume will remain stable. In fact, we have argued elsewhere (Mintzberg and Waters, 1982) that strategies appear not to be *conceived* in planning processes so much as elaborated from existing visions or copied from standard industry recipes (see Grinyer and Spender, 1979); planning thus becomes programming, and the planned strategy finds its origins in one of the other types of strategies described below.

Although few strategies can be planned to the degree described above, some do come rather close, particularly in organizations that must commit large quantities of resources to particular missions and so cannot tolerate unstable environments. They may spend years considering their actions, but once they decide to act, they commit themselves firmly. In effect, they deliberate so that their strategies can be rather deliberate. Thus, we studied a mining company that had to engage in a most detailed form of planning to exploit a new ore body in an extremely remote part of Quebec. Likewise, we found a very strong planning orientation in our study of Air Canada, necessary to co-ordinate the purchase of new, expensive jet aircraft with a relatively fixed route structure. Our study of the United States government's escalation of military activity in Vietnam also revealed a rather planned strategy. Once Lyndon Johnson announced his decision to escalate in 1965, the military planners took over and articulated the intentions in detail (or pulled out existing contingency plans), and pursued the strategy vigorously until 1968 when it became clear that the environment was less controllable than it had seemed (Mintzberg, 1978).

(Note the distinction here between unrealized strategy – that is, intentions not successfully realized – and realized strategy that is unsuccessful in its consequences. The intention to escalate was realized, in fact from Johnson's point of view, *over*-realized; it just did not achieve its objective. In contrast, John F. Kennedy's earlier intention to provide advisers to the Vietnam army was not realized to the extent that those advisers became combatants. It should be noted, however, that the degree of deliberateness is not a measure of the potential success of a strategy. In our research, we have come across rather emergent strategies as well as rather deliberate ones that have been highly successful (see the discussion of the experimental film strategy later in the text for an example of the former) and others of both types that have been dramatic failures.)

The entrepreneurial strategy

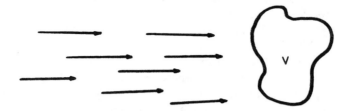

In this second type of strategy, we relax the condition of precise, articulated intentions. Here, one individual in personal control of an organization is able to impose his or her vision of direction on it. Because such strategies are rather common in entrepreneurial firms, tightly controlled by their owners, they can be called *entrepreneurial strategies*.

In this case, the force for pattern or consistency in action is individual vision, the central actor's *concept* of his or her organization's place in its world. This is coupled with an ability to impose that vision on the organization through his or her personal control of its actions (e.g. through giving direct orders to its operating personnel). Of course, the environment must again be co-operative. But entrepreneurial strategies most commonly appear in young and/or small organizations (where personal control is feasible), which are able to find relatively safe niches in their environments. Indeed, the selection of such niches is an integral part of the vision. These strategies can, however, sometimes be found in larger organizations as well, particularly under conditions of crisis where all the actors are willing to follow the direction of a single leader who has vision and will.

Is the entrepreneurial strategy deliberate? Intentions do exist. But they derive from one individual who need not articulate or elaborate them. Indeed, for reasons discussed below, he or she is typically unlikely to want to do so. Thus, the intentions are both more difficult to identify and less specific than those of the planned strategy. Moreover, there is less overt acceptance of these intentions on the part of other actors in the organization. Nevertheless, so long as those actors respond to the personal will of the leader, the strategy would appear to be rather deliberate.

In two important respects, however, that strategy can have emergent characteristics as well. First, as indicated in the previous diagram, vision provides only a general sense of direction. Within it, there is room for adaptation: the details of the vision can emerge *en route*. Secondly, because the leader's vision is personal, it can also be changed completely. To put this another way, since here the formulator is the implementor, step by step, that person can react quickly to feedback on past actions or to new opportunities or threats in the environment. He or she can thus reformulate vision, as shown in the figure below.

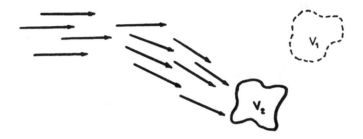

It is this adaptability that distinguishes the entrepreneurial strategy from the planned one. Visions contained in single brains would appear to be more flexible, assuming the individual's willingness to learn,[1] than plans articulated through hierarchies, which are comprised of many brains. Adaptation (and emergentness) of planned strategies are discouraged by the articulation of intentions and by the separation between formulation and implementation. Psychologists have shown that the articulation of a strategy locks it into place, impeding willingness to change it (e.g. Kiesler, 1971). The separation of implementation from formulation gives rise to a whole system of commitments and procedures, in the form of plans, programmes and controls elaborated down a hierarchy. Instead of one individual being able to change his or her mind, the whole system must be redesigned. Thus, despite the claims of flexible planning, the fact is that organizations plan not to be flexible but to realize specific intentions. It is the entrepreneurial strategy that provides flexibility, at the expense of the specificity and articulation of intentions.

Entrepreneurial strategies have appeared in our research, not surprisingly, in two companies that were controlled personally by their aggressive owners – one the food retail chain, the other the manufacturer of women's under-garments. Here, typically, when important aspects of the environment

---

[1] An interesting situation arises when the vision is beyond even the control of the individual himself, so that he or she pursues a pattern of action due to inner, subconscious forces (as, say, when the leader chooses to produce only unconventional products, perhaps because of a phobia about being ordinary). Such 'subconscious' strategies would probably be more difficult to change than those based on more conscious visions.

changed, strong new visions emerged rather quickly, followed by long periods of deliberate pursuit of these visions. But as both organizations grew and became more formalized, the visions became the basis for planning (programming), and thereafter decisive changes were less in evidence. This led us to suspect that planned strategies often follow entrepreneurial ones, based on the vision of leaders, sometimes ones who have departed the organization (see Mintzberg and Waters, 1982, 1984).

The ideological strategy

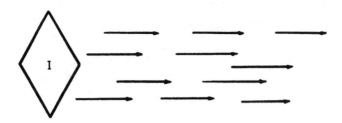

Vision can be collective as well as individual. When the members of an organization share a vision and identify so strongly with it that they pursue it as an ideology, then they are bound to exhibit patterns in their behaviour, so that clear realized strategies can be identified. These may be called *ideological strategies*.

Can an ideological strategy be considered deliberate? Since the ideology is likely to be somewhat overt (e.g. in programmes of indoctrination), and perhaps even articulated (in rough, inspirational form, such as a credo), intentions can usually be identified. The question thus revolves around whether these intentions can be considered organizational and whether they are likely to be realized as intended. In an important sense, these intentions would seem to be most clearly organizational. Whereas the intentions of the planned and entrepreneurial strategies emanate from one centre and are accepted passively by everyone else, those of the ideological strategy are positively embraced by the members of the organization.

As for their realization, because the intentions exist as a rough vision, they can presumably be adapted or changed. But collective vision is far more immutable than individual vision. All who share it must agree to change their 'collective mind'. Moreover, ideology is rooted in the past, in traditions and precedents (often the institutionalization of the vision of a departed, charismatic leader: one person's vision has become everyone's ideology). People, therefore, resist changing it. The object is to interpret 'the word', not to defy it. Finally, the environment is unlikely to impose change: the purpose of ideology, after all, is to change the environment or else to insulate the organization from it. For all these reasons, therefore, ideological strategy would normally be highly deliberate, perhaps more so than any type of strategy except the planned one.

We have not as yet studied any organization dominated by an ideology. But such strategies do seem to occur in certain organizations described in the literature, notably in certain Israeli kibbutzim, 'distinctive colleges', and some charitable institutions (see Clark, 1970, 1972; Sills, 1957; also Mintzberg, 1983: Chapters 11 and 21).

The umbrella strategy

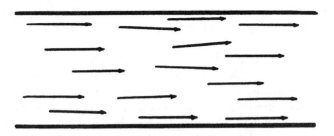

Now we begin to relax the condition of tight control (whether bureaucratic, personal or ideological) over the mass of actors in the organization and, in some cases, the condition of tight control over the environment as well. Leaders who have only partial control over other actors in an organization may design what can be called *umbrella strategies*. They set general guidelines for behaviour – define the boundaries – and then let other actors manoeuvre within them. In effect, these leaders establish kinds of umbrellas under which organizational actions are expected to fall – for example that all products should be designed for the high-priced end of the market (no matter what those products might be).

When an environment is complex, and perhaps somewhat uncontrollable and unpredictable as well, a variety of actors in the organization must be able to respond to it. In other words, the patterns in organizational actions cannot be set deliberately in one central place, although the boundaries may be established there to constrain them. From the perspective of the leadership (if not, perhaps, the individual actors), therefore, strategies are allowed to emerge, at least within these boundaries. In fact, we can label the umbrella strategy not only deliberate and emergent (intended at the centre in its broad outlines but not in its specific details), but also 'deliberately emergent' (in the sense that the central leadership intentionally creates the conditions under which strategies can emerge).

Like the entrepreneurial strategy, the umbrella one represents a certain vision emanating from the central leadership. But here those who have the vision do not control its realization; instead they must convince others to pursue it. The umbrella at least puts limits on the actions of others and ideally provides a sense of direction as well. Sometimes the umbrella takes the form of a more specific target, as in a NASA that concentrated its efforts during the 1960s on putting a man on the moon. In the light of this specific target, all kinds of strategies emerged, as various technical problems were solved by thousands of different specialists.

The architectural firm in our research provides a good example of umbrella strategy. The partners made it clear what kinds of buildings they wished to design: unique, excellent and highly visible ones that would 'celebrate the spirit of the community'. Under that umbrella, anything went – performing arts centres, office buildings, hotels, etc. The firm occasionally filled in gaps with smaller projects of a more mundane nature, but it never committed itself to a major undertaking that strayed from those central criteria (Mintzberg et al., 1986).[2]

We have so far described the umbrella strategy as one among a number of types that are possible. But, in some sense, virtually all real-world strategies have umbrella characteristics. That is to say, in no organization can the central leadership totally pre-empt the discretion of others (as was assumed in the planned and entrepreneurial strategies) and, by the same token, in none does a central leadership defer totally to others (unless it has ceased to lead). Almost all strategy making behaviour involves, therefore, to some degree at least, a central leadership with some sort of intentions trying to direct, guide, cajole or nudge others with ideas of their own. When the leadership is able to direct, we move towards the realm of the planned or entrepreneurial strategies; when it can hardly nudge, we move toward the realm of the more emergent strategies. But in the broad range between these two can always be found strategies with umbrella characteristics.

In its pursuit of an umbrella strategy – which means, in essence, defining general direction subject to varied interpretation – the central leadership must monitor the behaviour of other actors to assess whether or not the boundaries are being respected. In essence, like us, it searches for patterns in streams of actions. When actors are found to stray outside the boundaries (whether inadvertently or intentionally), the central leadership has three choices: to stop them, ignore them (perhaps for a time, to see what will happen), or adjust to them. In other words, when an arm pokes outside the umbrella, you either pull it in, leave it there (although it might get wet), or move the umbrella over to cover it.

In this last case, the leadership exercises the option of altering its own vision in response to the behaviour of others. Indeed, this would appear to be the

---

[2] Of course, to the extent that other architects in the firm embraced these criteria, instead of merely accepting them as the intentions of the central leadership, the strategy could have been labelled ideological.

place where much effective strategic learning takes place – through leadership response to the initiatives of others. The leadership that is never willing to alter its vision in such a way forgoes important opportunities and tends to lose touch with its environment (although, of course, the one too willing to do so may be unable to sustain any central direction). The umbrella strategy thus requires a light touch, maintaining a subtle balance between proaction and reaction.

The process strategy

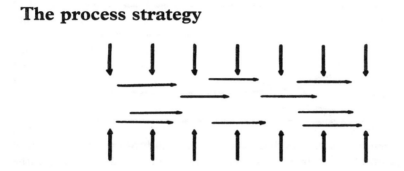

Similar to the umbrella strategy is what can be called the *process strategy*. Again, the leadership functions in an organization in which other actors must have considerable discretion to determine outcomes, because of an environment that is complex and perhaps also unpredictable and uncontrollable. But instead of trying to control strategy content at a general level, through boundaries or targets, the leadership instead needs to exercise influence indirectly. Specifically, it controls the *process* of strategy making while leaving the *content* of strategy to other actors. Again, the resulting behaviour would be deliberate in one respect and emergent in others: the central leadership designs the system that allows others the flexibility to evolve patterns within it.

The leadership may, for example, control the staffing of the organization, thereby determining who gets to make strategy if not what that strategy will be (all the while knowing that control of the former constitutes considerable influence over the latter). Or it may design the structure of the organization to determine the working context of those who get to make strategy. Thus, it was claimed recently that '75 per cent of the (Hewlett Packard) plan is devoted to the new product portfolio generation *process*'.[3]

Divisionalized organizations of a conglomerate nature commonly use process strategies: the central headquarters creates the basic structure, establishes the control systems and appoints the division managers, who are then expected to develop strategies for their own businesses (typically planned

---

[3] Statement by Thomas Peters at the Strategic Management Society Conference 'Exploring the Strategy-making Process', Montreal, 8 October, 1982; emphasis added.

ones for reasons outlined by Mintzberg, 1979: 384–392); note that techniques such as those introduced by the Boston Consulting Group to manage the business portfolios of divisionalized companies, by involving headquarters in the business strategies to some extent, bring their strategies back into the realm of umbrella ones.

The unconnected strategies

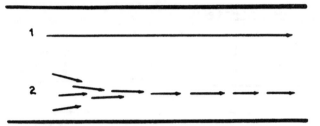

The *unconnected strategy* is perhaps the most straightforward one of all. One part of the organization with considerable discretion – a subunit, sometimes even a single individual – because it is only loosely coupled to the rest, is able to realize its own pattern in its stream of actions. Our clearest example of this appeared in the study of the National Film Board of Canada, a producer of primarily short films, where the central leadership seldom dictated the content of films. From the 1940s to the mid-1960s, the Film Board produced, among many others, a thin but steady stream of experimental films; after that, their number increased significantly. In fact, with one exception, every single film up to 1960 was made by one person, Norman McLaren, the Board's most celebrated film-maker. McLaren, in other words, pursued his own personal strategy – 'did his own thing', as the saying goes – for decades, quite independently of the activities of other film-makers.

How deliberate or emergent are these unconnected strategies? Since they come neither from a central leadership nor from intentions in the organization at large, they would seem to be relatively emergent from the perspective of the entire organization. But from the perspective of the unit or individual involved, clearly they can be deliberate or emergent, depending on the prior existence of intentions.

Identifying intentions is a tricky business in any context. Who can be sure that what was articulated was truly intended? Moreover, in the collective context, there is the problem of determining whose intentions really matter, and of dealing with conflicting intentions. These problems may be absent in the context of the individual, but they are replaced by others. For example, the individual pursuing a personal strategy is unlikely to have to articulate his or her intentions before actions are taken, and that can influence the very existence of intentions. Consider the experimental film strategy of Norman

McLaren. Was it deliberate? For McLaren himself, it could conceivably have been. That is, he may have developed a general intention to make a stream of experimental films, at least after his initial successes. But why should he have done so? Surely McLaren did not say to himself in 1943: 'I shall make experimental films for the next 30 years'. More likely, he just decided on one film at a time, in effect being deliberate about individual films (although these too may have emerged) but not about the pattern in the sequence of them.

The fact that a Norman McLaren has no need to articulate his intentions (unlike, at least in some cases, a leader in charge of other people) means that no one can ever be sure what he intended (or, more exactly, what he would have claimed he intended). To take another example, used in a previous paper to illustrate the definition of realized strategy (Mintzberg, 1978: 935), Picasso's blue period can be called a personal blue strategy, since there was consistency in his use of colour across a sequence of his paintings. But did Picasso 'decide' to paint blue for a given period of his life, or did he simply feel like using that blue each time he painted during these years?

The fact that neither a McLaren nor a Picasso had to explain their intentions to anyone (McLaren at least not beyond saying enough in his organizational context to get funding for a single film at a time) meant that neither was forced to think them through. This probably allowed those intentions to remain rather vague, to themselves as well as to others around them, and so probably encouraged a degree of emergentness in their behaviours.

The example of Norman McLaren is indicative of the fact that unconnected strategies tend to proliferate in organizations of experts, reflecting the complexity of the environments that they face and the resulting need for considerable control by the experts over their own work, providing freedom not only from administrators but sometimes from their own peers as well. Thus, many hospitals and universities appear to be little more than collections of personal strategies, with hardly any discernible central vision or umbrella, let alone plan, linking them together. Each expert pursues his or her own strategies – method of patient care, subject of research, style of teaching. On the other hand, in organizations that do pursue central, rather deliberate strategies, even planned ones, unconnected strategies can sometimes be found in remote enclaves, either tolerated by the system or lost within it.

As indicated in the previous diagram, unconnected strategies may be deliberate or emergent for the actors involved (although always emergent from the perspective of the organization at large). Also, although they are shown within an umbrella strategy, clearly they can fall outside of these, too. Indeed, some unconnected strategies directly contradict umbrella ones (or even more centrally imposed planned or entrepreneurial ones), in effect developing on a clandestine basis. Allison (1971), for example, describes how President Kennedy's directive to defuse the missile bases in Turkey during the Cuban Missile Crisis was deliberately ignored by the military leaders. We show such clandestine strategies in the figure below as a sequence of arrows breaking out of an umbrella strategy. These arrows signify that even though the strategy is likely to be deliberate from the point of view of its proponents, it cannot be articulated as such: they cannot reveal their intentions. To minimize their risk of exposure, they seek to realize intentions subtly, action by action, as if the strategy was emergent. Of course, that increases the chances that the intentions will get deflected along the way. If they do not, there is still the risk that the leadership will realize what is happening – will recognize the pattern in the stream of actions – and stop the strategy. The leadership can, however, play the game too, waiting to see what happens, knowing it too can learn from clandestine behaviour. If the strategy should prove successful, it can always be accepted and broadened – internalized in the system as a (henceforth) deliberate strategy. Our suspicion is that much strategic adaptation results from unconnected strategies (whether or not clandestine) that succeed and so pervade the organization.

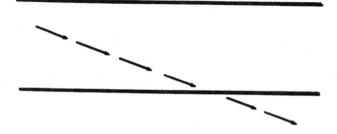

The consensus strategy

In no strategy so far discussed have we totally dropped the condition of prior intention. The next type is rather more clearly emergent. Here many different actors naturally converge on the same theme, or pattern, so that it becomes pervasive in the organization, without the need for any central direction or control. We call it the *consensus strategy*. Unlike the ideological strategy, in which a consensus forms around a system of beliefs (thus reflecting intentions widely accepted in the organization), the consensus strategy grows out of the mutual adjustment among different actors, as they learn from each other and from their various responses to the environment and thereby find a common, and probably unexpected, pattern that works for them.

In other words, the convergence is not driven by any intentions of a central management, nor even by prior intentions widely shared among the other actors. It just evolves through the results of a host of individual actions. Of course, certain actors may actively promote the consensus, perhaps even negotiate with their colleagues to attain it (as in the congressional form of government). But the point is that it derives more from collective action than from collective intention.

Our clearest example of a consensus strategy formed so fast that it seemed literally spontaneous. In the early 1950s, the National Film Board of Canada made its first film for television and in a matter of months the organization found itself concentrating two-thirds of its efforts in that medium. Despite heated debate and indications of managerial intentions to the contrary, one film-maker set the precedent by making that first film, and many of the others quickly followed suit. (In fact, the strategy lasted about 4 years and then disappeared just as spontaneously as it began.) Such spontaneity presumably reflects a strong drive for consistency (the Film Board having been groping for a new focus of attention for several years). As soon as the right idea comes along, the consensus crystallizes quickly, much as does a supersaturated solution the moment it is disturbed. We have been speculating on possible uses for the term intuition in a collective context; the spontaneous strategy might be a good example of 'organizational intuition'.

When the convergence is on a general theme rather than a specific activity (such as making films for television), the consensus is likely to develop more gradually: individual actions would take time to be understood and to pervade the organization as precedents. An electronics manufacturer may find itself concentrating on high quality products after it had achieved success with a number of such products, or a university may find itself over the years favouring the sciences over the humanities as its members came to realize that this is where its real strengths lie.

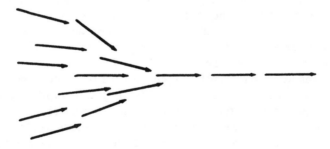

The imposed strategies

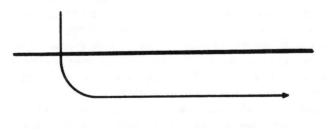

All the strategies so far discussed have derived in part at least from the will (if not the intentions) of actors within the organization. The environment has been considered, if not benign, then at least acquiescent. But strategies can be *imposed* from outside as well; that is, the environment can directly force the organization into a pattern in its stream of actions, regardless of the presence of central controls. The clearest case of this occurs when an external individual or group with a great deal of influence over the organization imposes a strategy on it. We saw this in our study of the state-owned Air Canada, when the minister who created and controlled the airline in its early years forced it to buy and fly a particular type of aircraft. Here the imposed strategy was clearly deliberate, but not by anyone in the organization. However, given its inability to resist, the organization had to resign itself to the pursuit of the strategy, so that it became, in effect, deliberate.

Sometimes the 'environment' rather than people *per se* impose strategies on organizations, simply by severely restricting the options open to them. Air Canada chose to fly jet aeroplanes and later wide-body aeroplanes. But did it? Could any 'world class' airline have decided otherwise? Again the organization has internalized the imperative so that strategic choice becomes a moot point. To draw from another of our studies, did Lyndon Johnson 'choose' to escalate the United States' involvement in Vietnam in 1965? Kennedy's earlier intended strategy of providing advisers for the South Vietnamese became an emergent strategy of engagement in a hot war, imposed by the environment (namely the actions of the Vietcong; of course, to the extent that the military advisers intended to fight, the strategy might be more accurately described as clandestine). The result was that by the time Johnson faced the decision to escalate, the pressures were almost inescapable. So he 'decided', and the strategy became a planned one.

Many planned strategies in fact seem to have this determined quality to them – pursued by organizations resigned to co-operating with external forces. One is reminded here of the king in the Saint-Exupéry (1946) story of *The Little Prince*, who only gave orders that could be executed. He claimed, for example, that he could order the sun to set, but only at a certain time of the day. The point is that when intentions are sufficiently malleable, everything can seem deliberate.

Reality, however, seems to bring organizations closer to a compromise position between determinism and free choice. Environments seldom pre-empt all choice, just as they seldom offer unlimited choice. That is why purely determined strategies are probably as rare as purely planned ones. Alternatively, just as the umbrella strategy may be the most realistic reflection of leadership intention, so too might the partially imposed strategy be the most realistic reflection of environmental influence. As shown in the figure below, the environment bounds what the organization can do, in this illustration determining under what part of the umbrella the organization can feasibly operate. Earlier we described the umbrella strategy of the architectural firm we studied. During one period in its history, it was repeatedly selected to design performing arts centres, even though it was prepared to work on a wide variety of building types. The environment (namely the clients) made its choices for it and so determined its specific strategy for a time, but only within the strategic umbrella acceptable to it. Just as we argued earlier that virtually all real-world strategies have umbrella characteristics, so too do we add here that virtually all have environmental boundaries.

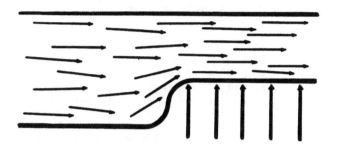

This completes our discussion of various types of strategies. Table 1 summarizes some of their major features.

Emerging conclusions

This paper has been written to open up thinking about strategy formation, to broaden perspectives that may remain framed in the image of it as an *a priori*, analytic process or even as a sharp dichotomy between strategies as either deliberate or emergent. We believe that more research is required on the process of strategy formation to complement the extensive work currently taking place on the content of strategies; indeed, we believe that research on the former can significantly influence the direction taken by research on the latter (and vice versa).

One promising line of research is investigation of the strategy formation process and of the types of strategies realized as a function of the structure and context of organizations. Do the various propositions suggested in this paper, based on our own limited research, in fact hold up in broader samples, for example, that strategies will tend to be more deliberate in tightly coupled, centrally controlled organizations and more emergent in decentralized, loosely coupled ones?

It would also be interesting to know how different types of strategies perform in various contexts and also how these strategies relate to those defined in terms of specific content. Using Porter's (1980) categories, for

Table 1   Summary description of types of strategies

Strategy	Major features
Planned	Strategies originate in formal plans: precise intentions exist, formulated and articulated by central leadership, backed up by formal controls to ensure surprise-free implementation in benign, controllable or predictable environment; strategies most deliberate
Entrepreneurial	Strategies originate in central vision: intentions exist as personal, unarticulated vision of single leader, and so adaptable to new opportunities; organization under personal control of leader and located in protected niche in environment; strategies relatively deliberate but can emerge
Ideological	Strategies originate in shared beliefs: intentions exist as collective vision of all actors, in inspirational form and relatively immutable, controlled normatively through indoctrination and/or socialization; organization often proactive vis-à-vis environment; strategies rather deliberate
Umbrella	Strategies originate in constraints: leadership, in partial control of organizational actions, defines strategic boundaries or targets within which other actors respond to own forces or to complex, perhaps also unpredictable environment; strategies partly deliberate, partly emergent and deliberately emergent
Process	Strategies originate in process: leadership controls process aspects of strategy (hiring, structure, etc.), leaving content aspects to other actors; strategies partly deliberate, partly emergent (and, again, deliberately emergent)
Unconnected	Strategies originate in enclaves: actor(s) loosely coupled to rest of organization produce(s) patterns in own actions in absence of, or in direct contradiction to, central or common intentions; strategies organizationally emergent whether or not deliberate for actor(s)
Consensus	Strategies originate in consensus: through mutual adjustment, actors converge on patterns that become pervasive in absence of central or common intentions; strategies rather emergent
Imposed	Strategies originate in environment: environment dictates patterns in actions either through direct imposition or through implicitly pre-empting or bounding organizational choice; strategies most emergent, although may be internalized by organization and made deliberate

example, will cost leadership strategies prove more deliberate (specifically, more often planned), differentiation strategies more emergent (perhaps umbrella in nature), or perhaps entrepreneurial? Or using Miles and Snow's (1978) typology, will defenders prove more deliberate in orientation and inclined to use planned strategies, whereas prospectors tend to be more emergent and more prone to rely on umbrella or process, or even unconnected, strategies? It may even be possible that highly deliberate strategy making processes will be found to drive organizations away from prospecting activities and towards cost leadership strategies whereas emergent ones may encourage the opposite postures.

The interplay of the different types of strategies we have described can be another avenue of inquiry: the nesting of personal strategies within umbrella ones or their departure in clandestine form from centrally imposed umbrellas; the capacity of unconnected strategies to evoke organizational ones of a consensus or even a planned nature as peripheral patterns that succeed pervade the organization; the conversion of entrepreneurial strategies into ideological or planned ones as vision becomes institutionalized one way or another; the possible propensity of imposed strategies to become deliberate as they are internalized within the organization; and so on. An understanding of how these different types of strategies blend into each other and tend to sequence themselves over time in different contexts could reveal a good deal about the strategy formation process.

At a more general level, the whole question of how managers learn from the experiences of their own organizations seems to be fertile ground for research. In our view, the fundamental difference between deliberate and emergent strategy is that whereas the former focuses on direction and control – getting desired things done – the latter opens up this notion of 'strategic learning'. Defining strategy as intended and conceiving it as deliberate, as has traditionally been done, effectively precludes the notion of strategic learning. Once the intentions have been set, attention is riveted on realizing them, not on adapting them.

Messages from the environment tend to get blocked out. Adding the concept of emergent strategy, based on the definition of strategy as realized, opens the process of strategy making up to the notion of learning.

Emergent strategy itself implies learning what works – taking one action at a time in search for that viable pattern or consistency. It is important to remember that emergent strategy means, not chaos, but, in essence, *unintended order*. It is also frequently the means by which deliberate strategies change. As shown in Figure 2, in the feedback loop added to our basic diagram, it is often through the identification of emergent strategies – its patterns never intended – that managers and others in the organization come to change their intentions. This is another way of saying that not a few deliberate strategies are simply emergent ones that have been uncovered and subsequently formalized. Of course, unrealized strategies are also a source of

STRATEGIC LEARNING

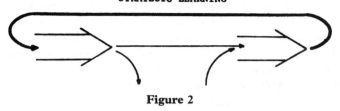

Figure 2

learning, as managers find out which of their intentions do not work, rejected either by their organizations themselves or else by environments that are less than acquiescent.

We wish to emphasize that emergent strategy does not have to mean that management is out of control, only – in some cases at least – that it is open, flexible and responsive, in other words, willing to learn. Such behaviour is especially important when an environment is too unstable or complex to comprehend, or too imposing to defy. Openness to such emergent strategy enables management to act before everything is fully understood – to respond to an evolving reality rather than having to focus on a stable fantasy. For example, distinctive competence cannot always be assessed on paper *a priori*; often, perhaps usually, it has to be discovered empirically, by taking actions that test where strengths and weaknesses really lie. Emergent strategy also enables a management that cannot be close enough to a situation, or to know enough about the varied activities of its organization, to surrender control to those who have the information current and detailed enough to shape realistic strategies. Whereas the more deliberate strategies tend to emphasize central direction and hierarchy, the more emergent ones open the way for collective action and convergent behaviour.

Of course, by the same token, deliberate strategy is hardly dysfunctional either. Managers need to manage too, sometimes to impose intentions on their organizations – to provide a sense of direction. That can be partial, as in the cases of umbrella and process strategies, or it can be rather comprehensive, as in the cases of planned and entrepreneurial strategies. When the necessary information can be brought to a central place and environments can be largely understood and predicted (or at least controlled), then it may be appropriate to suspend strategic learning for a time to pursue intentions with as much determination as possible (see Mintzberg and Waters, 1984).

Our conclusion is that strategy formation walks on two feet, one deliberate, the other emergent. As noted earlier, managing requires a light deft touch – to direct in order to realize intentions while at the same time responding to an unfolding pattern of action. The relative emphasis may shift from time to time but not the requirement to attend to both sides of this phenomenon.

We need to know more about the responding side of this directing/ responding dialectic. More specifically, we would like to know more about how managers track the realized strategies of their own organizations. A major component of that elusive concept called 'strategic control' may be in managers doing what we do as researchers: searching for patterns in streams of organizational actions. Pattern recognition is likely to prove a crucial ability of effective managers and crucial to effective organizations may be the facilitation of self-awareness on the part of all its members of the patterns of its own actions and their consequences over time. Strategic choice requires that kind of awareness; a high degree of it is likely to characterize effective managers and effective organizations.

References

Allison, G. T. *Essence of Decision: Explaining the Cuban Missile Crisis*, Little, Brown, Boston, 1971.

Brunet, J. P. H. Mintzberg and J. Waters. 'Does planning impede strategic thinking? The strategy of Air Canada 1937–1976,' in Lamb, R (ed.) *Advances in Strategic Management*, Volume 4, Prentice-Hall, Englewood Cliffs, N. J., 1986.

Chandler, A. D. *Strategy and Structure*, MIT Press, Cambridge, 1962.

Clark, B. R. *The Distinctive College*, Aldino, Chicago, 1970.

Clark, B. R. 'The organizational saga in higher education', *Administrative Science Quarterly*, 1972, pp. 178–184.

Galbraith, J. K. *The New Industrial State*, Houghton Mifflin, Boston, 1967.

Grinyer, P. H. and J. C. Spender. *Turnaround: the Fall and Rise of the Newton Chambers Group*, Association Business Press, London, 1979.

Kiesler, C. H. *The Psychology of Commitment: Experiments Linking Behaviour to Belief*, Academic Press, New York, 1971.

Miles, R. and C. Snow. *Organizational Strategy, Structure, and Process*, McGraw-Hill, New York, 1978.

Mintzberg, H. 'Research on strategy-making', *Proceedings of the 32nd Annual Meeting of the Academy of Management*, Minneapolis, 1972.

Mintzberg, H. 'Patterns in strategy formation', *Management Science*, 1978, pp. 934–948.

Mintzberg, H. *The Structuring of Organizations*, Prentice-Hall, Englewood Cliffs, N. J., 1979.

Mintzbeg, H. *Power in and Around Organization*, Prentice-Hall, Englewood Cliffs, N. J., 1983.

Mintzberg, H. and A. McHugh. 'Strategy Formation in Adhocracy', *Administrative Science Quarterly*, 1985.

Mintzberg, H. D. Raisinghani and A. Theoret. 'The Structure of 'unstructured' decision processes', Administrative Science Quarterly, 1976, pp. 246–275.

Mintzberg, H. and J. A. Waters. 'Tracking strategy in an entrepreneurial firm', *Academy of Management Journal*, 1982, pp. 465–499.

Mintzberg, H. and J. A. Waters. 'Researching the formation of strategies: the history of Canadian Lady, 1939–1976', in Lamb, R. (ed.) *Competitive Strategic Management*, Prentice-Hall, Englewood Cliffs, N.J., 1984.

Mintzberg, H., S. Otis., J. Shamsie and J. A. Waters. 'Strategy of design: a study of "architects in co-partnership" ', Grant, John (ed.) *Strategic Management Frontiers*, JAI Press, Greenwich, CT, 1986.

Porter, M. E. *Competitive Strategy: Techniques for Analyzing Industries and Competitors*, Free Press, New York, 1980.

Saint-Exupery, A. *Le Petit Prince*, English translation by Katherine Woods, Reynal and Hitchcock, New York, 1943.

Sills, D. L. *The Volunteers*, Free Press, New York, 1957.

Source: Mintzberg, Henry and Waters, James A. (1985) Of strategies, deliberate and emergent. *Strategic Management Journal*, **6**, 257–272.

Part Six

Beyond Social Engineering: Towards a Reflective Practice of Management

It is the mark of an educated man to seek in each inquiry the sort of precision which the nature of the subject permits.

Aristotle

11 Cartographic myths in organisations

Karl E. Weick

The purpose of this article is to provide a fuller appreciation of the nature of maps and mapping as a context for the studies of cognition and strategy. Traditionally maps have emphasized spatial relatedness (O'Keefe and Nadel, 1978, pp. 62 – 89). Maps are surrogates of space (Wilford, 1981, p. 13) and have been described informally as 'a sketch to communicate a sense of place, some sense of here in relation to there' (p. 7). A map of a city, a mall, a university campus is useless until one sees the comforting label, 'You are here'. Maps put people in their place, both literally and figuratively (p. 12). The concept of spatial relatedness is a quality that the human mind requires to comprehend anything, which is probably the reason why map metaphors abound (e.g. the purpose of this strategy is to map out the future).

Spatial relatedness is a vivid part of organizational life, as is evident in such words as above, below, near, far, vertical, full, empty, dense, open, closed, connected, crowded, center, periphery. Network theory (Monge and Eisenberg, 1987) is a theory of spatial relations.

Even though mapmakers keep emphasizing space, what is interesting about strategic maps in management is that they also seem to capture time. Maps which portray causality, predicate logic, or sequences, all capture temporal relations: if this (in the now), then that (in the future).

Not only do maps emphasize spatial relatedness, they also emphasize classification and the assignment of things to classes. 'Naming is always classifying, and mapping is essentially the same as naming' (Bateson, 1979, p. 30). The content of maps consists largely of differences. A map is 'some sort of effect summating differences, organizing news of differences in the "territory"' (Bateson, 1979, p. 110). You have to know something already in order to 'see' something different. This is a point we will encounter repeatedly. The problem with getting managers to think more globally, for example, may be that this task is difficult to map because there is nothing but difference.

Everything looks the same because it is all incomprehensible, so there is nothing to map. What a confused global thinker needs is patterns interspersed among the differences.

Maps and territories

The relationship between maps and classification is perhaps best known by social scientists through Korzybski's epigram, the map is not the territory (Korzybski, 1958 [1st edition in 1933]; Hampden-Turner, 1981). The key ideas behind this well-known phrase are summarized by Postman (1986).

Humans live in two worlds – the world of events and things (the territory) and the world of *words* about events and things (the map). The central question then is, how, by use of abstracting and symbolizing, do people map the territory? Abstracting is the process that enables people to symbolize, and is described as 'the continuous activity of selecting, omitting, and organizing the details of reality so that we experience the world as patterned and coherent' (p. 229). This process becomes necessary but inherently inaccurate, because the world changes continuously and no two events are the same. The world becomes stable only as people ignore differences and attend to similarities.

Even though the world is not the way people see it, people still get by because the names they have for it tell them what to expect and how to prepare for action (p. 229). Korzybski took the position that scientists were more aware of the abstracting process and more aware of the distortions in their maps, which meant they were more flexible than lay people in altering their symbolic maps to fit the world. Applied to managerial cognition, this line of reasoning would suggest that those managers who were more aware of the abstraction process and of the distortions it could create, would have more accurate maps [. . . .]

The practical advice that flows from sensitivity to map-territory issues focuses on changes in language behavior. The most compact example is Kellogg's (1987) effort to train himself to write and talk in E prime, a form of language which, among other things, eliminates any use of the verb 'to be' (basically am, is, was, are, were). Use of this verb form promotes the idea that the map IS the territory (e.g. John is smart = the smartness is in John, not in the eye of beholder). This construction makes the subject of the sentence disappear and the object is made to seem like the key actor. If avoidance of 'to be' forms is too difficult, one can always simply append 'to me' to any declarative statement (e.g. It seems to me John is smart). Another piece of advice is to punctuate any assertion with 'etc.', to remind ourselves that we have not said and cannot say everything that could be said about the territory.

The size of the managerial vocabulary becomes important to students of mapping because words have different degrees of richness and nuance and therefore may provide better or poorer approximations of the territory. Having been sensitized to the fact that the map is not the territory, one must also admit that some maps are better than others. Some media, those with many independent externally constrained elements, render the things they sense more accurately than do media having the opposite set of properties (few, dependent, internally constrained) (Heider, 1959; Weick, 1979, pp. 188–193).

The distinction between map and territory has typically had a cautionary ring, warning people not to treat nouns as anything but a crude static rendering of a much more complex changing territory. What is interesting about problems of strategic mapping in managerial life is that the distinction between map and territory sometimes disappears.

Managers sometimes blur the distinction because strategic thinking is often a right-brain activity. As Bateson (1979) notes, the distinction between map and territory is made by the left brain *but not* by the right brain (p. 30). He uses as his example, an issue which has a contemporary ring, flag desecration. '(W)ith the dominant hemisphere, we can regard such a thing as a flag as a sort of name of the country or organization that it represents. But the right hemisphere does not draw this distinction and regards the flag as sacramentally identical with what it represents. So "Old Glory" is the United States. If somebody steps on it, the response may be rage. And this rage will not be diminished by an explanation of map-territory relations. (After all, the man who tramples the flag is equally identifying it with that for which it stands.)'

Point? If, as Mintzberg (1976) says, intuiting and managing strategy is a right-brain activity, then maps *are* the territory, and it makes even more sense to talk about strategic mapping than Huff and her associates argue.

Managers also may blur the distinction between map and territory because much managerial life is socially constructed. A significant portion of the organization and its environment 'consists of nothing more than talk, symbols, promises, lies, interest, attention, threats, agreements, expectations, memories, rumors, indicators, supporters, detractors, faith, suspicion, trust, appearances, loyalties, and commitments, all of which are more intangible and more influenceable than material goods' (Weick, 1985, p. 128). In a socially constructed world, the map creates the territory, labels the territory, prefigures self-confirming perception and action.

Most map/territory discussions imply passive actors facing an intractable, material world which they register imperfectly and categorize crudely. Managerial life is often different, involving proactive people who enact, manipulate, influence, create, or construct territories that realize their maps.

And finally, managerial strategists may blur the distinction between map and territory because unique territories resemble one another at high levels of abstraction. When a specific territory is simplified and categorized, it becomes more like other territories in the same category. The map is not the territory when the territory is described with particulars, but it is more like the territory when those particulars are ignored and treated as non-existent.

Maps and action

Managerial maps differ from conventional spatial maps, not just in their unusual relationships to the territory, but also in the conditions of their use. These conditions often determine what is crucial in a map. For example, contrary to what might be suspected, accuracy is not always crucial in managerial maps. Three examples illustrate why. The first is my all time favorite map story.

A small Hungarian detachment was on military maneuvers in the Alps. Their young lieutenant sent a reconnaissance unit out into the icy wilderness just as it began to snow. It snowed for two days, and the unit did not return. The lieutenant feared that he had dispatched his people to their deaths, but the third day the unit came back. Where had they been? How had they made their way? Yes, they said, we considered ourselves lost and waited for the end, but then one of us found a map in his pocket. That calmed us down. We pitched camp, lasted out the snowstorm, and then with the map we found our bearings. And here we are. The lieutenant took a good look at this map and discovered, to his astonishment, that it was a map of the Pyrenees. (This story was related by the Nobel Laureate Albert Szent-Gyorgi and was turned into a poem by Holub, 1977.)

My favorite moral of the Pyrenees story is the advice, if you're lost any old map will do. For people who study maps, as well as those who claim to use them, a map provides a reference point, an anchor, a place to start from, a beginning, which often becomes secondary once an activity gets underway. Just as a map of the Pyrenees gets people moving so they find their way out of the Alps, a map of the wrong competitor can get people talking so they find their way into the right niche.

Accuracy is also not the dominant issue when the Naskapi Indians burn caribou bones to find game (Speck, 1977) or when the armed forces use tourist maps to find targets in Grenada (Metcalf, 1986).

In the case of the Naskapi, if you're lost and don't know where to hunt for game, any old input – including cracks in a bone – will do. Priests read cracks formed when caribou shoulder bones are heated over a fire and, on the basis of this information, forecast where game can be found. Once the prophecy is made, the hunters don't continue to sit around and argue about where to hunt. Instead, they get moving, which improves the chance that they will find some game. Furthermore, since they hunt in different places from day to day, they do not overhunt an area and they make it more difficult for animals to evade them.

In the case of Grenada, if you're lost and don't know where to attack, then again, any old input, including a tourist map made in 1895, will do (Metcalf, 1986, p 293). The invasion of Grenada happened so quickly that military cartographers were unable to prepare the usual detailed maps judged 'necessary' for a large-scale operation. Therefore, each unit initially used a different map of Grenada made by separate sources until enough copies of a common map were found, which turned out to be a tourist chart printed in London. Only after the initial assault was an 'official' map made available to everyone.

Parenthetically, managing may be a lot like the invasion of Grenada. Managers invade new markets before the cartographers hand them a map, and before people are entirely sure the invasion is legitimate. The invasion becomes the pretext to learn what is being invaded and what constitutes the legitimate grounds for the invasion. Furthermore, the fact that military units acted in a coordinated manner even though they were not working off a common map, suggests that a little organization and structure can go a long way.

The point of these three different examples can be understood in the context of Huff's question, is the idea of a map merely a useful metaphor or is information actually encoded in the form of maps? In the case of managerial mapping, both answers seem to be true. The issue is one of timing. With a map in hand, no matter how crude it is, people encode what they see to conform as closely as possible to what is on the map. The map prefigures their perceptions, and they see what they expect to see. But, as discrepancies accumulate, they pay closer attention to what is in their immediate experience, look for patterns in it, and pay less attention to the maps. The map in hand then becomes more metaphorical but, ironically, only because it was the means by which other, more current maps were formed. The map in hand calls attention to differences between it and that which is actually encoun-tered. It takes a map to make a map because one points out differences that are mapped into the other one. To find a difference, one needs a comparison and it is maplike artifacts which provide such comparisons.

Maps activate self-correcting action, so they are real starting points that soon become real fictions based on experience which serves to update a static representation of a changing world. Maps provide a frame, albeit a flawed (simplified) one, within which experience can be understood. Parts of the map confirm that experience, but more important, parts are discrepant with it. Discrepancies between maps and current experience stand out because comparison is made possible. The map deepens the appreciation of what is actually encountered, highlights it, punctuates it, but is also altered by it.

In each of the three examples, maps are important for reasons other than accuracy. The map calms the troops snowbound in the Alps and gets them moving toward home. The map makes a decision for the Naskapi and gets them moving toward game. The map coordinates the invasion forces in Grenada and gets them moving toward shore. In each case, it is the movement that is crucial to the resolution. Movement locates exit routes, game and the enemy.

Generalized to organizational settings, accuracy is seldom the highest priority in managing, as is demonstrated by the adequacy with which things get done in the face of inertia, satisfying, organized anarchies, ambiguity, lies, and overload. Strategy implementation is often judged successful when the organization is moving roughly in the same direction. Accuracy is nice, but not necessary, and the reason is that organizations generate action which creates its own substitutes for accuracy and learning.

Maps and sensemaking

Mapmaking resembles sensemaking, an assertion that can be illustrated by explanatory tradeoffs, patient files in a suicide-prevention clinic, and narrative fiction.

Both mapmaking and sensemaking involve a search for explanations. The explanations they turn up vary in their generality, accuracy, and simplicity. As Thorngate (1976) has argued, of the three criteria of simplicity, generality, and accuracy, only two can be achieved in any one explanation.

By definition a map starts simple. The simplification can be used as a crude guideline in several different settings (combination of simple and accurate). The tension and wonder in the Pyrenees story comes because the normal tradeoff among the three criteria is breached and all three are accomplished. The map of the Pyrenees is treated as if it was a map of the Alps, which makes the simplification more general. At the same time, the map of the Pyrenees gets people moving which makes the simplifications in the map more accurate as the map is updated by what the soldiers actually encounter. Simplicity, generality, and accuracy all exist at the same time. The misconception adds generality to the simplification at the same time that action adds accuracy to it.

In an odd way, the fact that the map is a simplification is the soldiers' salvation. Even though the map is of one mountain range, and the soldiers are in a different range, the common feature is that both settings are mountain ranges and fit the same category. The map contains both the particular and the general, as is true for any map. The particular becomes ground, the general becomes figure, and the map becomes the territory.

Managerial maps also resemble file folders in a suicide-prevention center (Garfinkel, 1967). Entries in these folders are crafted with an eye toward future questions that may be raised about them, questions that can only be dimly anticipated in the present. Therefore the folders must be capable of being read in several different ways. The contents of the folder are approximations, multiple stories awaiting the telling, documents in search of diverse underlying rationales which will shift the meaning of the fragments collected in the folder. An assortment of lines connecting nodes on a map often means just as many different things as do scraps of paper in a folder, as do cracks in a shoulder bone, as do tourist attractions in military maneuvers. The truth of the map lies in the action and in the conditions of use. To understand a map is not just to observe it lying passively on the desk in front of a researcher or lying open near a campfire in the Alps or lying embedded in dried shoulder bones in the Labrador Peninsula. The conditions under which the map was judged necessary, the conditions under which it was discovered, the project that its discovery interrupted – and either accelerated or slowed – the salient questions at the time of its discovery, the intentions, all inform it and render the debate over its ontological significance premature, if not misplaced.

Strategic sensemaking with maps also bears a close affinity to narrative sensemaking. The similarity can best be appreciated in the context of Bruner's (1986) discussion of virtual texts. Great storytelling consists of narratives that are powerful, not so much because they evoke a standard reaction, as because they recruit what is 'most appropriate and emotionally lively in the reader's repertory' (p. 35). To recruit personal interests, the stories must allow for rewriting by the reader. When stories retain this latitude and readers:

> begin to construct a virtual text of their own, it is as if they were embarking on a journey without maps – and yet, they possess a stock of maps that *might* give hints and besides they know a lot about journeys and mapmaking. First impressions of the new terrain are, of course, based on older journeys already taken. In time, the new journey becomes a thing in itself, however much its initial shape was borrowed from the past. The virtual text becomes a story of its own, its very strangeness only a contrast with the reader's sense of the ordinary. The fictional landscape, finally, must be given a 'reality' of its own – the ontological step. It is then that the reader asks the crucial interpretive question. 'what's it all about?' But what 'it' is, of course, is not the actual text – however great its literary power – but the text that the reader has constructed under its sway. And that is why the actual text needs the subjunctivity that makes it possible for a reader to create a world of his own. Like Barthes, I believe that the writer's greatest gift to a reader is to help him become a writer . . . . Beyond Barthes, I believe that the *great* writer's gift to a reader is to make him a *better writer*. (pp. 36–37)

If cognitive maps are imperfect renderings of territory, and if people have had extensive experience with other territories in their lives, then present maps which evoke earlier 'analogous' maps (Schutz, 1967, p. 90), create a composite virtual map that capitalizes on what the person already knows. And since personal past experience is the vehicle by which the gaps are filled, personal involvement in the present should be higher. A journey that starts without maps is not frightening as long as there are hints of earlier journeys that are similar.

Good strategies, like good fiction, invite rewriting and pull past experience into the present to construct virtual strategies. The crucial question then becomes one of the repertory available to the person doing the rewriting, the person's access to that repertory, and the organization's willingness to listen to what the person draws forward.

Strategies that encourage rewriting and increased involvement are likely to be those strategies that call forth the most relevant past experience. And those strategies most likely to do this are those whose outcomes can be envisioned most clearly. Clear outcomes are most likely to occur when the strategy is conceived in the future perfect tense as if it had already been accomplished, rather than in the future tense where it is visualized simply as an open-ended possibility, one of many possibilities.

Once the future project is visualized as if it were already finished, then the intermediate steps that must occur 'in-order-to' reach that end become clearer when people search through memory for 'analogous' completed projects and the steps by which they were completed. Current intermediate steps become meaningful because they are similar to the steps that earlier led to an outcome that resembles the outcome envisioned in the current strategy.

Maps enter into future perfect scenarios because they preserve means-end relationships derived from earlier experience. If we imagine experience stored in the form of sequences flowing from left to right, then means are toward the left side and ends are toward the right. When a future project is visualized in the future perfect tense, it becomes an 'accomplished' end which may bear some resemblance to an end already accomplished and stored at the right end of an existing map. Events to the left of that end are some of the means by which it was accomplished, and things that should be done in order to achieve the envisioned end.

Conclusion

Having reviewed several nuances of maps that become more visible when we view them in the context of organized life, we can now finally unpack the title of this introduction. When we say that people in organizations live by cartographic myths, we mean the following.

In the loosely coupled, chaotic, anarchic world of the organization, differences are everywhere and people need abstractions to smooth over the differences. People also need to be/become cartographers in order to fashion those disconnected abstractions into more plausible patterns. Having become cartographers, people then need to adopt the myth that their maps are a sufficiently credible version of the territory that they can now act intentionally. The key steps in this process have been summarized as follows:

> The important feature of a cause map [or any map] is that it leads people to anticipate some order 'out there'. It matters less what particular order is portrayed than that an order of *some* kind is portrayed. The crucial dynamic is that the prospect of order lures the manager into ill-formed situations that then accommodate to forceful actions and come to resemble the orderly relations contained in the cause map. The map animates managers, and the fact of animation, not the map itself, is what imposes order on the situation.
>
> Thus, trappings of rationality such as strategic plans are important largely as binding mechanisms. They hold events together long enough and tight enough in people's heads so that they do something in the belief that their action will be influential. The importance of presumptions, expectations, justifications, and commitments is that they span the breaks in a loosely coupled system and encourage confident interactions that tighten settings. *The conditions of order and tightness in organizations exist as much in the mind as they do in the field of action.* (Weick, 1985, pp. 127–128.

In the present discussion, I have argued that maps are intimately bound up with action, both the action that is ongoing when the map is first invoked, and the action that occurs subsequent to the discovery of the map. It is the tight coupling between maps and action that tightens the coupling between maps and the territory. Distortions of the territory that find their way into maps, find their way out again when maps are coupled with action. This line of reasoning suggests that studies in managerial cognition can be appreciated as commentaries on the resourcefulness with which managers and researchers alike abstract from territories which themselves are only imperfectly known and then use these abstractions to attack those imperfections and correct them. The cycle is a chronic process for both researchers and managers, although the demands for correction usually are more stringent for the researchers than for the managers [. . .]

References

Bateson, G. (1979) *Mind and Nature.* New York: Dutton.

Bruner, J. (1986) *Actual Minds, Possible Worlds.* Cambridge, MA: Harvard University Press.

Garfinkel, H. (1967) *Studies of Ethnomethodology.* Englewood Cliffs, NJ: Prentice-Hall.

Hampden-Turner, C. (1981) *Maps of the Mind.* New York: Collier.

Heider, F. (1959) Thing and medium. *Psychological Issues.* 1 (3), 1–34.

Holub, M. (1977) Brief thoughts on maps. *The Times Literary Supplement,* 4 February, p. 118.

Kellogg, E. W. (1987) Speaking in E-prime. ETC,: *A Review of General Semantics,* 44, (2), 188–128 .

Korzybski, A. (1958) *Science and Sanity*, 4th edition. Lakeville, CT: International Non-aristotelian Library Publishing Co.

Metcalf, J. (1986) Decision making and the Grenada rescue operation. In J. G. March and R. Weissinger-Baylon (eds), *Ambiguity and Command*, pp. 227–297. Marshfield, MA: Pitman.

Mintzberg, H. (1976) Planning on the left side and managing on the right. *Harvard Business Review*, July–August.

Monge, P. R. and Eisenberg, E. M. (1987) Emergent communication networks. In F. M. Jablin, L. L. Putnam, K. H. Roberts and L. W. Porter (eds), *Handbook of Organizational Communication*, pp. 304–342. Beverly Hills: Sage.

O'Keefe, J. and Nadel, L. (1978) *The Hippocampus as a Cognitive Map*. Oxford: Clarendon Press.

Postman, N. (1986) The limits of language. ETC, **43** (3), 227–233.

Schutz, A. (1967) *The Phenomenology of the Social World*. Evanston: Northwestern University.

Speck, F. G. (1977) *Naskapi*. Norman: University of Oklahoma.

Thorngate, W. (1976) Possible limits on a science of social behaviour. In L. H. Strickland, F. E. Abound and K. J. Gergen (eds.) *Social Psychology in Transition*, pp. 121–139. New York: Plenum.

Weick, K. E. (1979) *The Social Psychology of Organizing*. 2nd edition. Reading, MA: Addison-Wesley.

Weick, K. E. (1985) Sources of order in underorganized systems: themes in recent organizational theory. In Y. S. Lincoln (ed.), *Organizational Theory and Inquiry*, pp. 106–136. Beverly Hills, CA: Sage.

Wilford, J. N. (1981) *The Mapmakers*. New York: Knopf.

Source: Weick, Karl E. (1990) Introduction: Cartographic myths in organizations. In A. S. Huff (ed.), *Mapping Strategic Thought*, John Wiley, Chichester, pp. 1–10.

12 The value of humanities in executive development

Thomas Vargish

Twenty years ago, at the end of the first week of the first Dartmouth Institute, a mover and shaker among international bankers raised his hand and asked, 'What in hell are we doing here?' Courses in the humanities have long been offered in executive development programs, but their content and method-ology can seem anomalous because they do not contain a rationale for immediate practical application. In this paper I will try to frame an answer to the banker's question by showing that the humanities offer unique and intelligible benefits to the practice of management. The special province of the humanities is the study of *values* in their most basic and potent forms, and such study has an important relevance to the contemporary exercise of executive responsibility.

In executive education, every program, seminar, of course must offer a worthwhile approach to the art and science of management. Just as there are good reasons for courses in marketing or finance, reasons that derive from the actual needs of executives in their professional lives, so there are good reasons for courses in the liberal arts; they also meet practical needs. But the way in which liberal arts courses do this is very different from that of marketing and finance courses. This difference causes much confusion, especially in the relatively recent educational undertaking called executive development.

Built into most courses in professional schools, whether they are schools of business, medicine, law, or even graduate schools in the humanities, is the rationale for the existence of the course itself. Courses in pathology, torts, or finance teach students how to do something, how to reach a practical end, and they constantly affirm their relation to that goal. Most executive development courses also follow this pattern. But for executives (or doctors or lawyers) who suddenly find themselves in a liberal arts course reading Sophocles or Shakespeare, the rationale is not at all apparent.

There is a good reason for this. Assigning liberal arts courses a practical, immediate end would undermine their real value. This paradox lies at the heart of all higher learning: as soon as you give it an objective, a functionally defined goal, it ceases to produce the widely functional definitions that are its raison d'être. For example, a course that proposes to teach students to think philosophically is a contradiction in terms: one cannot think philosophically by aiming at a single goal (even if that goal is to think philosophically). Such absurd courses do in fact exist, but their claims are misleading. The power of authentic liberal arts courses is always latent, always potential. Their power can only be released in and through the minds of the individual participants. No professor can tell an executive when and how the material and methods of thought will prove their value, will become 'useful.' The liberal arts teacher knows that Sophocles and Shakespeare (themselves great students of the art and science of management) will help in the 'real world,' but their concrete application by any individual executive is unknown and may remain so. Relativity Theory or Cubism may teach an executive the breakthrough skill of counterintuitive thinking, but the crucial moment when this 'pays off' cannot be predicted.

Thus the material and methods of liberal arts courses must by nature be widely diffusive and highly personal in order to function properly in the practical, professional sphere as well as in personal life. On the one hand, the lack of a single aim or result obscures the value of the liberal arts. But on the other hand, the essentially diffusive and personal quality of application gives the liberal arts course its extraordinary depth, flexibility, and power. And these qualities are precisely the ones that executives who take and evaluate such courses consistently appreciate.

If liberal arts courses have a tendency to rise above the bottom line it is not because their proponents are superior to practical and professional considerations. For grudging competitiveness and unyielding professional ambition I will match liberal arts professors against any other group worldwide. The fact is that liberal arts courses *must* rise above the bottom line if they are to offer their distinctive value. To maintain the intimacy and flexibility from which they draw their power, they must resist any accounting that ties them to a single definition of intellectual profit.

The study of values

I am defending the humanities here for two reasons. First, they are my primary field of specialization, and second, they are the field most vulnerable to charges of irrelevance and impracticality. Most educated people recognize the importance of the natural sciences (at least in their technological applications) in our economic and political life. Most see the social sciences as usefully concerned with the continued functioning of our pluralistic democracy. If I can make a case for the humanities, my reasoning goes, then by extension I can make a case for the more obviously useful sciences and social sciences. Beyond this I have a secret and probably unprovable conviction that the study of the humanities at the highest level actually comprehends and prefigures study in the natural and social sciences. Or – to put it less imperialistically – real scientific knowledge and discovery is humanistic knowledge and discovery (I even know a few scientists who agree with this).

So what do the humanities do that the other areas of study and thought don't do? Humanities courses try to answer questions like, 'What in hell are we doing here?' When Shakespeare's Hamlet asks his well-known question, 'To be or not to be?' we understand it in a large, philosophical context. We do not ask him, 'To be or not to be *what?*' We allow for the range of his inquiry. We allow him to ask about the fundamental value of being alive. Hamlet goes on to conclude that there is no available practical answer: the human condition denies us the information to reach a bottom-line answer about the value of being. He concludes that we lack the resources to come to a conclusion – and, as he is tragically aware, the effect is to inhibit us from taking the gratifying practical action (killing the king). Does this mean that Hamlet's inquiry is without meaning? As with many executive decisions, Hamlet's restraint is a matter of personal judgment.

Hamlet's question – like the question 'What in hell are we doing here?' – is not about fact. No empirical conclusion or statistical summary will give the answer. These are questions about values, and the only division of learning that studies the nature of values is the humanities. I do not mean that other branches of learning do not *work with* values. Natural science is deeply committed to such values as accuracy and verification. The social sciences perpetually allude to values (liberty, equality, solidarity, free market economy, and so forth). But neither really asks what values are and how human beings apply them when they make choices and act. It is the humanities that tell us how people deal with what they most deeply feel and believe in their most intense expressions – in their art and science, in their ethical choices and moral lives. Such values are often quite different from the abstractions affirmed in political speeches and manifestos.

The word 'values' has many meanings. A true value may or may not be ethically positive. For example, many political officeholders use the phrase 'family values,' a mushy formulation aimed to strike a positive chord in voters. No doubt many of these politicians are sincere. But the phrase they choose to use is vague – 'family values.' Some officeholders who don't care at all about children or the family (to judge from their voting records) use these words. Similarly, many of the same people give the impression that they are talking about values when they affirm their support for 'the American way of life.' This formulation suggests a kind of national stew of values that can be stirred in various ways to engage the attention of American voters, and no doubt the stew consists of a number of common ingredients that give off an aroma recognizable by a majority of us.

But students of the humanities pursue something more specific and more primary than these vague slogans. Someone trained in the study of language

– that is, someone trained in the basic technology of the humanities – will look at the two phrases 'family values' and 'The American way of life' and recognize a similarity in their mode of expression. Deep down, beneath the putative affirmations, the words contain an element in common, an element that I call a 'value.' And that value is the *vagueness* itself. The phrases 'family values' and 'the American way of life' don't say anything explicit about vagueness, but they are characterized by and validate vagueness. The student of language and expression sees that our political leaders like such phrases not because they are devoted to family and country (they may or may not be) but because they like vague phrases that keep them out of trouble with voters. In a highly pluralistic society vagueness is a proven value when you run for office. The more you can disguise the actual ingredients of your candidacy, the fewer groups you will alienate. Many voters seem to sense and approve of this – as they approved in such numbers of President Reagan's soothing paternal generalizations. So an underlying *value* in such appeals, one that is not explicit but that is nevertheless closer to the true agendas of their usage than the values explicitly affirmed (whatever these may be), is their indefiniteness. The agenda for the politicians is to get elected, and the agenda for the voters is to elect somebody whose position does not separate them from each other by pressing specifics. Such agendas may be as important in American life as family or national identity. In this way indefiniteness, vagueness, or even evasiveness may be a *value* whether or not the person who holds it perceives or acknowledges it as such. Finally, we need to remember that we got to this conclusion by looking at the *language* of the politicians, their *habit of expression*. That is, we employed a distinctly humanistic mode of analysis. In this kind of analysis, values are the most primitive and primary dispositions, the most elemental social coordinates, the ultimate constituents of our actions.

Let me offer a somewhat fancier example of a distinctively humanities-based analysis. Let's take two primary values of postmodern literature (cutting-edge fiction roughly since World War II): *play* and *reflexivity*. The work of postmodern writers – Borges, Cortázar, Robbe-Grillet, Hawkes, for example – validates the ideas of *play* (actions and patterns that have immediate or formal rather than utilitarian value) and *reflexivity* (the idea that meaning is generated within closed systems, and not in relation to any external 'reality' – a derogated concept in postmodernism).[1] Thus a postmodern film or novel may show the same events happening over and over again (as in the works of Robbe-Grillet) with only slight but troubling and possibly sinister variations. The reader notices these variations and by a process of comparison arrives at the understanding that these are patterns whose importance derives only from their relation (play) to each other; there is no one 'true' (privileged) version of the events. Or the reader may observe a protagonist working toward a solution to a mystery (as in stories by Borges and Cortázar) only to realize that the mystery offers no 'solution' in the 'real,' external world (what world is that?) but contains meaning exclusively within the self-referential framework of the work of fiction. Thus in postmodern literature there is the latent but finally obvious equation of fiction with reality and of reality with fiction. This is a logical consequence of making play and reflexivity primary values.

It is true that cutting-edge fiction immediately affects quite limited numbers of people, and that only a few of these are corporate executives (although more than most liberal arts professors think). But fortunately for specialists in the humanities, the culture's dominant values are not field-specific. We can, for example, see the same tendencies surfacing in the media (as might be expected, there's a lag between avant-garde fiction and journalism). Until quite recently, the news on television or in the daily paper presented itself as an account of reality, a description of what was going on in the world. Of course many newspeople were openly critical or cynical about the degree of accuracy in news reports, but they still believed that the news had some connection with a real world independent of our perception of it. Many of us can remember Walter Cronkite ending his newscast every weekday with the endearing and somehow reassuring phrase, 'And that's the way it is . . . .' But recent years have seen a shift away from actual events and toward the *perception* of actual events. Dan Rather, Peter Jennings, and the others show less concern with actual U.S. policy and practice than with how people *judge* our policy and practice. The question is not so often what President Bush's stand on taxes really is but on how his stand is perceived by the person in the street, by right-wing Republicans, and so on. We appear to care less about the actual effects of our support of, say, Israel, than about how US voters *feel about* our support of Israel. In other words, the media shows a growing tendency to concern itself not with trying to describe actualities but with trying to describe the attitudes of the media audience. News organizations commonly conduct media polls (such as those by CBS/*New York Times* and NBC/*Wall Street Journal*) and report the results (which measure perceptions and attitudes) as *news*. Not only is the media in the business of describing perceptions, it is in the business of turning these descriptions into news itself. The whole industry increasingly seems to consist of the media's continuous self-reflection, its *play of reflexivity*. So that even devoted students of postmodernism long for the return of the media to its former mission of pretending to report real events from a real world. But reality – as students of postmodern literature know well and as newspeople seem at least to intuit – is fading as a *value*.

Postmodern money

Well, so what? What does all this have to do with the price of junk bonds (as my banker friend might well ask)? I answer that if certain values turn up in postmodern literature and the news media, they may very well turn up in contemporary finance, in what I'll call 'postmodern money.' What follows represents a deliberately high-risk investment in the methods of value analysis. As always, it is the reader (the investor) who will judge whether it performs well.

Widely evident in financial scandals of the last few years is an increasing departure from the investment community's connection with the productive energy of the economy. This connection was its link to the concrete (real) world of goods and services and was generally thought to justify speculation in the 'free' market. Such an ethos of work-ingenuity-risk used to constitute 'the American way of life.' Money (I was taught in my high school civics course) was invested in the production of goods and services, especially goods. Capital financed industry, which produced goods. Goods were freely traded, and the result was increasing national wealth. My civics teacher, dear old Adam Smith, told us that the production and exchange of goods eventually produced more capital; this capital could be reinvested; and the 'invisible hand' of free trade would see that all parties prospered.

Boy, have times changed! Postmodern investment couldn't care less what was actually being produced or traded. What turned out to be important was not building an industry but something much more simple: numbers. What counts in postmodern money is how much (or more accurately how *many*) you have. We don't care if it's airlines or biscuits. We can reduce it to a common point system (the points in this high scoring game are called dollars) and tell who's won. It's not the 'real world' (as in airplanes and passengers, farmers and grain supplies, books and readers) but the *game* that counts. One doesn't invest in an *industry*; one invests in an *opportunity*. One is not interested in producing *things*: that's not what *players* do because that's not how you *win*.

To the extent that this cartoon of postmodern money has validity, many members of the financial community deplore it. Unfortunately, however, the cartoon is accurate enough to describe the values (in our precise sense of the word) of a number of highflyers. I'm speaking of the bizarre collection of crooks and clowns who engineered the insider trading and S&L scandals. These people got absorbed in the game. They adopted the postmodern value of *play* with one important element left out. They became so self-referential, so solipsistically *reflexive*, that they lost sight of another key postmodern perception: that the absence of a privileged reality means that they didn't have it either. They believed their game comprehended all other games. In the end they seemed to be aware only of each other, the knowing few, the few with the privileged information. In the end they made up their own ethics. But – to keep the game metaphor, itself a value in our sense – the board was bigger than they thought. There turned out to be other agendas, competing interests, the requisite sucker majority – so some highflyers got caught. The comments of such players, many of them made in court, when analyzed to separate the euphemisms from the operative values, reveal a breathtaking lack of any sense of responsibility to the people defrauded and injured by their actions. And still less evident is any awareness of obligation to the systems (free enterprise capitalism, basic business ethics) to which they owe their wealth and power, the context of their *opportunities*.

Values like play and reflexivity in themselves are neither good nor bad. No doubt every period and culture contains its own highflyers and its own values whose misuse can sweep them away. But my point concerns what I see as a remarkable affinity between what has been going on in contemporary cutting-edge fiction, in the media, and in financial practice. We can see this affinity in the film *Wall Street*, which, though probably exaggerated, effectively sum-marizes the ethos of the hostile takeover. Here Michael Douglas plays the highflyer: Gekko is a genius not only at making the right deal at the right time but – like some of his prototypes in 'real' life – also brilliant at advocating his own methods. In one scene he goes before a meeting of shareholders and defends his tactics as good for the company and the economy. At the conclusion of his forceful speech the shareholders (and some members of the movie audience) applaud him. But later on he tells his young protégé that his words are merely moves in the game, that they have no reference to anything outside the game (such as the employees of an airline he has acquired). In so doing he offers a postmodern definition of reality. He says that he makes the news, that he is the news, that the news is whatever he says it is. Dealing as he does with the *perception* of value (the airline is worth whatever people think it is worth) he approaches *perception* directly. He bypasses the airline as a producer of valuable services. What might formerly have been thought of as the 'real' condition or value of the airline (its relation to employees, passengers, suppliers, assets, and the national transportation network), pales into irrelevance (becomes *unreal*) when compared to the value (in dollars, the points in the game) of the perceptions. Gekko sees himself as nothing less than the *creator* of his reality. He thus assumes an incomplete but authentically postmodern ethical posture. When he loses it's because he has mistaken his own game for the only game. In other words, he fails because he's not postmodern all the way, but (like the other criminal highflyers he's meant to stand for) gets trapped in his own solipsism, the victim of a primitive regression. He becomes a lizard, a gecko.

If I had space to present all the relevant material I have in hand (a lot), could I prove these connections between avant-garde literature, news media, and junk bonds? Certainly not: you don't *prove* values. But this does not mean that my evidence is 'soft', as is so often charged of the means by which we reach conclusions in the humanities. The materials I work with – words, events, values – are in many ways as hard and concrete in their identity, in their definition, as the empirical verification or statistical evidence of the natural and social sciences, or indeed of practical economics. If we want to compare the 'hardness' of our data (observe that in our information ethic, hardness is a positive value!), I'll put any text in my courses up against the annual report of any large corporation, and indeed against most analyses and reports that drive corporate policy. What I can't do (because the pedagogic technology of my discipline precludes it) is to forecast how, for example, my analysis of postmodern money might affect a particular executive's policy making. I can't do that because that action will take place in the executive's mind. But if I am correct in arguing that recent financial scandals represent not just the excesses of a few misguided spirits but instead the misapplication of widely shared changes in the general culture's value structure, then this argument might well affect the policy of government agencies and corporations. The important question becomes not whether I can 'prove' that my analysis is correct but whether it might help executives to have more contact with this kind of thinking. Do policy makers need to know this? Do policy makers who can think humanistically (as well as economically and technologically) have a better chance of making wise decisions?

Ethics anyone?

But (I can hear people asking) am I not really talking about *ethics*? Does not the real solution to the financial scandals lie much more simply in teaching business school graduate students courses in ethics, with maybe a refresher course for middle management? If the crooks and clowns of the S&L disaster had only had a good, solid course in ethics, starting, say, with Aristotle and moving up through Kant and on to current methods of evaluating stakeholder interests, wouldn't they have shunned the fraud that will cost taxpayers so dearly? It would, as Hemingway said in another context, be pretty to think so.

And some people do seem to think so, or at least to believe that certain adjustments to the business school curriculum may provide the answers. In a recent *New York Times* interview of three business school deans, Meyer Feldberg of Columbia asks, 'What is the correct mechanism for introducing morality and ethics into our curriculum, not just at the beginning but all the way through?' Later in the interview, Dean Rosenblum of Darden offers this hypothesis: 'We have concluded that ethics is a discipline much like marketing, or any other discipline . . . . We've decided to have a required course in ethics. But not a course that says this is right and that is wrong.' Dean Jacobs of the Kellogg Graduate School of Management argues, 'It is an irony that it was the scandals on Wall Street that caused us to be so concerned about the teaching [of] ethics on campus. But the scandals had nothing to do with ethics. They were simply against the law and that's different.'[2]

Before I venture to disagree with so much prestige and power I want to say exactly where I stand on the teaching of ethics. Ethics is a well-established branch of philosophy, a discipline in the division of the humanities. As a humanities professor I regularly help to teach senior executive seminars in business ethics. I not only believe in the value of such seminars but enjoy some of the more rewarding moments of my professional life in helping to design and conduct them. But I don't believe they really produce ethical profession-als. However able Columbia's business teachers may be, morality and ethics cannot be introduced by a 'mechanism,' curricular or otherwise. I can easily imagine that if Darden's faculty has concluded that 'ethics is a discipline much like marketing,' they don't talk much about 'this is right and that is wrong.' Finally, I believe that Dean Jacobs must have been misquoted when the *Times* has him saying that 'the scandals had nothing to do with ethics.' Even if that were credible, ethics has everything to do with the scandals – but not the ethics of a curricular 'mechanism,' not the ethics that is a discipline 'much like marketing.' What is being marketed here is not ethics, but business schools. This is not disingenuous of these deans. On the contrary, they are merely (and maybe a little casually) voicing a widespread assumption of US education: that if you find the right pedagogic technology you can teach anything. If only Ivan and Michael had heard my lecture on postmodern money!

But if ethics courses don't produce ethical executives then why offer courses or take seminars in business ethics? My answer is that ethics is valuable in the same way that other courses in the humanities are valuable, as a way of thinking about values. Ethics deals more directly with the process of moral choice than other courses, and it can offer methods for making such choices. But by itself it cannot teach anyone to make morally sound or ethically defensible decisions. Ethically defensible decisions are made by people who are morally fit, who have regularly practiced making ethically defensible decisions. When the fire starts, when the deal goes down, when pressure is on to bend the rules, nobody takes an ethics course. Executives act. That is why they are called *executives*. And only executives who have practiced thinking about values, who understand the full range of options, and who are not driven by cultural pressures (values) of which they are unconscious will make fully informed decisions.

I say 'fully informed' rather than 'morally right' because I know that it is possible for very alert people to make ethically indefensible decisions. They do it all the time. From the standpoint of ethics, many people who make such decisions know what they are doing and choose to go forward. They do this for the elementary reason that they want something and are willing to take unethical action in order to get it. When these unethical actions are also against the law, as of course a great many of them are, then we call these people criminals. Breaking the law *always* raises ethical issues though it may in specific cases be ethically defensible. The action I choose to take depends on the values I hold and the clarity of my conscious relation to them. To the extent that I know myself, I believe that I would not break the law to take unfair advantage of other traders in the marketplace, but I can imagine circumstances in which I would choose to break the law (to protect myself or someone I love from permanent harm, for example).

What one chooses to do depends in the end on the unimaginably complicated interaction of value structures at play inside the mind with the

being a workaholic. Presumably workaholics work addictively because they like it better than anything else. But Captain Vere's disease has us going *against* what we love and what we like. In this ethos, you know you are fulfilling your responsibilities when you are feeling pain. The Captain Veres of this world know that executing Billy (which of course stands for taking the action we find most distasteful) is right because it's the decision that hurts the most. Pain becomes a positive value.

All this might be ironically amusing if it were not so costly and so common. The most widespread executive problem in 1990, according to my humanistic calculation, was not ethical ignorance or moral laxity (though these weaknesses continued to attract attention). The chief problem for most executives that comes to light in my courses is that they have not taken the time or have not found the techniques to reconcile the values of their professional context with the values of their personal and private sphere. This is a loss. The professional ethos would benefit enormously from a massive injection of the kinds of values that most executives feel able to acknowledge only in a domestic context – their affective, emotional lives. In this regard, the workplace is said to be progressing, but in practice it shows itself liable to massive regressions. As women and minorities especially know, it is still usually a mistake to show your true feelings at the office. Discipline must be maintained.

The value disorder that Melville diagnosed in Captain Vere over a hundred years ago pursues us still. What is the cure? Again, this is the *application* of our analysis and as we know by now that always takes place in the minds of individuals. But in a general way we could say that Vere would have benefited from greater latitude in his thinking, a latitude that would allow for a direct connection with his emotional life. Instead of confining his consideration of the difficult situation before him to the letter of the Mutiny Act, he would have done well to open the doors of his mind to a wider range of influences. He represents the pitiful but familiar spectacle of an executive actually *narrowing* the range of his options. Executives often describe this as a failure of nerve. At his moral core the hero is a coward. Despite the fact that his subordinates suggest to him other sources of value – religion, civil law, natural law, natural pity – he goes at first by the book and then beyond the book of discipline. In the end his supreme value is airless, dissociated, pointless. What, we ask, is he fighting for? What is his business?

Who needs it?

It should be clear by now that I believe the humanities, and by extension the liberal arts, to be essential to serious executive education. And in order to deliver their special benefits, liberal arts courses must remain free from the constraint of predefined practical objectives. But because their overall purpose is to provide methods of thought and substantive content that will help executives be better executives, these courses must be designed with them in mind. Courses developed for undergraduates, for graduate students in professional schools, or simply for adults who want to continue their liberal arts education, however excellent in themselves, are not sufficiently focused on executive concerns. Humanities courses designed specifically for executive development deal with values central to the practice of management. They treat such resonant themes as the exercise of power and its correlative responsibilities, or the nature of authority, its sources, archetypes, and embodiments.[3] The challenge to executives lies in acknowledging the substance of humanistic thinking and practicing its techniques; the challenge to educators is to focus that thinking on areas of executive experience.

Provided these conditions are met, the returns can be considerable. They are suggested, I hope, in my examples of 'postmodern money' and 'Captain Vere's disease,' but I owe the following list of benefits largely to appraisals from executive participants themselves. They have found:

- a widening of the perceived range of options and choices, both in the culture at large and in their relation to it;
- increased awareness of the integrity or unity of their experience and of connections between experiences in areas too often kept separate (e.g., personal-professional; aesthetic-technical);
- a consciousness of values otherwise latent and unperceived, in the general culture and in themselves;
- an increased perception of social and cultural direction or drift and an awareness of what is happening in worlds outside their own professions;
- increased ethical awareness (though not necessarily moral improvement) gained from practice in thinking about values and choices; and
- an opportunity to exercise influence or control in matters where such opportunity would previously have gone unperceived.

I think that such benefits justify the presence of the humanities in executive education. It is true that the questions we began with persist: How do these enlargements translate into better figures on the bottom line? What are we doing here? But now I can say with assurance that such questions, in order to contain value, must remain open.

References

1 I owe the identification of these values in postmodern literature to E. Ermarth's *Sequel to History* (Princeton, New Jersey: Princeton University Press), forthcoming, fall 1991.

2 J. Kurtzman, 'Shifting the Focus at B-Schools,' *New York Times*, 31 December 1989.
3 Examples from the MIT Sloan School of Management's Program for Senior Executives.

Source: Vargish, Thomas (1991) The value of humanities in executive development, *Sloan Management Review*, **32** 83–91.

13 Teaching artistry through reflection-in-action

Donald A. Schön

Knowing-in-action

I use the term *professional artistry* to refer to the kinds of competence practitioners sometimes display in unique, uncertain, and conflicted situations of practice. Note, however, that their artistry is a high-powered, esoteric variant of the more familiar sorts of competence all of us exhibit every day in countless acts of recognition, judgment, and skillful performance. What is striking about both kinds of competence is that they do not depend on our being able to describe what we know how to do or even to entertain in conscious thought the knowledge our actions reveal. As Gilbert Ryle observed, 'What distinguishes sensible from silly operation is not their parentage but their procedure, and this holds no less for intellectual than for practical performances. "Intelligent" cannot be defined in terms of "intellectual" or "knowing *how*" in terms of "knowing *that*"; "thinking what I am doing" does not connote "both thinking what to do and doing it." When I do something intelligently . . . I am doing one thing and not two. My performance has a special procedure or manner, not special antecedents' (1949, p. 32). For similar reasons, my late friend Raymond M. Hainer spoke of 'knowing more than we can say,' and Michael Polanyi, in *The Tacit Dimension* (1967), coined the term *tacit knowledge*.

Polanyi wrote, for example, about the remarkable virtuosity with which we recognize the faces of people we know. He pointed out that, when we notice a familiar face in a crowd, our experience of recognition is immediate. We are usually aware of no antecedent reasoning, no comparison of *this* face with images of other faces held in memory. We simply see the face of the person we know. And if someone should ask us how we do it, distinguishing one particular face from hundreds of others more or less similar to it, we are likely to discover that we cannot say. Usually we cannot construct a list of features particular to *this* face and distinct from the other faces around it; and even if we could do so, the immediacy of our recognition suggests that it does not proceed by a listing of features.

Polanyi has also described our ordinary tactile appreciation of the surfaces of materials. If we are asked what we feel when we explore the surface of a table with our hand, for example, we are apt to say that the table feels rough, smooth, cool, sticky, or slippery; but we are unlikely to say that we feel a certain compression or abrasion of our fingertips. Nevertheless, it must be from this kind of feeling that we get to our appreciation of the qualities of the table's surface. In Polanyi's words, we perceive *from* fingertip sensations to the qualities of the surface. Similarly, when we use a stick to probe, say, a hole in a stone wall, we focus, not on the impressions of the stick on the fingers and palm of our hand, but on the qualities of the hole – its size and shape, the surfaces of the stones around it – which we apprehend through these tacit impressions. To become skillful in the use of a tool is to learn to appreciate, directly and without intermediate reasoning, the qualities of the materials that we apprehend *through* the tacit sensations of the tool in our hand.

Often such processes of recognition or appreciation take the form of normative judgments. In the very act by which we recognize something, we also perceive it as 'right' or 'wrong.' Chris Alexander (1968) has described how craftsmen recognize the mismatch of an element to an overall pattern – his most famous example is the making of Slovakian peasant shawls – without the slightest ability or need to describe in words the norms they see as violated. And Geoffrey Vickers (1978), commenting on Alexander's example, has gone on to observe that, not only in artistic judgment but in all our ordinary judgments of the qualities of things, we can recognize and describe deviations from a norm very much more clearly than we can describe the norm itself.

This capacity seems to have a great deal to do with the way we learn new skills. A tennis teacher of my acquaintance writes, for example, that he always begins by trying to help his students get the feeling of 'hitting the ball right.' Once they recognize this feeling, like it, and learn to distinguish it from the various feelings associated with 'hitting the ball wrong,' they begin to be able to detect and correct their own errors. But they usually cannot, and need not, describe what the feeling is like or by what means they produce it.

Skilled physicians speak of being able to recognize a particular disease, on occasion, the moment a person afflicted with it walks into their office. The recognition comes immediately and as a whole, and although the physician may later discover in his examination of the patient a full set of reasons for his diagnosis, he is often unable to say just what clues triggered his immediate judgment.

Chester Barnard wrote, in the appendix to *The Functions of the Executive* (1938/1968), about our 'non-logical processes,' by which he meant the skillful judgments, decisions, and actions we undertake spontaneously, without being able to state the rules or procedures we follow. A boy who has learned to throw a ball, for example, makes immediate judgments of distance and coordinates them with the bodily movements involved in the act of throwing, although he cannot say how he does so or perhaps even name the distance he estimates. A high school girl who has learned to solve quadratic equations can spontaneously perform a series of operations without being able to give an accurate description of the procedures she follows when she does so. A practiced accountant of Barnard's acquaintance could 'take a balance sheet of considerable complexity and within minutes or even seconds get a significant set of facts from it' (p. 306), although he could not describe in words the judgments and calculations that entered into his performance.

In similar fashion, we learn to execute such complex performances as crawling, walking, juggling, or riding a bicycle without being able to give a verbal description even roughly adequate to our actual performance. Indeed, if we are asked to say how we do such things, we tend to give wrong answers which, if we were to act according to them, would get us into trouble. When people who know how to ride a bicycle are asked, for example, how to keep from falling when the bicycle begins to tilt to their left, some of them say that they regain their balance by turning the wheel to their right. If they actually did so, they would be likely to fall; fortunately, however, the know-how implicit in their actions is incongruent with their description of it.

I shall use *knowing-in-action* to refer to the sorts of know-how we reveal in our intelligent action – publicly observable, physical performances like riding a bicycle and private operations like instant analysis of a balance sheet. In both cases, the knowing is in the action. We reveal it by our spontaneous, skillful execution of the performance; and we are characteristically unable to make it verbally explicit.

Nevertheless, it is sometimes possible, by observing and reflecting on our actions, to make a description of the tacit knowing implicit in them. Our descriptions are of different kinds, depending on our purposes and the languages of description available to us. We may refer, for example, to the sequences of operations and procedures we execute; the clues we observe and the rules we follow; or the values, strategies, and assumptions that make up our 'theories' of action.

Whatever language we may employ, however, our descriptions of knowing-in-action are always *constructions*. They are always attempts to put into explicit, symbolic form a kind of intelligence that begins by being tacit and spontaneous. Our descriptions are conjectures that need to be tested against observation of their originals – which, in at least one respect, they are bound to distort. For knowing-in-action is dynamic, and 'facts,' 'procedures,' 'rules,' and 'theories' are static. When we know how to catch a ball, for example, we anticipate the ball's coming by the way we extend and cup our hands and by the on-line adjustments we make as the ball approaches. Catching a ball is a continuous activity in which awareness, appreciation, and adjustment play their parts. Similarly, sawing along a penciled line requires a more or less continuous process of detecting and correcting deviations from the line. Indeed, it is this on-line anticipation and adjustment, this continuous detection and correction of error, that leads us, in the first place, to call activity 'intelligent.' Knowing suggests the dynamic quality of knowing-in-action, which, when we describe it, we convert to knowledge-in-action.

Reflection-in-action

When we have learned how to do something, we can execute smooth sequences of activity, recognition, decision, and adjustment without having, as we say, to 'think about it.' Our spontaneous knowing-in-action usually gets us through the day. On occasion, however, it doesn't. A familiar routine produces an unexpected result; an error stubbornly resists correction; or, although the usual actions produce the usual outcomes, we find something odd about them because, for some reason, we have begun to look at them in a new way. All such experiences, pleasant and unpleasant, contain an element of *surprise*. Something fails to meet our expectations. In an attempt to preserve the constancy of our usual patterns of knowing-in-action, we may respond to surprise by brushing it aside, selectively inattending to the signals that produce it. Or we may respond to it by reflection, and we may do so in one of two ways.

We may reflect *on* action, thinking back on what we have done in order to discover how our knowing-in-action may have contributed to an unexpected outcome. We may do so after the fact, in tranquility, or we may pause in the midst of action to make what Hannah Arendt (1971) calls a 'stop-and-think.' In either case, our reflection has no direct connection to present action. Alternatively, we may reflect in the midst of action without interrupting it. In an *action-present* – a period of time, variable with the context, during which we can still make a difference to the situation at hand – our thinking serves to reshape what we are doing while we are doing it. I shall say, in cases like this, that we reflect-*in*-action.

Recently, for example, I built a gate out of wooden pickets and strapping. I had made a drawing and figured out the dimensions I wanted, but I had not reckoned with the problem of keeping the structure square. As I began to nail the strapping to the pickets, I noticed a wobble. I knew the structure would become rigid when I nailed in a diagonal piece, but how could I be sure it would be square? There came to mind a vague memory about diagonals: in a rectangle diagonals are equal. I took a yardstick, intending to measure the diagonals, but I found I could not use it without disturbing the structure. It occurred to me to use a piece of string. Then it became apparent that, in order to measure the diagonals, I needed a precise location at each corner. After several trials, I found I could locate the center point at each corner by constructing diagonals there (see illustration). I hammered in a nail at each of the four center points and used the nails as anchors for the measurement string. It took several minutes to figure out how to adjust the structure so as to correct the errors I found by measuring. And then, when I had the diagonals equal, I nailed in a piece of strapping to freeze the structure.

Here, in an example that must have its analogues in the experiences of amateur carpenters the world over, my intuitive way of going about the task led me to a surprise (the discovery of the wobble), which I interpreted as a problem. In the midst of action, I invented procedures to solve the problem, discovered further unpleasant surprises, and made further corrective inventions, including the several minor ones necessary to carry out the idea of using string to measure the diagonals. We might call such a process 'trial and error.' But the trials are not randomly related to one another; reflection on each trial and its results sets the stage for the next trial. Such a pattern of inquiry is better described as a sequence of 'moments' in a process of reflection-in-action:

- There is, to begin with, a situation of action to which we bring spontaneous, routinized responses. These reveal knowing-in-action that may be described in terms of strategies, understandings of phenomena, and ways of framing a task or problem appropriate to the situation. The knowing-in-action is tacit, spontaneously delivered without conscious deliberation; and it works, yielding intended outcomes so long as the situation falls within the boundaries of what we have learned to treat as normal.
- Routine responses produce a surprise – an unexpected outcome, pleasant or unpleasant, that does not fit the categories of our knowing-in-action. Inherent in a surprise is the fact that it gets our attention. For example, I might not have been surprised by the wobble in my gate because I might not have attended to it; the structure might not have ended up square, and I might not have noticed.
- Surprise leads to reflection within an action-present. Reflection is at least in some measure conscious, although it need not occur in the medium of words. We consider both the unexpected event and the knowing-in-action that led up to it, asking ourselves, as it were, 'What is this?' and, at the same time, 'How have I been thinking about it?' Our thought turns back on the surprising phenomenon and, at the same time, back on itself.

- Reflection-in-action has a critical function, questioning the assumptional structure of knowing-in-action. We think critically about the thinking that got us into this fix or this opportunity; and we may, in the process, restructure strategies of action, understandings of phenomena, or ways of framing problems. In my example, the surprise triggered by my observation of the wobble led me to frame a new problem: 'How to keep the gate square?'

- Reflection gives rise to on-the-spot experiment. We think up and try out new actions intended to explore the newly observed phenomena, test our tentative understandings of them, or affirm the moves we have invented to change things for the better. With my measuring-string experiment, I tested both my understanding of squareness as equality of diagonals and the effectiveness of the procedures I had invented for determining when diagonals are equal. On-the-spot experiment may work, again in the sense of yielding intended results, or it may produce surprises that call for further reflection and experiment.

The description I have given is, of course, an idealized one. The moments of reflection-in-action are rarely as distinct from one another as I have made them out to be. The experience of surprise may present itself in such a way as to seem already interpreted. The criticism and restructuring of knowing-in-action may be compressed into a single process. But regardless of the distinctness of its moments or the constancy of their sequence, what distinguishes reflection-in-action from other kinds of reflection is its immediate significance for action. In reflection-in-action, the rethinking of some part of our knowing-in-action leads to on-the-spot experiment and further thinking that affects what we do – in the situation at hand and perhaps also in others we shall see as similar to it.

The distinction between reflection- and knowing-in-action may be subtle. A skilled performer adjusts his responses to variations in phenomena. In his moment-by-moment appreciations of a process, he deploys a wide-ranging repertoire of images of contexts and actions. So a baseball pitcher adapts his pitching style to the peculiarities of a particular batter or situation in a game. In order to counter an opponent's changing strategies, a tennis player executes split-second variations in play. We can say, in cases like these, that the performer responds to *variation* rather than *surprise* because the changes in context and response never cross the boundaries of the familiar.

However, in a kind of process that may look from the outside like the ones described above, a skilled performer can integrate reflection-in-action into the smooth performance of an ongoing task. I recently heard the story of a cellist who had been called to join in performing a new piece of chamber music. Because of illness, he missed the first few rehearsals and finally put in an appearance the day before the performance was to take place. He sat down with the other musicians and sight-read his way through the difficult part, playing it so well that the conductor had no need to reschedule the performance. As the cellist sight-read the score, he could not have known for certain where the piece was heading. Yet he must have sensed at each moment the direction of its development, picking up in his own performance the lines of development already laid down by others. He must have encountered surprises in response to which he formed, on-line, an interpretation guided by his emerging sense of the whole. And the execution of this feat left him with a newly developed understanding of the piece and how to play it that he would reveal as knowing-in-action on the day of the performance.

When good jazz musicians improvise together, they similarly display reflection-in-action smoothly integrated into ongoing performance. Listening to one another, listening to themselves, they 'feel' where the music is going and adjust their playing accordingly. A figure announced by one performer will be taken up by another, elaborated, turned into a new melody. Each player makes on-line inventions and responds to surprises triggered by the inventions of the other players. But the collective process of musical invention is organized around an underlying structure. There is a common schema of meter, melody, and harmonic development that gives the piece a predictable order. In addition, each player has at the ready a repertoire of musical figures around which he can weave variations as the opportunity arises. Improvisation consists in varying, combining, and recombining a set of figures within a schema that gives coherence to the whole piece. As the musicians feel the directions in which the music is developing, they make new sense of it. They reflect-in-action on the music they are collectively making – though not, of course, in the medium of words.

Their process resembles the familiar patterns of everyday conversation. In a good conversation – in some respects predictable and in others not – participants pick up and develop themes of talk, each spinning out variations on her repertoire of things to say. Conversation is collective verbal improvisation. At times it falls into conventional routines – the anecdote with side comments and reactions, for example, or the debate – which develop according to a pace and rhythm of interaction that the participants seem, without conscious deliberation, to work out in common within the framework of an evolving division of labor. At other times, there may be surprises, unexpected turns of phrase or directions of development to which participants invent on-the-spot responses.

In such examples, the participants are *making* something. Out of musical materials or themes of talk, they make a piece of music or a conversation, an artifact with its own meaning and coherence. Their reflection-in-action is a reflective conversation with the materials of a situation – 'conversation,' now, in a metaphorical sense. Each person carries out his own evolving role in the collective performance, 'listens' to the surprises – or, as I shall say, 'back talk' – that result from earlier moves, and responds through on-line production of new moves that give new meanings and directions to the development of the artifact. The process is reminiscent of Edmund Carpenter's description of the Eskimo sculptor patiently carving a reindeer bone, examining the gradually emerging shape, and finally exclaiming, 'Ah, seal!'

Like knowing-in-action, reflection-in-action is a process we can deliver without being able to say what we are doing. Skillful improvisers often become tongue-tied or give obviously inadequate accounts when asked to say what they do. Clearly, it is one thing to be able to reflect-in-action and quite another to be able to reflect on our reflection-in-action so as to produce a good verbal description of it; and it is still another thing to be able to reflect on the resulting description.

But our reflection on our past reflection-in-action may indirectly shape our future action. The reflections of a Monday morning quarterback may be full of significance if the person reflecting is the quarterback who will play – and play differently because of his Monday morning quarterbacking – in next Saturday's game. As I think back on my experience with the wooden gate, I may consolidate my understanding of the problem or invent a better or more general solution to it. If I do, my present reflection on my earlier reflection-in-action begins a dialogue of thinking and doing through which I become a more skillful (though still amateur) carpenter. Indeed these several levels and kinds of reflection play important roles in the acquisition of artistry.

Practice

So far in this article, I have shifted focus from the specialized and esoteric artistry of professional practice to the more mundane – but no less remarkable – artistry of everyday life. I have done so in order to show that knowing-in-action and reflection-in-action enter into experiences of thinking and doing that everyone shares; when we learn the artistry of a professional practice – no matter how disjunct from ordinary life it may at first appear to be – we learn new ways of using *kinds* of competences we already possess.

Nevertheless, the context of a professional practice is significantly different from other contexts; and the roles of knowing- and reflection-in-action in professional artistry, correspondingly different.

Everett Hughes defined a professional as one who makes a claim to extraordinary knowledge in matters of great human importance (Hughes, 1959). He saw the professional's claim to extraordinary knowledge as bound up in a paradigmatic bargain with society. In return for access to his special knowledge, the professional is accorded a special mandate for social control in matters of his expertise, a license to determine who shall enter his profession, and a relatively high degree of autonomy in the regulation of his practice. Thus, in close association with the very idea of a profession, we find the idea of a community of practitioners whose special knowledge sets them off from other individuals in relation to whom they hold special rights and privileges.

A professional practice is the province of a community of practitioners who share, in John Dewey's term, the traditions of a calling. They share conventions of action that include distinctive media, languages, and tools. They operate within particular kinds of institutional settings – the law court, the school, the hospital, and the business firm, for example. Their practices are structured in terms of particular kinds of units of activity – cases, patient visits, or lessons, for example – and they are socially and institutionally patterned so as to present repetitive occurrences of particular kinds of situations. A 'practice' is made up of chunks of activity, divisible into more or less familiar types, each of which is seen as calling for the exercise of a certain kind of knowledge.

Practitioners of a profession differ from one another, of course, in their subspecialties, the particular experiences and perspectives they bring to their work, and their styles of operation. But they also share a common body of explicit, more or less systematically organized professional knowledge and what Geoffrey Vickers has called an 'appreciative system' – the set of values, preferences, and norms in terms of which they make sense of practice situations, formulate goals and directions for action, and determine what constitutes acceptable professional conduct.

A professional's knowing-in-action is embedded in the socially and institutionally structured context shared by a community of practitioners. Knowing-in-*practice* is exercised in the institutional settings particular to the profession, organized in terms of its characteristic units of activity and its familiar types of practice situations, and constrained or facilitated by its common body of professional knowledge and its appreciative system.

So much we can say without making explicit reference to a particular epistemology of professional practice. Beyond this point, however, our view of a practitioner's knowing will greatly affect our descriptions of the functions and interactions of professional knowledge and professional artistry.

From the perspective of *technical rationality*, a competent practitioner is always concerned with instrumental problems. She searches for the means best suited to the achievement of fixed, unambiguous ends – in medicine, health; in law, success at litigation; in business, profit – and her effectiveness is measured by her success in finding, in each instance, the actions that produce the intended effects consistent with her objectives. In this view, *professional* competence consists in the application of theories and techniques derived from systematic, preferably scientific research to the solution of the instrumental problems of the practice.

From this perspective, we can distinguish two kinds of practice situations and two kinds of knowing appropriate to them.

There are familiar situations where the practitioner can solve the problem by routine application of facts, rules, and procedures derived from the body of professional knowledge. In city planning, for example, there are rules of thumb by which a planner can calculate, under a given zoning bylaw, the number of parking spaces required for each living unit in an apartment building. In medicine, there are routine diagnostic work-ups of patients and routine prescriptions for familiar, uncomplicated complaints.

There are also unfamiliar situations where the problem is not initially clear and there is no obvious fit between the characteristics of the situation and the available body of theories and techniques. It is common, in these types of situations, to speak of 'thinking like a doctor' – or lawyer or manager – to refer to the kinds of inquiry by which competent practitioners bring available knowledge to bear on practice situations where its application is problematic. In this sense, the familiar law school drill takes students through a process that begins with a statement of 'the facts of the case' and proceeds through characteristic patterns of reasoning to determine what legal questions are centrally at stake in the case and what judicial precedents are most pertinent to it. Similarly, medical students learn to 'take a present illness' where, starting from standardized observations, physical examinations, interviews, and laboratory tests, the student must reason his way to a plausible diagnosis of the patient's illness and a proposed strategy of treatment.

From the perspective of technical rationality, 'thinking like a – ' must be thought to consist in rule-governed inquiry. The competent practitioner is seen as following rules for data gathering, inference, and hypothesis testing, which allow him to make clear connections between presenting situations and the body of professional knowledge, where such connections are initially problematic. Such rules are presumed to be explicable, where they are not already explicit. The currently popular 'expert systems,' in clinical medicine as in other fields, are attempts to make explicit the information bases, rules, and procedures by which professional knowledge is applied to particular problematic cases (Kassirer and Gorry, 1970).

Within this framework, there is little room for professional artistry, except as a matter of style grafted onto technical expertise. One might recognize the existence of professional artists capable of making sense of unique or uncertain situations, but there is no way to talk sensibly about their artistry – except, perhaps, to say that they are following rules that have not yet been made explicit.

On the alternative epistemology of practice suggested here, professional artistry is understood in terms of reflection-in-action, and it plays a central role in the description of professional competence.

On this view, we would recognize as a limiting case the situations in which it is possible to make a routine application of existing rules and procedures to the fact of particular problematic situations. Beyond these situations, familiar rules, theories, and techniques are put to work in concrete instances through the intermediary of an art that consists in a limited form of reflection-in-action. And beyond these, we would recognize cases of problematic diagnosis in which practitioners not only follow rules of inquiry but also sometimes respond to surprising findings by inventing new rules, on the spot. This kind of reflection-in-action is central to the artistry with which practitioners sometimes make new sense of uncertain, unique, or conflicted situations. For example:

- A physician, aware that about 85 percent of the cases that come into her office are not 'in the book,' responds to a patient's unique array of symptoms by inventing and testing a new diagnosis.
- A market researcher, monitoring consumers' reactions to a new product, discovers that they have seen in the product uses he never intended and responds by rethinking the product in terms of the consumers' discoveries.

In such cases, the practitioner experiences a surprise that leads her to rethink her knowing-in-action in ways that go beyond available rules, facts, theories, and operations. She responds to the unexpected or anomalous by restructuring some of her strategies of action, theories of phenomena, or ways of framing the problem; and she invents on-the-spot experiments to put her new understandings to the test. She behaves more like a researcher trying to model an expert system than like the 'expert' whose behavior is modeled.

Underlying this view of the practitioner's reflection-in-action is a *constructionist* view of the reality with which the practitioner deals – a view that leads us to see the practitioner as constructing situations of his practice, not only in the exercise of professional artistry but also in all other modes of professional competence.

Technical rationality rests on an *objectivist* view of the relation of the knowing practitioner to the reality he knows. On this view, facts are what they are, and the truth of beliefs is strictly testable by reference to them. All meaningful disagreements are resolvable, at least in principle, by reference to the facts. And professional knowledge rests on a foundation of facts.

In the constructionist view, our perceptions, appreciations, and beliefs are rooted in worlds of our own making that we come to *accept* as reality. Communities of practitioners are continually engaged in what Nelson Goodman (1978) calls 'worldmaking.' Through countless acts of attention and inattention, naming, sensemaking, boundary setting, and control, they make and maintain the worlds matched to their professional knowledge and know-how. They are in transaction with their practice worlds, framing the problems that arise in practice situations and shaping the situations to fit the frames, framing their roles and constructing practice situations to make their role-frames operational. They have, in short, a particular, professional way of seeing their world and a way of constructing and maintaining the world as they see it. When practitioners respond to the indeterminate zones of practice by holding a reflective conversation with the materials of their situations, they remake a part of their practice world and thereby reveal the usually tacit processes of worldmaking that underlie all of their practice.

Practicum

When someone learns a practice, he is initiated into the traditions of a community of practitioners and the practice world they inhabit. He learns their conventions, constraints, languages, and appreciative systems, their repertoire of exemplars, systematic knowledge, and patterns of knowing-in-action.

He may do so in one of several ways. Rarely, he may learn the practice on his own, as people sometimes learn hunting, carpentry, or the criminal trades. He may become an apprentice to senior practitioners, as many craftsmen, industrial workers, and professionals still do. Or he may enter a practicum.

Picking up a practice on one's own has the advantage of freedom – freedom to experiment without the constraints of received views. But it also has the disadvantage of requiring each student to reinvent the wheel, gaining little or nothing from the accumulated experience of others. Apprenticeship offers direct exposure to real conditions of practice and patterns of work. But most offices, factories, firms, and clinics are not set up for the demanding tasks of initiation and education. Pressures for performance tend to be high; time, at a premium; and mistakes, costly. Senior professionals have learned, in addition, to expect apprentices to come equipped with rudimentary practice skills. Nevertheless, many novices still learn through apprenticeship, and many senior practitioners and critics of professional education still see it as the method of choice.

A practicum is a setting designed for the task of learning a practice. In a context that approximates a practice world, students learn by doing, although their doing usually falls short of real-world work. They learn by undertaking projects that simulate and simplify practice; or they take on real-world projects under close supervision. The practicum is a virtual world, relatively free of the pressures, distractions, and risks of the real one, to which, nevertheless, it refers. It stands in an intermediate space between the practice world, the 'lay' world of ordinary life, and the esoteric world of the academy. It is also a collective world in its own right, with its own mix of materials, tools, languages, and appreciations. It embodies particular ways of seeing, thinking, and doing that tend, over time, as far as the student is concerned, to assert themselves with increasing authority.

When a student enters a practicum, she is presented, explicitly or implicitly, with certain fundamental tasks. She must learn to recognize competent practice. She must build an image of it, an appreciation of where she stands in relation to it, and a map of the path by which she can get from where she is to where she wants to be. She must come to terms with the claims implicit in the practicum: that a practice exists, worth learning, learnable by her, and represented in its essential features by the practicum. She must learn the 'practice of the practicum' – its tools, methods, projects, and possibilities – and assimilate to it her emerging image of how she can best learn what she wants to learn.

The work of the practicum is accomplished through some combination of the student's learning by doing, her interactions with coaches and fellow students, and a more diffuse process of 'background learning.'

Students practice in a double sense. In simulated, partial, or protected form, they engage in the practice they wish to learn. But they also practice; as one practices the piano, the analogues in their fields of the pianist's scales and arpeggios. They do these things under the guidance of a senior practitioner – a studio master, supervising physician, or case instructor, for example. From time to time, these individuals may teach in the conventional sense, communicating information, advocating theories, describing examples of practice. Mainly, however, they function as coaches whose main activities are demonstrating, advising, questioning, and criticizing.

Most practicums involve groups of students who are often as important to one another as the coach. Sometimes they play the coach's role. And it is through the medium of the group that a student can immerse himself in the world of the practicum – the all-encompassing worlds of a design studio, a musical conservatory, or psychoanalytic supervision, for example – learning new habits of thought and action. Learning by exposure and immersion, *background* learning, often proceeds without conscious awareness, although a student may become aware of it later on, as he moves into a different setting.

Our view of the work of the practicum and the conditions and processes appropriate to it depends in part on our view of the kinds of knowing essential to professional competence. The types of knowing described in the previous section, and the different perspectives on them set forth there, suggest different conceptions of a practicum.

If we see professional knowledge in terms of facts, rules, and procedures applied nonproblematically to instrumental problems, we will see the practicum in its entirety as a form of technical training. It will be the business of the instructor to communicate and demonstrate the application of rules and operations to the facts of practice. One might imagine, on this view, a practicum for learning a computer language, techniques of analytic chemistry, or methods of statistical analysis. Students would be expected to acquire the material by reading, listening and watching, familiarizing themselves with examples of practice problems matched to the appropriate categories of theory and technique. Coaching would consist in observing student performance, detecting errors of application, pointing our correct responses.

If we see professional knowing in terms of 'thinking like a' manager, lawyer, or teacher, students will still learn relevant facts and operations but will also learn the forms of inquiry by which competent practitioners reason their way, in problematic instances, to clear connections between general knowledge and particular cases. The standard drills of the law school classroom and the medical clinic exemplify this view. In a practicum of this kind, there is presumed to be a right answer for every situation, some item in the corpus of professional knowledge that can be seen, eventually, to fit the case at hand. But, depending on one's view of 'thinking like a – ,' coaches may emphasize either the *rules* of inquiry or the reflection-in-action by which, on occasion, students must develop new rules and methods of their own.

If we focus on the kinds of reflection-in-action through which practitioners sometimes make new sense of uncertain, unique or conflicted situations of practice, then we will assume neither that existing professional knowledge fits every case nor that every problem has a right answer. We will see students as having to learn a kind of reflection-in-action that goes beyond statable rules – not only by devising new methods of reasoning, as above, but also by constructing and testing new categories of understanding, strategies of action, and ways of framing problems. Coaches will emphasize indeterminate zones of practice and reflective conversations with the materials of a situation.

It is important to add that the third kind of practicum need not obviate the work of the first and second. Perhaps we learn to reflect-in-action by learning first to recognize and apply standard rules, facts, and operations; then to reason from general rules to problematic cases, in ways characteristic of the profession; and only then to develop and test new forms of understanding and action where familiar categories and ways of thinking fail.*

Practicums of the third kind exist, in greater or lesser degree, in the deviant traditions of studio and conservatory. They are sometimes also found in association with apprenticeships or – less often, and usually without formal legitimacy or status – in the clinics, workshops, and internships of professional schools. These practicums are reflective in that they aim at helping students learn to become proficient at a kind of reflection-in-action. They are reflective in the further sense that they depend for their effectiveness on a reciprocally reflective dialogue of coach and student.

---

* There are two points here, and they are of equal importance. The first is that the knowing-in-action characteristic of competent practitioners in a professional field is not the same as the professional knowledge taught in the schools; in any given case, the relationship of the two kinds of knowledge should be treated as an open question. Ordinary knowing-in-action may be an application of research-based professional knowledge taught in the schools, may be overlapping with it, or may have nothing to do with it. This point is similar to the one made by Charles Lindblom and David Cohen in *Usable Knowledge* (1979).

The second point is that competent professional practitioners often have the capacity to generate new knowing-in-action through reflection-in-action undertaken in the indeterminate zones of practice. The sources of knowing-in-action include this reflection-in-action and are not limited to research produced by university-based professional schools.

References

Alexander, C. *Notes Toward a Synthesis of Form*. Cambridge, Mass.: Harvard University Press, 1968.

Arendt, H. *The Life of the Mind*. Vol. 1: *Thinking*. San Diego, Calif.: Harcourt Brace Jovanovich, 1971.

Barnard, C. *The Functions of the Executive*. Cambridge, Mass.: Harvard University Press, 1968. (Originally published 1938.)

Goodman, N. *Ways of World Making*. Indianapolis: Hackett, 1978.

Hughes, E. 'The Study of Occupations.' In R. K. Merton, L. Broom, and L. S. Cottrell, Jr. (eds.), *Sociology Today*. New York: Basic Books, 1959.

Kassirer, J., and Gorry, G. A. 'Clinical Problem-Solving: A Behavioral Analysis.' *Annals of Internal Medicine*, 1970, **89**, 245–255.

Lindblom, C. E., and Cohen, D. K. *Usable Knowledge: Social Science and Social Problem-Solving*. New Haven, Conn.: Yale University Press, 1979.

Polanyi, M. *The Tacit Dimension*. New York: Doubleday, 1967.

Ryle, G. *The Concept of Mind*. London: Hutchinson, 1949.

Vickers, G. Unpublished memorandum, Massachusetts Institute of Technology, 1978.

Source: Schön, Donald A. (1987) Teaching artistry through reflection-in-action. In D. A. Schön, *Educating the Reflective Practitioner*, Jossey-Bass, San Francisco, pp. 22–40.

Index